EDUCATOR'S INTERNET
COMPANION™

EDUCATOR'S INTERNET
COMPANION™

CLASSROOM CONNECT'S COMPLETE GUIDE TO EDUCATIONAL RESOURCES ON THE INTERNET

By the staff of
Classroom Connect,
the premier
Internet newsletter
for K–12 educators

Gregory Giagnocavo, Editorial Director

Tim McLain, Writer

Vince DiStefano, Writer

Chris Noonan Sturm, Senior Editor

Wentworth Worldwide Media, Inc.
1866 Colonial Village Lane
Lancaster, PA 17601
(717) 393-1000
Email: connect@classroom.net
URL: http://www.classroom.net

Library of Congress Cataloging-in-Publication Data

Educator's Internet companion / by the staff of Classroom connect ; Gregory Giagnocavo, director ;
    Tim McLain, writer, Vince DiStefano, writer ; Chris Noonan Sturm, editor.
        p.   cm.
    Includes index.
    ISBN 0-13-569484-1 (alk. paper)
      1. Education—Computer network resources—Directories. 2. Internet (Computer network)—
Directories. I. Giagnocavo, Gregory. II. McLain, Tim. III. DiStefano, Vince. IV. Sturm, Chris
Noonan. V. Classroom connect.
LB1044.87.E37 1996
025.06'37—dc20
                                     96–15627

> *Dedicated to educators everywhere working to bring the Internet revolution to schools, children, and their communities.*

Typesetters: *Eileen Mauskapf, Sheryl Mills*

Indexer: *Christa N. Shoreman*

Project manager: *Dorissa Bolinski*

Editorial/production supervision: *Craig Little*

Cover design director: *Jerry Votta*

Cover design: *Talar Agasyan*

Manufacturing manager: *Alexis R. Heydt*

Acquisitions editor: *Mary Franz*

From the
publishers of

   and

Prentice Hall PTR
Prentice-Hall Inc.
A Simon & Schuster Company
Upper Saddle River, New Jersey 07458

The publisher offers discounts on this book when ordered in bulk quantities. For more information, contact
Corporate Sales Department, Prentice Hall PTR, 1 Lake Street, Upper Saddle River, NJ 07458.
Phone: 800-382-3419; Fax: 201-236-7141; email: corpsales@prenhall.com

All terms mentioned in this book that are known to be trademarks or service marks have been appropriately
capitalized.

Printed in the United States of America
10   9   8   7   6   5   4   3   2   1

ISBN 0-13-569484-1

Prentice-Hall International (UK) Limited, *London*
Prentice-Hall of Australia Pty. Limited, *Sydney*
Prentice-Hall Canada Inc., *Toronto*
Prentice-Hall Hispanoamericana, S.A., *Mexico*
Prentice-Hall of India Private Limited, *New Delhi*
Prentice-Hall of Japan, Inc., *Tokyo*
Simon & Schuster Asia Pte. Ltd., *Singapore*
Editora Prentice-Hall do Brasil, Ltda., *Rio de Janeiro*

C O N T E N T S

Thirty lesson plans that integrate the Internet into the curriculum and put students and teachers online.

Chapter 2: VIRTUAL TOURS   67

A walk through eight Internet sites for educators.

Chapter 3: EDUCATIONAL RESOURCES   105

An extensive list of educational Internet sites of value to educators and students.

Chapter 4: WORLD WIDE WEB TOUR   179

Snapshots of 50 of the best educational World Wide Web sites.

Chapter 5: FUNDING SOURCES   207

How to find the money to finance school telecommunications programs, including lists of sources of government and corporate grants.

APPENDIXES   219

GLOSSARY   257

INDEX   263

P R E F A C E

VIRTUAL CLASSROOMS

Unleashing the Internet for K–12 education

We are witnessing the greatest explosion of change to affect the field of education in decades, perhaps in all history. This change is the Internet.

The Internet is the world's largest computer network, connecting more than 4 million computers in over 160 countries. More than 30 million people—increasing at a rate of one million per month—are estimated to have access to the Internet. Millions of them are passionately involved in education and research.

Until late 1993, the Internet's unexciting, text-based appearance and cryptic commands were too unwieldy for everyday use, particularly in the classroom. Investigating the hard-to-decipher variations of Internet connectivity and climbing the steep learning curve required to master Internet commands understandably discouraged many in education from exploring the Internet's educational possibilities. This hampered the rate of adoption of Internet use in the classroom.

But the technology landscape has recently erupted with new and exciting changes. Advances in the software used to navigate the Internet have opened its vast potential to even the most computer-phobic. In particular, the World Wide Web, known as the "Web," has almost single-handedly re-invented the concept of how people can and will use the Internet. Web "browser" software such as Mosaic and Netscape has given computer users around the world graphical, point-and-click access to millions of documents on the Internet. This new software is so simple, anyone who can maneuver a mouse already knows how to use it. Educators and students who taste the Web will be captivated by its multimedia features—pictures, graphics, text, sound, and video clips. With a simple click, its "hypertext" capability immediately presents you with information located on computers throughout the world.

But that's only part of what the Web has done to simplify Internet use. Web browser software also incorporates traditional Internet navigation tools such as ftp (file transfer), telnet, gopher, email, WAIS, and newsreader, which are usually used as individual pieces of software. Rapid software enhancements and improvements mean the Internet community will soon have access to Web software that seamlessly handles every navigation tool—including two-way email—all combined in one easy-to-use interface—the World Wide Web. This technology leap will accelerate the Internet's impact on education. Students and teachers, who are often awestruck after their first Internet session using the Web, will want more of this state-of-the-art yet 20-year-old, Internet technology.

Of course, this new technology will not automatically or magically change education for the better. Getting connected to the Internet won't instantly make the job of the educator easier, nor will students suddenly become smarter, brighter, or more eager to learn. But to succeed in the new information society we—parents, teachers, students, and administrators—**must** become part of the information stream. It may take a little effort on the part of all of us. But do it we must.

Why? Because the new information society will place demands on all of us, especially today's students, that were unknown a decade ago. We have an obligation to do all we can to prepare our children to function and thrive in this new, global information environment.

The Internet as an agent of change

The education process cannot depend solely upon the teacher-as-expert model. Education is more than a one-to-one, or even one-to-many communication experience. No longer is the teacher the dispenser of knowledge. Rather, the teacher is the learned, guiding hand in the student's process of the discovery of knowledge.

The Internet is a timely tool for educators who are reforming education. If we believe information is the bedrock of knowledge, understanding, and power, then universal access to worldwide databases and up-to-the-minute, global information and people-to-people networking is crucial to providing students with educational challenges.

Using the Internet, we can teach students to search, retrieve, collect, and exchange information. More importantly, they will learn to analyze, write about, and then publish information on any imaginable topic. This cycle of information gathering, analyzing, writing, and publishing is important in the new information age already upon us. From elementary school to high school, from school-to-work programs to higher education, teaching the value of the Internet will be a key component to success and achievement in the job market of the future.

Raising curiosity seekers

Einstein was on to something. While he had a high respect for knowledge, Einstein has been quoted saying that "Curiosity is more important than knowledge." Through history it has been the "curious ones" who have discovered and invented, painted and authored, and been purveyors of rich veins of new ideas, discourse, and thought.

Perhaps we need to keep in mind that "curiosity is the mother of knowledge" as we encourage students to develop the skills they'll need to become successful, lifelong learners. No longer can we consider that a person "finishes" school and "completes" his or her education upon graduation.

Using the Internet, the curious person will stay on top of international news, track and discover developing trends, communicate and collaborate with peers and professional associates, and gather, analyze, and synthesize data and information from around the world in real time, parlaying that into career-enhancing knowledge. Those who aren't "curious," who are content to rest on the knowledge base of yesterday—of their school years—will be ill-equipped to compete with tomorrow's knowledge workers in an information-based society. The Internet is the backbone, the pipeline, that will open the world to anyone with the tiniest spark of curiosity.

The Internet as a library resource

Recent studies by Lance[1] and Krashen[2] have explored the impact of the availability of library resources and voluntary student reading on academic achievement. These in-depth studies, published in 1993, came to a powerful conclusion: student achievement is directly linked to the availability of resource materials and an active School Library Media Center. They further confirmed the results of the study, *Becoming a Nation of Readers,*[3] that reported that students who are encouraged to explore and read on their own do better academically in almost all fields of study.

The Internet, the "ultimate" library resource, can assist students in wonderful ways. Its powerful, global resource can facilitate these positive factors in your school and for your students. How much more effective libraries and schools become, how much more successful students can become, when the Internet is offered as part of the student's available resources!

What's a teacher to do?

What can teachers do on the Internet? The possibilities are endless. Download your choice of millions of files consisting of reports, research, software programs, pictures, and graphics. Send email around the world in seconds to join classroom projects, participate in collaborative research, communicate with peers, or pose your difficult questions to several "Ask an Expert" programs. Most exciting of all, you can use the World Wide Web to search for and retrieve information in all its multimedia glory. Use the Web to visit cities, medical centers, research labs, huge databases, zoos, and museums around the world. From inner-city schools to Antarctica base stations, the Web takes you there in an instant. You and your students will want to become an integral part of this rich, ever-changing information stream by mounting your own files and graphical Web pages on the Internet for the world to see.

Student empowerment through Internet publishing

Electronic publishing via the Internet is extremely valuable at all grade levels. Students search for and find information from physical libraries and from online sources. They gather text, graphics, and video clips, as well as email discussions from mailing lists and newsgroups and responses from peers, teachers and experts from around the world. Then, students compile and study the information, write reports, and publish them on the Internet and in multimedia presentations.

The Internet enhances and expands the learning process as students realize that others in the global Internet community and locally are viewing and using these published reports as part of *their* educational experience. What a thrill to see first-hand the sense of excitement and empowerment that students feel as they receive comments and field questions from Internet-using students in other states, provinces, and countries. Consider this sense of accomplishment, but magnify it many times, when a special needs, handicapped, or learning-disabled student is involved. When these students realize that millions of Internet users are prepared to accept them solely for their words, ideas, and opinions, they feel accepted and empowered in a new way. That moment can become an epiphany of sorts, a watershed event in their educational experience as well as their life's journey, confirming the value of the Internet as a vital educational resource for educators and students.

The Internet and the community

A sense of community will play an increased role in enriching students' educational experience, largely facilitated by telecommunications and the Internet. K–12 educators should do what they can to encourage local community members to realize they play a role in education, and that they share the responsibility for passing on to students the value of experience, knowledge, and an excitement for learning and excellence. This community—of educators, parents, students, business people, professionals, retired persons, and residents—can provide valuable input and feedback, expert and professional advice, historical perspective, seasoned opinion, and tales of experience that simply aren't in any textbook.

Once again, the Internet can help in this effort. With the Internet, schools can extend the sense of local community to one of a far-reaching, even global, nature. Electronic mail and file transfers take but a few seconds to travel across town or across the world. Recent photographs and those hidden from view for dozens of years can be transferred, shared, and published on the Internet. Electronic mailing lists on any topic and email projects of every type are used to share information otherwise not easily available. Those with impaired ability to travel can freely "visit" area classrooms, museums, and historic sites, or with a click of a mouse do the same in hundreds of communities scattered across the globe. The Internet facilitates community empowerment and learning for all its members. And community involvement among educators, parents, and others can be a powerful, positive factor in K–12 and lifelong education.

The Internet here and now

The Internet isn't a fad. It isn't just another new piece of technology such as a fax machine or laser disk player. And it isn't a "thing" or a "place" or "something to do." It's much more, almost indescribably more. It's as if it were a living, breathing organism, and in a way, it is. To me, and to hundreds of thousands of "curious" educators, the Internet is the world's largest community of users dedicated to common goals: the free exchange of information and the enrichment the lifelong (K–99) educational experience for millions of students and adults everywhere.

The Internet is here and it is available now. It isn't magical. But, it has the power to enhance and transform the educational process. As an educator, parent, or student, you simply must get involved with the Internet.

Let's all work our hardest to implement the Internet and adopt it as a necessity in education at every level.

Gregory Giagnocavo
Editorial Director
Email to: jgg@classroom.net

P.S.
About *Educator's Internet Companion*

If you are one of the estimated 23 million already "online," the *Educator's Internet Companion* will help you get the most out of what is available on the Internet. If you aren't yet online, we hope this guide will encourage you to immediately make efforts to "get connected" to the Internet. And for the many readers who are new to the Internet, we've included Appendixes on Internet basics.

In deciding on the material for *Companion*, we selected the very best education-related resources we could find, including many with links to other rewarding online resources. However, we simply didn't have the room to include all the terrific resources and interesting sites we discovered. And since the nature of the Internet is constant change, many more sites and resources will debut online each time you logon to the Internet. That's all the more exciting, because you're sure to find dozens of great new resources that suit your needs.

The resources we present in *Companion* and in our *Classroom Connect* newsletter, and the new ones you'll discover on your own, will add excitement and value to the teaching experience for you and your students. When you find something on the Internet that you'd like to share, send email to the editor, Chris Noonan Sturm, at **cnsturm@classroom.net**.

References

[1]Lance, Keith Curry, Lynda Welborn, and Christine Hamilton-Pennell. *The Impact of School Library Media Centers on Academic Achievement.* Hi Willow Research and Publishing (1993; ISBN 0-931510-48-1; $25), P.O. Box 266, Castle Rock, CO 80104.

[2]Krashen, Stephen. *The Power of Reading.* Libraries Unlimited, Inc. (1993; ISBN 1-56308-006-0; $13.50), P.O. Box 6633, Englewood, CO 80155.

[3]*Becoming a Nation of Readers*, Richard Anderson, Chairman (1983; U.S. Department of Education).

INTRODUCTION

The Internet is the fastest growing communications medium—*ever*.

Use of this global network connecting more than 4 million computers and 30 million people has exploded faster than the printed word, recorded sound, motion pictures, and television—*even if current growth estimates are too high.*

Many leading kindergarten through grade 12 schools are part of this explosive growth. Why? Because schools who use the Internet do not simply bring children into the future of information technology. They turn their students into something education reformers have been talking about for years—lifelong learners.

Teachers who work the Internet into their curricula—not for its own sake but to teach students how to use the network to find and use information to reach a goal—turn students into independent learners rather than rapt, or not so rapt listeners.

Starting the revolution without schools?

The 105,544 public and private K–12 schools in the United States cannot afford to be left behind during this technological revolution. Evidence of a growing separation of our society into technological haves and have-nots requires that children of all backgrounds have access to an information technology that is sweeping through all levels of government, business, and education.

Is the Internet really that pervasive? Yes, and more so every day. The Supreme Court, NASA, the White House, the Smithsonian Institution, Congress, and the United Nations have gone online to make archives of information available to *anyone*—not just reporters, researchers, or people with the time to travel to Washington, D.C. or New York City. Your local library, city hall, and county government will be next.

More businesses are opening up shop on the Internet every day. The Cable News Network, a flower shop, local car dealers, bookstores, real estate brokers, travel agents are just a few examples. And since the Internet has its roots in research institutions, many colleges and universities have been online for more than two decades.

A Numbers Explosion

The Internet is exploding so quickly that statisticians can't keep up. These numerical snapshots show a revolution in the making:

- The Internet grows by at least 10 percent a month.
- At least 160 countries are connected to the Internet.
- Almost 200 U.S. daily newspapers offer electronic versions on the Net.
- Schools in 41 states are fully connected to the Internet. The states with the most "wired" schools are: Arkansas (140); California (64); Pennsylvania (45); Florida (44); New York (43); Tennessee (25); Oregon (20).
- As many as 8,000 K–12 schools were estimated to be on the Net as of Winter 1996, a number estimated to be growing by 15 percent a month.

States and schools push to get online

More states are recognizing that their K–12 schools need access to the Information Superhighway. Some are wiring every new school building with fiber optics, simplifying educators' often daunting problem of finding the phone lines to get on the Internet. Other states are appropriating money for schools to acquire the phone lines they need. Still others are taking the small but very helpful step of giving teachers access to 800 numbers they can use to dial into free Internet access.

More often than not, however, schools are not waiting for the education bureaucracy to bring the fast-developing Internet to them. Technology committees of parents and educators are meeting to write proposals for grant money to wire their schools. Successful proposals bring in tens of thousands of dollars.

In many schools, an Internet "missionary" such as a computer teacher, a library/media person, a principal, or a technologically-oriented parent rounds up a few volunteers, some computer hardware, and patches in a phone line just to get things started. Some schools even roll a computer from classroom to classroom on a cart and plug the phone line into the wall to get students online. Often, the missionary's first step is on a commercial online service such as America Online or Prodigy. But the use of such services can be expensive, while use of the Internet is virtually free once schools have access.

Teachers take students around the world

What do educators do with the Internet after they've met the challenges of setting it up? Besides teaching students to search for, find, and use information, they bring students into contact with people they would never have otherwise met. While the Net is comprised of mountains of information, it's also made of *people* of all races, creeds, cultures, and colors—and they all have personal stories and knowledge to share. Because the culture of the Internet is one of a free sharing of information, busy professionals, renowned experts worldwide, and countless others dispense their knowledge with no expectation of payment, except perhaps thanks. That is a worthwhile lesson in itself for young people.

With the Internet, teachers can make class and individual student projects global affairs. Teachers match students with email penpals anywhere in the world to collect weather data, to learn about world cultures, or to practice Spanish with native speakers. Students can join a global project to correspond with explorers in the Arctic or Central American jungles. They can invite a scientist or writer to visit them electronically to exchange questions and answers. The possibilities are limitless. The challenge for teachers is to somehow structure this huge and exciting resource into their students' everyday classroom lives.

How *Classroom Connect* helps educators

This book and the newsletter *Classroom Connect* can help educators bring the Internet to their students. The newsletter helps teachers *apply* the Internet in the K–12 classroom. Few people have the time simply to wander around the Internet (or "Net") and find what is valuable to them. *Classroom Connect* keeps teachers abreast of new educational Internet resources. This book, by the staff of *Classroom Connect,* shows educators and students where to go on the Net to find the resources and information they need. More important, it helps teachers take this knowledge into the classroom and work it into lesson plans.

The Internet is changing and growing all the time. According to one estimate, more than 40,000 new Internet services and information locations come online *each month*. Educators and students have an incredible opportunity to benefit from and even shape this evolving electronic community.

Chris Noonan Sturm
Senior Editor
Email to: cnsturm@classroom.net

A B O U T   T H I S   B O O K

The *Educator's Internet Companion* is a practical guide and a rich resource for K–12 educators who want to apply the Internet in the classroom. Here's what you will find in each chapter and in the appendixes.

The chapters

Chapter 1: Lesson Plans
Over and over, teachers say their most pressing need is lesson plans incorporating the Internet. That's why we started the book with more than two dozen of them. They cover all grade levels and the major subject areas: English, history, mathematics, science, and social studies. They're in alphabetical order by subject and include a computer screen capture from one of the sites in the plan.

Chapter 2: Virtual Tours
The richest Internet sites for K–12 education are so huge that simply navigating *them* can be daunting. This chapter walks you through eight of these sites step-by-step. Each tour employs a different Internet navigation tool, such as gopher or telnet, so you learn not just about the site but also how to use the navigation tool.

Chapter 3: Educational Resources
The number of Internet sites, mailing lists, and newsgroups of value to educators is growing all the time. Here is a list of the best of them.

Chapter 4: World Wide Web Tour
The Web is the fastest growing segment of the Internet—and is the form the network will take in the future. The top 50 Web sites for K–12 education are displayed and described in this chapter for the first time anywhere.

Chapter 5: Funding Sources
How do you find the money to connect your school to the Internet? Government agencies, foundations, and corporations offer millions of dollars in grant money to schools with well-organized plans to bring the Internet into the classroom. Here is a list of contacts for tapping this grant money, as well as tips on school-business partnerships and grassroots fund raising.

Appendixes and glossary

Before diving into the book's chapters, newcomers to the Net might want to visit the appendixes and glossary to bring themselves up to speed on Internet terminology and how the Net works.

Appendix A: The Internet Defined
A description of the network, Internet addresses, and netiquette.

Appendix B: Internet Tutorials

An explanation of how to use different tools to navigate and search the Internet. Email, gopher, telnet, ftp, mailing lists, newsgroups, World Wide Web, Internet Relay Chat (IRC), and searching tools such as Archie, Veronica, and WAIS are covered.

Appendix C: Acceptable Use Policies

Schools must have a policy setting the rules of Internet use before putting students online. Here's how to begin.

Appendix D: Commercial Online Services

Brief descriptions of the major services.

Glossary

Terms educators need to know to understand this book and the Internet.

The Editor's Choice

This book is crammed with so many Internet resources that we want to make sure you don't miss those that are "musts" for educators. Look for stars with the words "Editor's Choice" above the heading for certain sites. These are resources the *Classroom Connect* staff has deemed particularly valuable to K–12 educators.

Conventions used

To make finding Internet addresses and directories easier, we've set them off from other text in this book.

- Internet addresses are in **bold** type. That includes email, gopher, telnet, ftp, and World Wide Web sites.
     Example: **Email to: connect@classroom.net**
- Internet addresses include the navigation method (such as gopher), followed by a colon. *Do not* type the words before the colon when entering the address. In the example below, you type only
  riceinfo.rice.edu
     Example: **Gopher to: riceinfo.rice.edu**
- Directions that require you to type a command are in **bold.**
     Example: Type **B Taxes** and hit return.
- Names of directories, subdirectories, filenames, and menu items are in *italics*.
     Example: Look in the *pub/clipart* subdirectory
- Names of mailing lists are in all caps.
     Example: NATIVELIT-L
- Remember that the Internet is an evolving entity. Change is its nature. Some addresses may change after publication of this book.

"Children in grade school today will need new skills to be information workers in the twenty-first century. The challenge is to create the curriculum to nurture such skills."

Libby Black
Boulder Valley School District

L E S S O N   P L A N S

Curricula that put students online

I t's one thing for a teacher to know how to navigate the Internet and find educational treasures—and quite another to incorporate it into classroom activities in a meaningful way.

Educators using the Internet crave hands-on, step-by-step methods for integrating the network into their curricula. That's what these lesson plans are for: to empower teachers to fulfill their educational objectives for students while learning to use the Internet and its resources. Many of these plans feature simple exercises that get teachers and students online—they're starting points.

How to use these plans

These 30 lesson plans cover a variety of subjects and grade levels and they've been arranged in alphabetical order by subject. Each plan includes objectives, materials, procedures, and addresses of Internet resources, including a computer screen capture. The suggested grade levels are simply guidelines, and most of these plans can be modified for use in other grades. Some plans also feature extensions for advanced students. You can use these lessons and projects as they are, modify them to meet your needs, or augment them with Internet resources of your own.

To really enrich students and to use the Internet in the most worthwhile way, educators should weave the use of Internet resources into *their own* lesson plans. But, that requires a healthy knowledge of what's out there on the Net, plus the time to navigate to various sites and check out their usefulness. Teachers can rely on these plans to get started and may photocopy them for classroom use.

Remember: the best lesson plans do not use the Internet as an end in itself. Rather, they employ it as a means to an end, incorporating its resources as an extra tool to attain a larger educational goal.

To use these plans most effectively, you should be familiar with the basics of Internet tools and navigation techniques. The Internet tutorials in Appendix B include a refresher course in Internet basics.

American History (Colonial)

Students are required to conduct research in a library and on the Internet, to write from a point of view other than their own, to work in teams, and to use a desktop publishing program.

GRADE LEVELS: 5–7

OBJECTIVES:
• Research colonial American life using the Internet.
• Compose, edit, and illustrate two letters: one from the point of view of a youngster living in colonial times to a modern-day student; another from the modern-day student explaining twentieth century life to the colonial counterpart.
• Learn to gopher and telnet. Learn the basics of HTML (Hypertext Markup Language) and how to mount the final project on the World Wide Web (optional).

MATERIALS:
• Personal computer with an Internet connection, including telnet and gopher access
• Word processor and simple desktop publishing program
• A graphical Web browser and a SLIP or PPP Internet account for the World Wide Web page optional extension

PROCEDURE:
1. Research life in colonial America by using the library's reference books and several online historical document sites. Telnet to the University of Kansas History Network Resources site.

Telnet to: hnsource.cc.ukans.edu (See Figure 1.1)
Login as **history** and follow the menu directions.

FIGURE 1.1

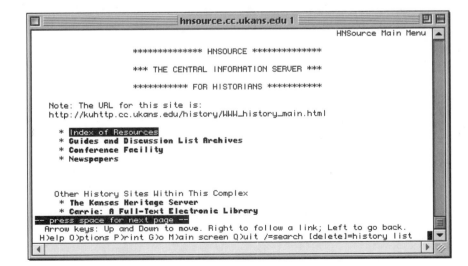

```
                         hnsource.cc.ukans.edu 1

                                                        HNSource Main Menu

           ************** HNSOURCE **************

           *** THE CENTRAL INFORMATION SERVER ***

           ********** FOR HISTORIANS **********

      Note: The URL for this site is:
      http://kuhttp.cc.ukans.edu/history/WWW_history_main.html
            *  Index of Resources
            *  Guides and Discussion List Archives
            *  Conference Facility
            *  Newspapers


         Other History Sites Within This Complex
            *  The Kansas Heritage Server
            *  Carrie: A Full-Text Electronic Library
      -- press space for next page --
       Arrow keys: Up and Down to move. Right to follow a link; Left to go back.
      H)elp O)ptions P)rint G)o M)ain screen Q)uit /=search [delete]=history list
```

Also gopher to the North Carolina State University Library for related documents.

Gopher to: vega.lib.ncsu.edu

Look in *USA, Colonial*

2. Review the fundamentals of point-of-view writing, including how to write from another's perspective, and the type of language and tone that would be typical of colonial times.

3. Based on the research, discuss as a group what should go into the letter written by the colonial. Have several groups prepare letters using word processors, and incorporate clip art or art created by the students.

4. Repeat step two and have students write a letter back to the colonial student from a twentieth century point of view.

EXTENSION:

Work with your school's technology coordinator to learn how to create and mount World Wide Web pages. If the school does not have a Web server, retrieve instructional materials from this site for tutorials and the software needed to create one at your school.

URL: http://www.ncsa.uiuc.edu/General/Internet/WWW/HTMLPrimer.html

If your school does not have full Internet access, approach a network in the area and ask if they'll sponsor a Web server for the school. Teachers can also send a request on the Internet asking for a site to mount the school's Web page.

Notes:

American History (General)

Students are required to retrieve clip art from the Internet, work in teams, construct a timeline, and write a very brief report about a period in American history.

GRADE LEVELS: 8–9

OBJECTIVES:
• Research a specific period of American history.
• Visualize the sequence of important events in a specific period of American history.
• Practice using file transfer protocol and gopher to find and download graphics and programs, and practice using gopher and WAIS Internet search tools.

MATERIALS:
• Personal computer with an Internet connection and ftp access (gopher, WAIS software, World Wide Web, or telnet access optional)
• A graphics viewer to view clip art; an unzip program
• Graphics-capable printer
• Construction paper, tape or tacks, string or yarn

PROCEDURE:
1. Choose a specific period of American history, e.g., the Great Depression or the Civil War. Have each student select an important event or date from that period from the textbook. More than one student can use a specific date.
2. Divide the class into small teams. Have each team work together to find clip art on the Internet that creatively represents each member's events. Students can use gopher and ftp to to access collections of clip art.
New York State Education Department
Gopher to: unix5.nysed.gov
Look in *K–12 Resources, Arts and Humanities*
Classroom Connect
Ftp to: ftp.classroom.net
Look in the *wentworth/clipart* subdirectory
Yale University
Ftp to: haskell.cs.yale.edu
Look in the *pub/clipart* subdirectory
If your school computers don't have a graphics viewer, which you need to view the art on a computer, you can download one from this ftp site. (These are appropriate for DOS or Mac computers.)
University of California at Oakland
Ftp to: oak.oakland.edu (See Figure 1.2)
Look in the *SimTel/msdos/graphics* or *SimTel/msdos/gif* subdirectories
If you don't already have an unzip program, you'll need a program called *unzip.exe* to decompress graphic viewer programs that you download for Windows.
Ftp to: ftp.classroom.net
Look in the *wentworth/Internet-Software/IBM* subdirectory for *unzip.exe*
3. Have each student print and label his or her graphic and use a word processor to write and attach a paragraph describing the significance of the event.

4. As a group, use construction paper and tape to create a wall-sized timeline. Mark off each year on the timeline, and have students place their pages on appropriate points. Use a piece of string to branch off pages from the timeline.

5. Give students time to examine their classmates' work and ask questions. Conclude with a general review of each date in the historical period.

FIGURE 1.2

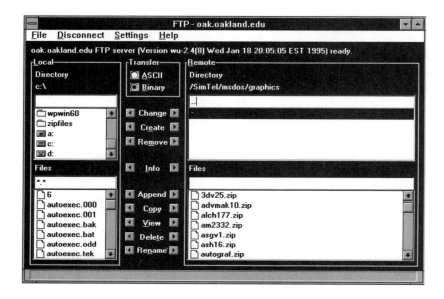

EXTENSION:

Have each student conduct more research about the event using a gopher-based Veronica search or WAIS. Try a variety of keywords, ranging from general (World War II) to more specific (Women's Suffrage). Students can add the information to their timeline or give a brief oral presentation. They can use gopher to conduct a Veronica search.

Gopher to: veronica.scs.unr.edu

They can also access LC Marvel, which has history texts and links to other historical information. Library of Congress

Gopher to: marvel.loc.gov

Notes:

American History (The Sixties)

Students are expected to find original government documents on the Internet, design a questionnaire and do five interviews, make a presentation of their findings, and write a paper.

GRADE LEVELS: 8–12

OBJECTIVES:
• Use the Internet to find information about the Vietnam War era in U.S. history.
• Develop a questionnaire to distribute to people who lived through the era or to use as the basis for personal interviews.
• Communicate with a distant class via email.

MATERIALS:
• Personal computer with an Internet connection, including gopher, ftp, and email access
• Unbiased documentaries, movies, books, or other presentation materials about the war

PROCEDURE:
1. Complete your regular examination of the Vietnam War era. If time permits, show the PBS documentary "Vietnam" or "Vietnam: The Ten Thousand Day War."
2. Have students use the Internet to augment their studies by finding relevant original documents and other materials from the Vietnam era.
  Gopher to: wiretap.spies.com
  Look in *Government, US-History, Vietnam*
  Ftp to: ftp.msstate.edu
  Select the *Docs/History/USA/Vietnam* subdirectory
  Gopher to: umslvma.umsl.edu
  Look in *The Library, Government Information, Background Notes, Vietnam*
  Gopher to: apollo.umd.edu
  Look in *Background Information, Factbook93, Countries, Vietnam*
3. Teach students how to create research surveys or questionnaires so they can gather accounts from people who lived through this period in American history. Make sure they include basic biographical questions such as residence, age, sex, occupation, etc. Review the basic types of questions used for such interviews (e.g., yes/no, open-ended, leading) and techniques of probing for responses. Each student should ask a minimum of ten questions.
4. Have students locate at least five people who were 15 years old or older during the Vietnam War era. Instruct them to try for as broad a cross-section as possible, e.g., someone who did military service, a high school student, a homemaker, a blue-collar worker, etc. Students can interview subjects in person, over the phone, by email, or via mailing list. Remind them that they will be required to turn in their notes.
5. To find interviewees online, subscribe to the Vietnam War and Sixties mailing lists. Students can post their questions to the list themselves, but the instructor should scan the discussion printouts ahead of time to make sure students aren't exposed to inappropriate materials. Here's how to subscribe to VWAR-L or SIXTIES-L mailing lists.
  Email to: VWAR-L@LISTSERV.NET or SIXTIES-L@LISTSERV.NET
  Type **SUBSCRIBE VWAR-L <your name>** or **SUBSCRIBE SIXTIES-LL <your name>** in the body of the message.

6. Have students make a brief presentation on the results of their interviews. Their presentations should include the questions asked, specific responses, and descriptions of the interviewees' reactions to the war.

7. After each student has made his or her presentation, ask for volunteers to answer questions such as: What was the emotional state of the respondee? Did the interviews affect you or make you feel a certain way? What conclusions can we draw based upon these interviews? Do you feel differently about the war and the Sixties?

8. Ask students to write a brief thought-reaction paper based on their new knowledge of this period of American history. Have them send thank you notes to their interviewees, by email whenever possible.

EXTENSION:

Subscribe to the International Email Classroom Connections mailing list and try to locate a Vietnamese class to correspond with. Have the students write the query (follow the guidelines you'll receive after your subscription is entered). Decide as a class which topics or questions you'd like to pursue. Examples include: What are you learning about the Vietnam War in your history classes? Do you know anyone who remembers living in the war era? What sort of feelings do people have today about the Sixties?

Email to: iecc-request@stolaf.edu

Type **subscribe** in the body of the message.

Notes:

American History (Women's Studies)

Students are expected to use the Internet to research women's issues and examine historical, constitutional, biographical, and current material and then to write a paper.

GRADE LEVELS: 6–12

OBJECTIVES:
• Gather information about the women's suffrage movement and other historical, gender-related constitutional issues.
• Find biographical information about important women in American history.
• Keep up to date with current women's issues.
• Practice using the Internet to search for and retrieve information.

MATERIALS:
• Personal computer with an Internet connection, including gopher, World Wide Web, telnet, and email access
• Word processor and printer

PROCEDURE:
1. Midway through your study of women's issues or the suffrage movement, have students go online to access an electronic version of the U.S. Constitution. Review critical amendments and sections pertaining to women's rights.
   Cornell Law School
   URL: http://www.law.cornell.edu/constitution/constitution.overview.html
2. Then, students should look for two kinds of information: historical information about notable women and the suffrage movement as well as classic texts dealing with gender issues such as rights to property; and, information about current women's issues, such as the glass ceiling. Here are some starting points.
   InforMN's Women's Studies Database
   URL: http://www.inform.umd.edu/EdRes/Topic/WomensStudies/
   Notable Women
   Gopher to: gopher.emc.maricopa.edu
   Look in *Information Commons, Notable Women*
   The University of Wisconsin System Women's Studies Librarian
   URL: http://www.library.wisc.edu/libraries/
   WomensStudies/

FIGURE 1.3

9

Information on Women in Science, Health, and Technology
> **Gopher to: library.berkeley.edu**
> Look in *Research Databases and Research by Subject, Women's/Gender Studies*

3. Students should pick a topic based on their Internet research and their interests for a brief thought-reaction paper. Topics can range from "The Poetry of Important Women in American History," "What would Elizabeth Cady Stanton be doing today?", or "Women In Today's Congress." Students can use the school library to find information not online.

4. Students should check to see if their topics are being addressed through current legislation about gender issues. They can search these sites.

Thomas Web
> **URL: http://thomas.loc.gov/**
CapWeb: A Guide to the U.S. Congress
> **URL: http://policy.net/capweb**

EXTENSIONS:

1. Students who want to become more involved in women's issues can access the Women's Net Web site. They'll find contact information for dozens of national and international organizations. Give extra credit to students who write to and receive information from groups that interest them.
> **URL: http://www.igc.apc.org/womensnet/**

2. Have students write letters or send email to members of Congress and the president about women's issues important to them. For postal and email addresses for members of Congress, return to the Thomas Web site, or try these sites.
> **Gopher to: marvel.loc.gov**
Select the *U.S. Congress, Congressional Directories* menu
> **Email to: president@whitehouse.gov**

Notes:

Astronomy

Students are expected to use the Internet for research, to track solar flare activity, to correspond via email with a distant class, and to write a paper.

GRADE LEVELS: 8-12

OBJECTIVES:
• Use the Internet to learn about the Aurora Borealis, the Northern Lights.
• Investigate the effects of solar activity on the Earth, and describe the process that causes the Aurora Borealis.

MATERIALS:
• Personal computer with an Internet connection, including gopher, finger, email, ftp, and World Wide Web access

PROCEDURE:
1. Have students go online to learn all they can about the Aurora Borealis. Give them a list of questions to guide their research, including "What does the name *Aurora Borealis* mean?", "What causes Northern Lights?", "What are solar flares?", "Why is the effect visible only in certain locations?", and "What folklore is associated with the Aurora Borealis?" Instruct them to look for images of the Northern Lights.
   The Northern Lights Planetarium, Norway
   URL: http://www.uit.no/npt/homepage-npt.en.html (See Figure 1.4)

FIGURE 1.4

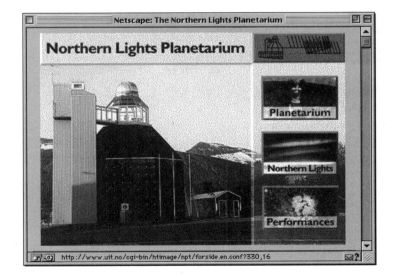

NASA SpaceLink
> **Telnet to: spacelink.msfc.nasa.gov**
> Select *Instructional Materials, Curriculum Materials* subdirectories

2. Track current solar flare and auroral activity by accessing Internet resources. Keep a log of the activity.

National Weather Service
> **Gopher to: ashpool.micro.umn.edu**
> Look in *Weather, Earthquakes-Tropical Storms-Auroral Activity*
> **Finger: aurora@xi.uleth.ca, solar@xi.uleth.ca** or **daily@xi.uleth.ca**

3. Contact and establish email correspondence with a class in Alaska or Canada. (See mailing list section of Chapter 3, Educational Resources.) Have students tell the Canadian or Alaskan students what they've learned about the Northern Lights and ask them questions. Ask students in the partner class to describe the Aurora Borealis and if they can send a videotape to your class.

4. Have students write a paper based on their findings, and include graphics they may have discovered. Material gathered from their email correspondence, such as personal observations of the effect, can be included.

EXTENSIONS:

1. Take a virtual field trip to observatories and planetariums to learn about their functions, see the facilities and equipment, and view some of their images, including downloadable .jpg and .gif images and moving picture or .mpeg clips. For an mpeg player:
> **Ftp to: ftp.classroom.net**
> Go to the *wentworth/Internet-Software/IBM* subdirectory. Select the *vmpeg.zip* file.

2. Have students write a brief thought-reaction paper describing what it would be like to be an astronomer. Would they consider it as a career? Why or why not?
> **URL: http://www.uit.no./npt/homepage-npt.en.html**

Northern Lights Planetarium
> The Anglo-Australian Observatory
> > **URL: http://www.aao.gov.au/images.html**
> National Optical Astronomy Observations
> > **URL: http://argo.tuc.noao.edu:80/nsokp/nsokp.html**
> Mount Wilson Observatory
> > **URL: http://www.mtwilson.edu**(See Figure 1.5)
> Dominion Radio Astrophysical Observatory
> > **URL: http://www.drao.nrc.ca**
> National Radio Astronomy Observatory
> > **URL: http://info.aoc.nrao.edu**

**FIGURE
1.5**

Chemistry (Hazardous Materials)

Students are expected to use the Internet for research, to design a database, to work in teams, and to write a report.

GRADE LEVELS: 9-12

OBJECTIVES:
• Identify hazardous chemicals commonly found in household products.
• Use gopher and the World Wide Web to find information about chemicals and their properties.
• Create a database using the results of the research on household chemicals.
• Learn about current plans for environmentally-sound disposal, recycling, or management of toxic chemicals.

MATERIALS:
• Personal computer with an Internet connection, including gopher, World Wide Web, and email access
• Database or graphing program

PROCEDURE:
1. Have students brainstorm about the products in their homes that they think might contain hazardous chemical substances. Have each student examine the labels on products at home during the next week and make a list of ingredients for several of them. Include cleaners, sprays, drain openers, bug sprays, and so forth. The list should include each product's name and household purpose, as well as contents. If ingredients aren't listed and time permits, students may write the manufacturer for content information.

2. Go over the findings in class and eliminate duplications to create a master list of products and chemicals to include in a database. Discuss as a class the fields to include in the database. Examples include names of the products, common uses, typical storage location in households, hazardous chemical ingredients, and non-hazardous ingredients. Help students design the database file.

3. Divide the class into small teams and give each one a portion of the database to complete. Students will need to find out which ingredients are hazardous and which are not.

The following Internet sites have specific information about various chemicals or dangerous substances.
Clearinghouse for Chemical Information Instructional Materials
   URL: http://www.rpi.edu:80/dept/chem/cheminfo/chemres.html#ccim
National Library of Medicine
   Gopher to: gopher.nlm.nih.gov
   Look in *teh, TEHIP Factsheets*
List of Carcinogens
   Gopher to: gopher.niehs.nih.gov
   Look in *NTP, ARC*
University of Virginia EcoGopher
   Gopher to: ecosys.drdr.virginia.edu (See Figure 1.6)
   Look in *Library, General, EPA Chemical Substance Factsheets*
Extremely Hazardous Substance List
   Gopher to: gopher.epa.gov
   Look in *Rules, Environmental Subset, EPA-WASTE, 1994, October, Day-12, pr-14*

4. After the database is complete, go online to find information about environmentally-sound disposal, recycling, or management of toxic chemicals and write a follow-up report. What steps are governments taking to address this issue? What responsibility does industry have to produce safer chemicals or use better disposal

methods? How much would such programs cost? Access the text of the agenda of the United Nations Environmental Conference.

Gopher to: gopher.inform.umd.edu

Look in *Educational Resources, Academic Resources By Topic, United States And World, World, International_Agencies, United Nations, EnvironConf, Agenda21, toxic-chemicals*

More information is also available at EcoGopher.

Gopher to: ecosys.drdr.virginia.edu

Look in *information, uva, recycling, Resource Recovery & Recycling Program*

FIGURE 1.6

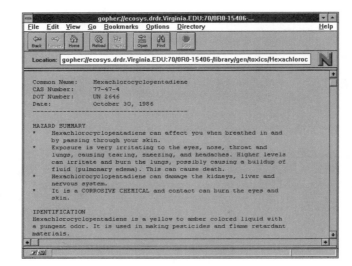

EXTENSIONS:

1. Have the class debate this question: How realistic is the United Nations agenda? Factors that could affect this include the economic consequences of implementing environmental programs, cultural differences, and the difficulty of enforcing international environmental laws. Have several students record the debate and use word processors to create text transcripts for the next step in the extension.

2. As a class, send email to members of Congress expressing concern about hazardous chemicals in household products. Use your research findings to offer solutions. Attach relevant materials such as your database, follow-up report on handling and disposal of chemicals, and debate transcripts. Instruct students on how to attach files to email messages. Use postal mail to reach members who aren't online, and include a brief paragraph explaining to the member why he or she should get an email account. Email this mailbot to find email addresses of members of Congress.

Email to: info@classroom.net

Type **send congress** in the body of the message.

Gopher to: vega.lib.ncsu.edu

Look in *Library, Disciplines, Government, Congress-Directory* and also *Library, Reference, Directories, Addresses, Finding-Addresses*

3. Send an email letter of support and a request for updated information to the U.N. Conference on the Environment and Development.

Email to: unced@igc.org

Chemistry (Periodic Table)

Students are expected to use the Internet for research, to contact chemistry professionals online, and to write a report.

GRADE LEVELS: 9-12

OBJECTIVES:
• Use the Internet to find information about the Periodic Table of the Elements and specific elements and chemical bonds.
• Learn about new developments in chemistry.
• Use online tools to communicate with chemistry professionals.

MATERIALS:
• Personal computer with an Internet connection, including telnet, gopher, World Wide Web, newsgroup, and email access
• Word processor and graphics-capable printer
• Desktop publishing or presentation software

PROCEDURE:
(Note: Because of the extensive Internet searching required for this project, teachers may want to make it a term or year-long assignment.)

1. After the class learns about and understands the Periodic Table of the Elements, show students how the field of chemistry is constantly evolving. Give examples of new uses or findings for elements. Or, discuss recent discoveries uncovering new knowledge of how elements or chemicals interact.

2. Assign each student one element from the Periodic Table. Instruct them to look for basic information such as atomic weight, density, reactivity, and general descriptions. They will also search for new findings about elements and how elements are used in day-to-day life. They will prepare a report on their findings.

If necessary, teach students to use the various Internet tools and remind them to adhere to the rules of netiquette. They can start with these online resources and can also use Internet search tools such as WAIS and Veronica.

Chemistry Resources on the Internet via Marvel
    Gopher to: marvel.loc.gov
    Look in *global, sci, chem, guides*
Davidson Library, University of California Santa Barbara
    Gopher to: ucsbuxa.ucsb.edu:3001 (See Figure 1.6)
    Look in *The Subject Collections, Chemistry*
Chemistry and Materials via NASA SCAN
    Gopher to: gopher.sti.nasa.gov
    Look in *NASA SCAN, Current Issue of SCAN by subject categories, 23, Chemistry and Materials*
Chemistry resources via University of California, Berkeley
    URL: http://www.cchem.berkeley.edu (See Figure 1.7)
U.S. Environmental Protection Agency Chemical Substance Fact Sheets
    Gopher to: ecosys.drdr.virginia.edu
    Look in The *Library, General, EPA Chemical Substance Factsheets*

WebElements
  URL: http://www2.shef.ac.uk/chemistry/web-elements/web-elements-home.html
Naval Research Laboratory
Science and Engineering at Washington University
  Telnet to: library.wustl.edu
  Select the *Resources by Subject, Science and Engineering* menu
American Chemical Society
  Gopher to: acsinfo.acs.org

FIGURE 1.7

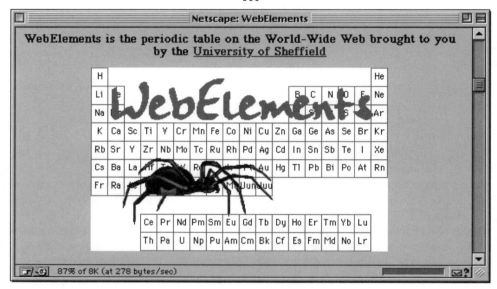

3. Besides accessing these online materials, students can use more interactive resources such as newsgroups and mailing lists to get information directly from experts.

Mailing Lists:
  Subscribe to these moderated chemistry-related mailing lists to find contacts for information about the elements. Read the list rules and regulations you will receive after subscribing.

BIOPI-L	Biology Teaching Enhancement
CHEMED-L	Chemistry Education
CHMINF-L	Chemical Information Sources
SAIS-L	Science Awareness and Promotion

Newsgroups:

     k12.chat.teacher

     sci.chem

     sci.chem.organomet

     sci.engr.chem

     sci.polymers

4. Have students organize their research and develop outlines for their papers. Review each student's outline to make sure he or she has enough relevant information to complete the project. Give students plenty of time to complete the papers.

EXTENSIONS:

1. If your school has access to presentation software such as Linkway, Powerpoint, or Astound, have each student convert his or her report into a computerized presentation. They can then incorporate text, graphics, sound, and video. Students could also design more basic presentations using desktop software, a color printer, and overhead transparencies.

2. Discuss as a class the value of using the Internet for researching and communicating chemistry information. For example, how did finding data online differ from, say, using more traditional reference works such as *The Handbook of Chemistry and Physics*? How do the multimedia capabilities of the Internet enhance or detract from the study of chemistry?

Notes:

Economics (Stocks)

Students are required to pick stocks, track their progress via the Internet, and try an online stock market simulation.

GRADE LEVELS: 11-12

OBJECTIVES:
• Understand how the stock market works and what factors affect it.
• Participate in simulated market transactions and track progress of investments.
• Practice using the Internet to find information on specific topics.

MATERIALS:
• Personal computer with an Internet connection, including World Wide Web, gopher, and telnet access
• Word processor and printer

PROCEDURE:
1. Provide an overview of how the stock market works. Explain the traditional methods of tracking stock activity, such as newspapers and brokerage services.

2. Have each student pick one to five stocks to monitor for several weeks. Each student should keep a log of their stocks' activities. Use these Internet resources to access up-to-date stock market information and news that could affect their holdings.

MIT Stock Market Data
URL: http://www.ai.mit.edu/stocks.html

Quote.com
URL: http://www.quote.com (See Figure 1.8)

FIGURE 1.8

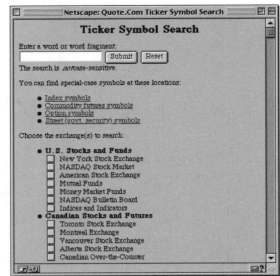

3. Using the same selected stocks, have students try out an online, interactive stock market simulation via the PAWWS Portfolio Management Challenge, a free financial service on the World Wide Web. Or use stock market simulations found in most commercial online services. Students will buy, sell, and value their portfolios for a specified period of time. Students should carefully read the rules and instructions first. Each student should print out their stock information and keep it in a binder.

PAWWS Portfolio Management Challenge

URL: http://pawws.secapl.com/G_phtml/top.html

Click on *Portfolio Management Challenge* for an overview, then jump back to play the simulation. Teachers may want to review these materials first.

4. At the end of the simulation, the class should examine each student's results and announce the "Financial Wizard" award winner.

EXTENSIONS:

1. Invite a local stock broker or financial analyst, preferably one knowledgeable about financial resources on the Internet, to speak to the class. Compose a list of questions to ask in class or send a list to the volunteer before the visit.

2. Explore other sources of information about the stock market and economics in general at the Economics Area of Sam Houston State University's Gopher Server. Using all the resources in this plan, have students publish their own directory of online financial information.

Gopher to: niord.shsu.edu

Look in *Economics*

Notes:

Endangered Species

Students are expected to use the Internet for research, to create a database, and to make an oral presentation using multimedia tools.

GRADE LEVELS: 10-12

OBJECTIVES:
• Use the Internet to find information about endangered species.
• Learn the differences between the term *extinct, endangered,* and *threatened.*
• Learn about the wide variety of organisms that are threatened and about specific endangered or threatened species.
• Understand the relationship between humans and extinction.
• Practice using email, telnet, and gopher.

MATERIALS:
• Personal computer with an Internet connection, including email, telnet, and gopher access
• Database program
• Graphing program
• Simple desktop publishing program

PROCEDURE:
1. Find definitions of *extinct, endangered,* and *threatened* by telnetting to the Aquatic Conservation Network.
Telnet to: freenet.carleton.ca
Login: **guest**
Go to *5. Social Services, Health, and Environment; 1. The Environment; 13. Table of Contents for Environment.* Choose the menu item for the ACN.
2. Ask students what they know about extinct or endangered species, and record results on a list.
3. Create a database of endangered species. Decide on fields to include in the database. Be sure to include the reason the species became endangered. Limit the database to type of animal or geographic location, if necessary. Students can use gopher to find the information they need.
Ecogopher at University of Virginia
Gopher to: ecosys.drdr.virginia.edu
NASA
Gopher to: quest.arc.nasa.gov
4. Ask each student to pick one organism from the database to research more extensively. Have them make an oral presentation about their organism, preferably using multimedia tools such as slides or video.
5. Group organisms in the database by cause of endangerment to determine the number endangered by each cause. Graph data using a simple computer graphing program.
6. Discuss the causes of endangerment and how humans contribute.
7. Find information about the Endangered Species Act and other legislation by gophering to the Library of Congress.
Gopher to: marvel.loc.gov

EXTENSIONS:

1. Share findings with others by joining the Envirolink Network. Telnet to the network and follow the instructions to access Envirolink's resources.

Telnet to: envirolink.org (See Fig. 1.9)

FIGURE 1.9

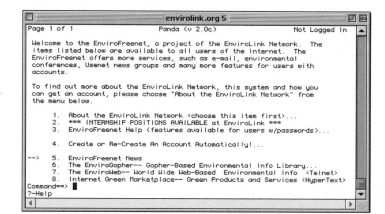

```
┌─────────────────────────────────────────────────────────────┐
│ □▤              envirolink.org 5                    ▣▤ │
│ Page 1 of 1              Panda (v 2.0c)         Not Logged In ▲│
│ Welcome to the EnviroFreenet, a project of the EnviroLink Network.  The │
│ items listed below are available to all users of the Internet.  The │
│ EnviroFreenet offers more services, such as e-mail, environmental │
│ conferences, Usenet news groups and many more features for users with │
│ accounts.                                                      │
│                                                                │
│ To find out more about the EnviroLink Network, this system and how you │
│ can get an account, please choose "About the EnviroLink Network" from │
│ the menu below.                                                │
│                                                                │
│    1.   About the EnviroLink Network <choose this item first>... │
│    2.   *** INTERNSHIP POSITIONS AVAILABLE at EnviroLink *** │
│    3.   EnviroFreenet Help (features available for users w/passwords)... │
│                                                                │
│    4.   Create or Re-Create An Account Automatically!... │
│                                                                │
│ -->  5.   EnviroFreenet News                                  │
│      6.   The EnviroGopher-- Gopher-Based Environmental Info Library... │
│      7.   The EnviroWeb-- World Wide Web-Based Environmental Info  <Telnet> │
│      8.   Internet Green Marketplace-- Green Products and Services <HyperText> ▼│
│ Command==> ▮                                                   │
│ ?-Help                                                         ▼│
│ ◄                                                            ► │
└─────────────────────────────────────────────────────────────┘
```

2. Have students email members of Congress for more information about current legislation. Use email to obtain a list of members of Congress with Internet email addresses.

Email to: info@classroom.net

Type **send congress** in the body of your message.

3. Produce ads or "advertorials" promoting conservation on a desktop publishing system. Try to have a representative few included in the school newspaper or perhaps even the local paper.

Notes:

Geography

Students are required to do research using the Internet, work in teams, and write a paper about a city's geography.

GRADE LEVEL: 2–6

OBJECTIVES:
• Understand the concept of longitude and latitude.
• Use Internet resources to find the coordinates of various locations around the world.
• Work cooperatively with other students.

MATERIALS:
• Personal computer with an Internet connection, including gopher, ftp, and World Wide Web access
• Teacher-prepared worksheets with a list of coordinates to identify and a list of locations for which to find coordinates.

PROCEDURE:
1. Define *latitude* and *longitude.* Explain or ask the class to discuss how these concepts are used every day (e.g., boats, airplanes, cartography, satellite communications). If time permits, provide a brief account of the development of this navigational tool.

2. Divide the class into small teams. Give each a handout containing 10–20 (depending on the size of teams) coordinates of cities around the world.

3. Have each team use the Internet to find information to help them match the coordinates with their respective cities. They can connect to the U.S. Geographic Name Server.
   URL: http://www-lib.iupui.edu/erefs/geogname.html
   Look in *Libraries and Information Access, Reference Sources, U.S. Geographic Names Database*
   Students can also use two World Wide Web sites—one maintained by Xerox and another called City.net, a guide to communities around the world.
   Xerox Palo Alto Research Center
   URL: http://pubweb.parc.xerox.com/map/
   City.net Guide
   URL: http://www.city.net (See Fig. 1.10)
   The CIA World Factbook also contains lots of pertinent information. Let students download it via ftp and instruct them how to search text by keyword to find the data they need. The complete file is quite large, however, so it may take several minutes to download.
   CIA World Factbook
   Gopher to: wiretap.spies.com
   Look in *Electronic Books at Wiretap*

4. Give each team a list of cities without coordinates, which they must find. They can use the Internet resources cited previously or try this ftp site, a FreeNet in Canada, where students can find the specific latitude/longitude for a given location.
   Ftp to: ftp.cs.toronto.edu
   Select the *doc/geography/USLat-Long* subdirectory
   Also see the *doc/geography/CIA_World_Map* subdirectory

5. When the teams have completed both worksheets, have each student pick one city from the list. Using the previously mentioned or different Internet resources, have them write a brief report about the city's geography. Students with very specific questions or who want to tap a human resource can ask for help from subscribers to these geography mailing lists.

GEOGRAPH is a global email conference for general or topical discussions about geographical issues.

GEOGRAPHY is a global list for all geographers.

> **Email to: Listserv@searn.sunet.se**
>
> Type **SUBSCRIBE <GEOGRAPH** or **GEOGRAPHY> <your name>** in the message body.

FIGURE 1.10

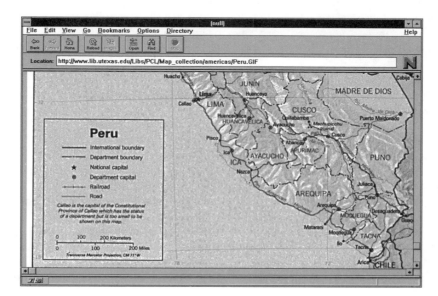

Notes:

Geography (Maps)

Students are expected to use the Internet to find maps, to compose email offline, and to correspond with a distant partner class.

GRADE LEVELS: 3–5

OBJECTIVES:
• Practice using email or telecommunications software.
• Communicate with a distant class via email.
• Use the Internet to find maps and practice using them to find specific locations.
• Practice using a word processor.

MATERIALS:
• Personal computer with an Internet (or commercial online service) connection, including email, World Wide Web, and ftp access
• Graphics viewer
• Word processor and printer

PROCEDURE:
1. Prior to beginning this lesson, find a class of roughly the same size to communicate with via email, preferably one in a faraway state or in another country. Post queries to the appropriate education newsgroups or mailing lists (See mailing list and newsgroup sections of Chapter 3, Educational Resources.)

2. Inform students they will exchange email with a distant class to find out how much alike or different they are from students from other regions or countries. Make sure they know how to use a word processor to compose email offline.

3. To help students understand the partner class' location, have small groups use the Internet to find maps to help them pinpoint the location of their partner class. Have students print, color, illustrate, and label the maps, and redraw them on large posterboards. Display the maps in a prominent location so students see where the partner class is situated and can grasp the geographical distance between the classes. These sites feature maps.

URL: http://pubweb.parc.xerox.com/map/
URL: http://www.cp.tn.tudelft.nl/maps.html
URL: http://www.vtourist.com/
URL: http://www.neosoft.com/citylink
Ftp to: gatekeeper.dec.com
Look in the *pub/maps* subdirectory
URL: http://www.usgs.gov/

If time permits, try using an Internet search tool to find maps and geographical information about the location of the partner class. Enter **map and** and then the name of the city, state, or country where they live as your keywords.

Gopher to: veronica.scs.unr.edu
URL: http://www.webcrawler.com/

4. After students are familiar with the location of the partner class, let each student pick a question to ask one of the students. Here are some samples.

What time do you usually get up in the morning? What do you eat for breakfast?

What kinds of clothes do you wear to school?

What time do you go to school?

How far do you live from your school? How do you get there? How long does it take?

When does your school year begin and end?

What's the first thing you do when you get to school?

What do you like to study most of all? What's your favorite class?

What's the hardest subject you have at school?

What sports do you like to play at school?

What's your favorite lunch menu?

What do you usually do after school but before dinner?

What time do you usually go to bed?

What's the weather like where you live?

What's the geography like where you live?

Have each student use a word processor to compose the email offline. Email the messages to the partner class, which should randomly distribute them. Each student in the partner class should return an email with an answer to the question, plus a new question (each response should be no less than 100 words). Students should keep printed versions of all question and answer exchanges.

5. After each student has asked and answered a question, go over the results as a class. Ask students to talk about things they had in common, and things that were different. Were there any surprises?

EXTENSION:

Students can continue to exchange email throughout the year for a variety of purposes. They can exchange ideas for papers, help each other with math or other homework problems, or simply write back and forth for fun. For extra credit, have students write a brief paper at the end of the school year on how their online friendships progressed or what new things they learned by communicating with their distant friends.

Notes:

Geography (The States)

Students are expected to use the Internet to do research and to use a variety of tools to write and illustrate a book.

GRADE LEVELS: 3–6

OBJECTIVES:
• Create an A-Z illustrated handbook about a specific state using a computer.
• Practice finding information on the Internet.

MATERIALS:
• Personal computer with an Internet connection, including gopher, World Wide Web, and email access
• Word processor and simple illustration or layout software
• Graphics-capable printer
• Paper, markers, and other art supplies

PROCEDURE:
1. Students will each make a book about a state of their choosing and pretend their books are to educate students visiting the United States for the first time.

Each page of a student's book will represent a letter of the alphabet and will present a fact that begins with that letter. The fact can be several paragraphs, a picture, or an illustration on a topic relevant to that state. For example, the "A" page for Florida might have a student's drawing of alligators; the "A" page for Pennsylvania might have a picture of an Amish buggy; and the "A" page for Ohio might include a list of facts about "Akron," the state capital. Students can include whatever they want, but they must explain how it is relevant to their state.

2. Have students use the Internet and the school library to find information about their state. Be flexible about how they create their books—students can draw pictures or use photographs taken during a vacation to the state. Challenge them to come up with creative entries. These Internet resources can help.

U.S. States via EINet Galaxy World Wide Web page

URL: http://galaxy.einet.net/galaxy/Community/US-States.html (See Figure 1.11)

FIGURE 1.11

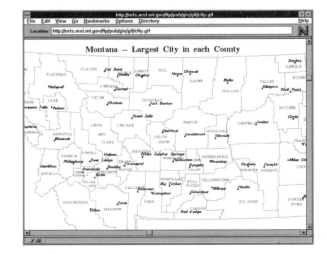

U.S. Census
> **Gopher to: riceinfo.rice.edu**
> Look in *Information by Subject Area, Census*

Bureau of Economics Gross State Products
> **Gopher to: una.hh.lib.umich.edu**
> Look in *GSP*
> (See Figure 1.12)

FIGURE 1.12

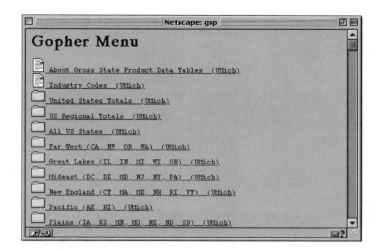

Students can also use Internet search tools such as Veronica or WAIS to find information by doing keyword searches.

3. Instruct students to employ a variety of tools to complete their books. They can use word processors, illustration or desktop publishing software, graphics downloaded from the Internet, colored markers, or other art supplies.

4. Give each student a folder or binder for his or her work. Set aside class time so students can exchange books before taking them home.

EXTENSIONS:

1. As a class, discuss the various entries for each student's book. Which pages could only belong to a certain state? Could any pages fit into almost any state's book?

2. Find partner classes overseas who would like to learn more about the individual states. Send them copies of the students' work. You could also set up email or Internet Relay Chat conversations between your students and students from the states they studied. (See Appendix B for Internet Relay Chat instructions.)

Geography (Travel)

Students are expected to discuss how to prepare travel and tourism information, use the Internet to find travel information about a specific location, create a travel schedule, create brochures using a word processor and desktop publishing program, and do a brief presentation.

GRADE LEVELS: 7-12

OBJECTIVES:
• Discuss travel and tourism and explore the geography of specific locations via the Internet.
• Practice writing in promotional style.

MATERIALS:
• Personal computer with Internet access, including Web and gopher software
• Word processor and graphics-capable printer
• Desktop publishing or graphics viewer program
• Overhead projector, presentation software, posterboard and markers, or other multimedia tools

PROCEDURE:
1. Tell students that they are going to become travel agents and create travel brochures and presentations for imaginary clients. Groups or individual students can choose places they've always wanted to visit. Or, they can explore the resources listed in step three to help them decide.

2. As a class, review some important considerations before preparing the travel materials. What information would potential travelers want? How effective are graphics or photos? Should the brochures include any "negative" information (e.g., crime rates or unfavorable currency rates)? Should they cover language barriers or local customs?

3. Have students use the Internet to find as much information about the travel destination as possible. They should download and print as much data as they can, keeping it in a binder for future reference. They can start at these sites.

Elnet Galaxy's Travel Index
   URL: http://galaxy.einet.net/galaxy/Leisure-and-Recreation/Travel.html (See Figure 1.13)
Foreign Languages for Travelers
   URL: http://www.travlang.com/languages
International Travel Tips
   Gopher to: uabdpo.dpo.uab.edu
   Look in *Information, Travel*
U.S. State Department Travel Advisories
   Gopher to: gopher.stolaf.edu
   Look in *Internet Resources, State Department Travel*
Advisories
GNN Travel Center
   URL: http://nearnet.gnn.com/meta/travel/
   index.html

**FIGURE
1.13**

CIA World Factbook
Gopher to: wiretap.spies.com
Look in *Electronic Books at Wiretap*

4. Each group or student should pick travel dates for their imaginary clients, then create a schedule with departure/arrival dates and times. Use the Internet as much as possible to find actual flight, ship, train, or bus schedules, or ask local travel agents to provide information.

Airline Information
Gopher to: cs4sun.cs.ttu.edu
Look in *Reference Shelf, Airline Toll-Free Numbers*

Amtrak Online
Gopher to: gwis.circ.gwu.edu
Look in *General Information, Train Schedules*

Oceanic Ship Information/Cruise Schedule Databases
Gopher to: diu.cms.udel.edu
Look in *Ship Schedules*

5. Give the students one week to use information in their binders to help them create their brochures. Have them use a word processor and desktop publishing software. Emphasize the importance of organized, professional-looking work. To find examples of travel brochures they can access these Internet resources.

Moon Travel Handbook
URL: http://www.book.uci.edu/Books/Moon/moon.html

Aspen Snowmass OnLine
URL: http://www.infosphere.com/aspenonline/

Aalborg Guide to Denmark
URL: http://www.info.denet.dk/denmark.html

A Personal Guide to Paris
URL: http://meteora.ucsd.edu/~norman/paris/Expos/PersonalView

6. Have each student pass out copies of his or her brochure and do a brief presentation for the class. Have students ask the presenter questions to test his or her knowledge of the travel destination.

EXTENSIONS:

1. Invite a travel agent to speak to the class. Give the agent copies of each student's travel brochure in advance, and ask him or her to provide a "professional critique." Students should also come to class with questions about being a travel agent.

2. Have students write a brief report about one of these topics:
• Of all the destinations, which one would you choose for your vacation and why?
• What did you like best about being a travel agent? What did you like least?
• Do you think the Internet will change the travel industry? Why?

Notes:

Geology (Earthquakes)

Students are expected to discuss earthquakes, use the Internet regularly to access earthquake information, use maps, and use email to correspond with a distant class.

GRADE LEVELS: 3–5

OBJECTIVES:
• Discuss what earthquakes are, what causes them, and how they're predicted and measured.
• Access earthquake information using the Internet.
• Find areas in the United States and around the world at greater risk of earthquakes.
• Associate earthquake locations with plate boundaries.

MATERIALS:
• Personal computer with an Internet connection, including gopher, email, and finger access
• United States and world maps

PROCEDURE:
1. Post United States and world maps on the classroom wall.

2. Survey students to learn what they know about earthquakes. Provide an overview of what causes earthquakes, their effects, and how scientists monitor and predict earthquake activity. Discuss relevant terms such as geology, seismic activity, plates, the Richter scale, and fault lines.

3. Use the Internet to access earthquake information on a regular basis and mark on the maps areas experiencing seismic activity.

University of Tennessee Department of Geological Sciences
Gopher to: tanasi.gg.utk.edu
Look in *Earthquakes*

St. Olaf College
Gopher to: gopher.stolaf.edu
Look in *Internet Resources, Weather and Geography*

Northwestern University Geology Department
Gopher to: earth.nwu.edu
Look in *Seismology Resources*

Pacific Northwest Seismograph Network
Finger: quake@geophys.washington.edu

Center for Wave Phenomena
Gopher to: cwp.mines.colorado.edu:3852

4. Look for and describe patterns of earthquake occurrences in the United States and around the world. Compare your earthquake map to another map showing the positions of plate boundaries.

5. Find a class in a quake-intensive state or country to communicate with via email. (See Chapter 3, Educational Resources, for mailing lists you can use to post queries.) Have students ask teachers and students in the other class what it's like to experience a quake. Was it frightening? Do they worry about earthquakes? What precautions do they have to take?

EXTENSIONS:
1. Study the geography and geology of the San Andreas Fault. Use the previous gopher sites to obtain data

about quakes along the fault. Find historical documentation of infamous earthquakes occurring along the fault line, such as the 1903 San Francisco quake.

2. Visit this site to access up-to-date information about the more recent Northridge earthquake.

California State University Northridge

Gopher to: huey.csun.edu

Look in *The Campus at California State University Northridge, Academic, Schools, Departments and Services, School of Science and Math, Geological Sciences, Latest Earthquake Information*

Notes:

Global Warming

Students are expected to use gopher and find information, to organize information, to write an essay, to exchange ideas via email, and to publish a report.

GRADE LEVELS: 6–9

OBJECTIVES:
• Find information on global warming on the Internet via gopher.
• Explain the process that heats the lower atmosphere.
• List the ways that humans contribute to global warming.

MATERIALS:
• Personal computer with an Internet connection, including gopher and email access
• A word processor

PROCEDURE:
1. Connect to the Internet. Have students find information about global warming by accessing the EcoGopher at the University of Virginia.
   Gopher to: ecosys.drdr.virginia.edu (See Figure 1.14)
   Look in *The Library* to start the search

FIGURE 1.14

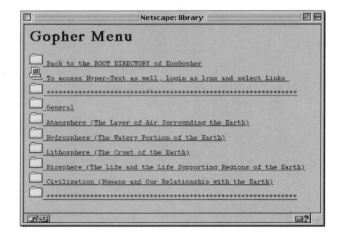

Netscape: library

Gopher Menu

Back to the ROOT DIRECTORY of EcoGopher

To access Hyper-Text as well, login as lynx and select Links

****

General

Atmosphere (The Layer of Air Surrounding the Earth)

Hydrosphere (The Watery Portion of the Earth)

Lithosphere (The Crust of the Earth)

Biosphere (The Life and the Life Supporting Regions of the Earth)

Civilization (Humans and Our Relationship with the Earth)

****

Also use the gopher at the Finnish Research Programme at the Academy of Finland.
   Gopher to: gopher.aka.fi
   Look in *The Finnish Research Programme on Climate Change*
2. Based on information from the gopher sites, have students compile a list of human activities that contribute to global warming. Discuss the Greenhouse Effect's consequences on the environment.
3. Using a word processor, have students write a story describing life on Earth if the temperature increased a few degrees.

4. Hold a "world conference" with classes from two other countries through Kidsphere, a mailing list providing an international forum for students and teachers to discuss ongoing projects. Trade ideas about what could be done about global warming.

Email to: kidsphere-request@vms.cis.pitt.edu

Type **subscribe kidsphere <your name>** in the body. Leave the subject line blank.

5. Publish a report on the conference results.

EXTENSIONS:

1. Send the president of the United States a copy of your report and express your concerns.

Email to: president@whitehouse.gov

2. Gopher to the Environmental Protection Agency site for related resources.

Gopher to: gopher.epa.gov

Look in *What's New on the EPA Servers* ànd *What's Hot on the EPA Servers*

Notes:

Government (American and Soviet)

Students are required to download materials from the Internet, discuss the style and rhetoric of political writings, use a word processor, search the Internet via keywords, and write a paper about Russia and the former U.S.S.R.

GRADE LEVELS: 7-12

OBJECTIVES:
• Learn the differences between the values in the *Communist Manifesto* and the Declaration of Independence, and how they were characterized through the relations between the two governments and societies during the Cold War years.
• Compare and contrast the tone and language of the U.S. and Soviet government documents.
• Explore the Soviet Archives Exhibit via the Internet to learn how Communist theory translated into everyday Soviet life.
• Write a paper about one subject in Russian history or culture.
• Practice using the Internet as a research tool.

MATERIALS:
• Personal computer with Internet access, including World Wide Web, gopher, and ftp software
• Word processor

PROCEDURE:
1. Provide a brief overview of the events leading to the development of Communism, and then the Cold War. Students should be familiar with the Declaration of Independence and the evolution of the U.S. Constitution.
2. Find and download the complete text of the *Communist Manifesto* by gophering to this location.
Gopher to: wiretap.spies.com
Look in *The Library, Classics*
For U.S. historical documents, look in *Government Documents, U.S. Historical Documents*
Have students examine the dictionary meaning of *manifesto*. Identify language in the document that qualifies the work as such and have students find key points and phrases from the document. As a class, discuss the tone, language, and euphemisms in the writing. Provide them with keywords such as "liberty," "property," "rights," and "labor." Instruct them to use the word processor's "search" or "find" function to jump to noteworthy sections.
3. Use the World Wide Web to visit the first floor of the Library of Congress' Soviet Archives to see how ideas in the *Manifesto* translated into everyday life. For example, discuss how the language and ideas found in the *Manifesto* led to living conditions not necessarily envisioned by its authors.
URL: http://sunsite.unc.edu/expo/soviet.exhibit/soviet.archive.html (See Figure 1.15)
Have students discuss how the ideas expressed in the Constitution and the Declaration of Independence are translated in everyday life in the United States. Have students give examples for both countries.
4. Visit the second floor of the exhibit to read about Soviet-American relations during the Cold War.
5. Create a list of possible essay or term paper subjects. Have each student or small teams of students choose one. Topics could include the lives of Marx or Engels, living conditions under Stalin, Russian culture, the Soviet-U.S. nuclear arms race, the economic consequences of communism, the attempted coup of 1991, or any topic covered in the Soviet Archives.

FIGURE 1.15

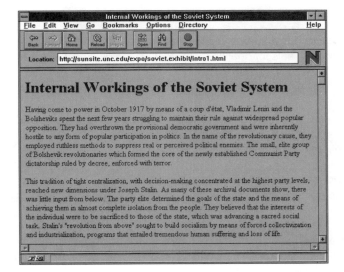

6. Have students use the Internet to research their topics. A good place to start is this home page on the Web.

ElNet's Galaxy Home Page

URL: http://galaxy.einet.net/galaxy.html

Scroll to the bottom to find the search interface. Enter a keyword, click on the World Wide Web and Gopher buttons, and select a maximum number of "hits" (resources found on the Internet) to return. Students may need to practice selecting keywords until they find enough leads for research.

(Note: Some search results will point to non-Web Internet addresses. If the school's Web browser doesn't support ftp, telnet, or gopher file types, launch those applications separately.)

Here are more Internet sites about Russia.

Window to Russia

URL: http://www.kiae.su/www/wtr/

St. Petersburg Web

URL: http://www.spb.su/

State Department Travel Advisory for Russia

Gopher to: gopher.stolaf.edu

Look in *Internet Resources, US-State-Department, Travel-Advisories, Current-Advisories, Russia*

Dazhdbog's Grandchildren (Russian culture and heritage)

URL: http://sunsite.oit.unc.edu/sergei/Grandsons.html

USA-Russia Friends and Partners Project

URL: http://april.ibpm.serpukhov.su:80/friends

Novgorod on the Web

URL: http://www.city.net/countries/russia/novgorod/

Health and Nutrition

Students are required to clip ads from print media, work in teams, use gopher to research food and nutrition, use software to plan nutritional meals for one week, do cost estimates, and make a presentation.

GRADE LEVELS: 3–6

OBJECTIVES:
• Find information about the food groups in the Food Guide Pyramid.
• List foods that fulfill nutritional requirements for protein, carbohydrates, fat, minerals, and vitamins.
• Design a balanced menu.
• Practice using the Internet to find information and download software.
• Find and try interesting food recipes.

MATERIALS:
• Personal computer with an Internet connection, including gopher, ftp, and telnet access
• Printer
• Magazine or newspapers with food advertisements

PROCEDURE:
1. Several weeks before beginning the project in class, have students collect food ads from newspapers or magazines.
2. Have teams of students use gopher to find information about the Pyramid food groups and to list the foods that fill certain nutritional requirements. Direct them to find as much specific data on proteins, carbohydrates, fats, vitamins, and minerals as they can. Allow them plenty of time to explore the following resources.
Penn State's PENpages
Gopher to: penpages.psu.edu (See Figure 1.16)
Look in *Alphabetical Keyword List, F, Food Guide* and *Food Guide Pyramid*
Also look in *Alphabetical Keyword List, N, Nutrient*

FIGURE 1.16

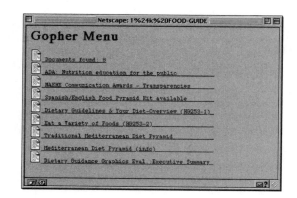

FDA's New Nutritional Pyramid Chart

Telnet to: fedworld.gov

If this is your first visit to this site, follow the simple login instructions. Select *Consumer Information Center's BBS* and look for the *pyramide.txt* file.

The following gopher site is also helpful.

Gopher to: unix5.nysed.gov

Look in *K–12 resources, Health-PhysEd-HomeEd, Home Economics*

Students can also find plenty of information on diet and nutrition by searching the Electronic Newsstand:

Gopher to: gopher.enews.com

Look in *Search All Electronic Newsstand Articles by Keyword*

Keywords they could use for the search include Nutrition, Diet, Food, Recommended Daily Allowance (RDA), and Vitamins.

Note: If you have access to a major commercial online service, have students search that database as well. The services offer plenty of information about diet and nutrition.

3. Meet with each team to find out what they have discovered. Explain to each group that it will plan a three-meal-a-day, nutritionally-balanced menu for one week. Help students download and set up free menu planning and shopping software via ftp. DOS computer users can find the software at this site.

Ftp to: ftp.cia.indiana.edu

Go to *pub/pc/win3/misc* subdirectory

4. Use the food advertisements the class gathered to help each team figure the cost of its proposed menu. Have each team use the software to create and print menus, then have them present the menus to the class with explanations of their selections.

EXTENSION:

Have students find unusual but nutritional recipes on the Internet to download, print, and take home to use. Ask them to write a brief report about the recipe. Was the meal tasty? Satisfying? Hard to prepare?

Ftp to: oak.oakland.edu

Select the *SimTel/win3/food* subdirectory and look for *ucook10a.zip* and *ucook10b.zip*

Gopher to: spinaltap.micro.umn.edu

Look in *Fun, Recipes*

Gopher to: gdim.geod.emr.ca

Look in *Vegetarian Info, Recipes*

Ftp to: newton.uiowa.edu

Select the *pub/software/medical-health/gut_buster.hqx* subdirectory

Notes:

Life in Space

Students are expected to use the Internet to research life on the space shuttle, to analyze and discuss findings, to write a descriptive paragraph, to draw pictures, and to create a scrapbook.

GRADE LEVELS: K–3

OBJECTIVES:
• Use the Internet to find information about the space shuttle and life in space.
• List things humans need to live on the space shuttle.
• Describe daily life on the space shuttle.
• Learn how to use gopher and finger programs to retrieve information.

MATERIALS:
• Personal computer with an Internet connection, gopher, and finger software
• Freeze dried food and Tang
• VCR
• Model of the space shuttle

PROCEDURE:
    1. Watch a taped or live space shuttle launch.
    2. Examine a model of the shuttle and talk about the purpose of its various parts.
    3. Use the finger command to find current news about NASA and the space shuttle over several days.
    Finger: nasanews@space.mit.edu
After reading the text, talk about the astronauts' daily activities and post a brief article daily for the rest of the school.
    4. Have students draw a picture of the shuttle orbiting Earth. Talk about what the astronauts had to take with them to survive. List the things humans need to live and put them in order from most to least important.
    5. Learn about the food astronauts take on shuttle flights by accessing NASA SpaceLink documents via gopher server or World Wide Web.
    Gopher to: spacelink.msfc.nasa.gov (See Figure 1.17)
    Look in *Instructional materials, Interdisciplinary*

**FIGURE
1.17**

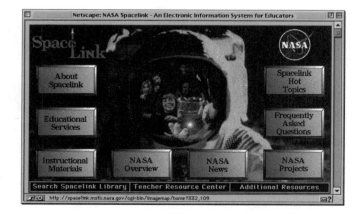

URL: http://spacelink.msfc.nasa.gov/Instructional.Materials/Interdisciplinary.Materials/

Based on the information, define dehydrated food and discuss why food on the shuttle must be dehydrated.

6. Make a meal from freeze dried food, serving Tang as a beverage. If real freeze dried foods are unavailable, use dried fruits and beef jerky.

7. Have students draw a picture of the meal. Include a paragraph explaining how it tasted. Combine the pictures from step four and this step to create a mini-space shuttle scrapbook for each student.

Notes:

Mathematics

Students are required to use the library to do preliminary research, to construct a database, to work in teams to find information on the Internet, to search the Internet using Veronica or WAIS, and to use email to exchange results with classes in other countries.

GRADE LEVELS: 7-10

OBJECTIVES:
• Use the Internet to search for information on the history of mathematics.
• Practice using gopher and telnet to collect, organize, store, and retrieve data.
• Create a database of information about mathematicians.
• Use email to communicate with distant classes.
• Work cooperatively in teams.

MATERIALS:
• Personal computer with an Internet connection, including email, gopher, and telnet access
• Word processor and database programs

PROCEDURE:
1. One month before beginning the lesson, telnet to the Cleveland Freenet and register as a new user.
Telnet to: freenet-in-a.cwru.edu
or **freenet-in-b.cwru.edu**
or **freenet-in-c.cwru.edu**
Login: Type **2** to enter as a visitor.
Look for *Academy One*, an experimental program designed to meet the information and communication needs of students and educators, on the menu. Register your class as an Academy One school. Using the Academy One database, find and print a list of Academy One schools outside the U.S.
2. Discuss why it's important to learn about the cultural and historical evolution of mathematics. Talk about how people of diverse backgrounds and cultures shaped the modern study of mathematics.
3. Have students use library materials to compile a list of important figures in the history of mathematics. Establish project teams and divide the list among them.
4. As a class, discuss what kinds of information students found during their research that they would like to include in a database. Possible fields include date of birth and death, nationality, occupations, interesting facts, and mathematical "claims to fame." If necessary, demonstrate how to create a database document with blank entry fields. Print and make copies for students to use while gathering information.
5. Have students logon to the Internet to find the information they need to complete their databases. First search all of gopherspace.
Gopher to: veronica.scs.unr.edu
To do a WAIS search of the World Wide Web, telnet or point the Web browser to a WAIS server and enter the appropriate keywords for which to search.
Telnet to: sunsite.unc.edu
Login: **wais**
or **URL: http://wais.com**
Have students access other online resources to complete their databases.

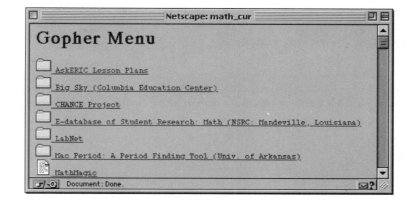

**FIGURE
1.18**

Database of Student Research in Math
> **Gopher to: hub.terc.edu** (See Figure 1.18)
> Look in *Resources for Mathematics and Science Education, Mathematics*

History of Math
> **Gopher to: gopher.cic.net**
> Look in *cicnet-gophers, K–12-gopher, Classroom, History of Math*

MathSource Gopher
> **Gopher to: gopher.wri.com** (See Figure 1.19)

**FIGURE
1.19**

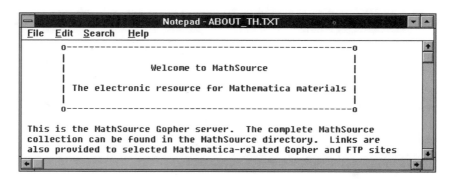

University of California at Santa Barbara
> **Gopher to: ucsbuxa.ucsb.edu:3001**
> Look in *The Subjects Collections, Mathematics and Statistics*

6. After the teams complete the project, have one member make an oral presentation to the class on interesting things the team learned about their mathematicians.

7. Instruct students how to use a word processor to compose email messages offline. Have them write messages to the schools on the Academy One list of schools outside the U.S. Students should:
- Introduce themselves.
- Explain the results of the project.
- Ask students in the other class if they would like to contribute information about mathematicians from their country to be added to the database.

Be sure to send a copy of the complete database to all schools that participate. If possible, practice using the email program's attach file or encode feature to send a non-text document via email. (Databases constructed using software such as Lotus are non-text documents.)

EXTENSION:

Post a short message to a few professional newsgroups (e.g., discussion groups for lawyers, doctors, engineers, journalists) or interview local professionals asking for examples of how they use mathematics in their professions.

Notes:

Plant Anatomy

Students are required to work in teams, to conduct research with printed and Internet resources, to write figuratively, and use illustration software.

GRADE LEVELS: 9-10

OBJECTIVES:
• Use the Internet to find information about plant anatomy.
• Think creatively to find analogies between plant parts and everyday objects or activities.
• Use ftp to download software for illustrating analogies.
• Work cooperatively with other students in teams.

MATERIALS:
• Personal computer with an Internet connection, including World Wide Web, ftp, and gopher access; Usenet newsgroup access (optional)
• Word processor
• Graphics-capable printer

PROCEDURE:
    1. Students must define "analogy" and come up with several of their own analogies for the next class.
    2. Divide the class into teams of three students. List the following plant parts (and more, if desired) on a bulletin or chalk board.

roots	vascular cambium
flowers	casparian strip
stems	latent bud
phloem	leaves
seeds	xylem

3. Explain that the purpose of the project is to write analogies for these plant parts. Here's an example:

Leaves of green plants are analogous to factory assembly lines. The epidermis is like the outer wall; palisade cells are like assembly lines; chloroplasts are like workers moving from place to place along those assembly lines, using energy (carbon dioxide and water) to bring together raw materials to produce a finished product, glucose. Glucose is then transferred via a conveyor belt, the phloem, to the warehouse or root. And as in real factories (unless there are second or third shifts), production stops at night.

Each team selects one plant part and finds as much information as it can using texts, library materials, and Internet resources. Allow sufficient time for teams to gather enough materials to use to create their analogies. For information on plant anatomy, students can access these World Wide Web sites.
    Dictionary of Cell Biology
        URL: http://mblab.gla.ac.uk/~julian/Dict.html
    Biodiversity and Biological Collections
        URL: http://muse.bio.cornell.edu/

Students can gopher to the Missouri Botanical Garden Gopher.
Gopher to: mobot.org (See Figure 1.20)

FIGURE 1.20

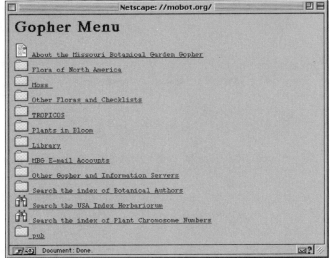

They can also gopher to the Smithsonian Institution Natural History Gopher.
Gopher to: nmnhgoph.si.edu (See Figure 1.21)
Look in *Botany at SI*

FIGURE 1.21

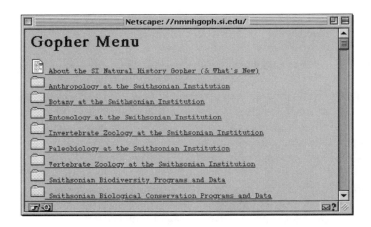

4. After they've gathered enough information, have the teams brainstorm and write their analogies. Teams should preferably bring their research to class and compose the analogy together on word processors (see extension). Each analogy should be no more than one page. For help with using figurative language, students can access the World Wide Web.

IBM Writing Project
   URL: http://www.ucet.ufl.edu/
Purdue University Online Writing Lab (OWL)
   URL: http://owl.trc.purdue.edu/

5. If you do not have illustration software, ftp to the following site and download a free program. Have the teams illustrate and label the plant part and its analogous counterpart. Make copies of each group's text and illustrations and distribute to the class.

For IBM-compatible users:

Ftp to: oak.oakland.edu

Look in the *SimTel/win3/graphics* subdirectory for an index file to help you find software.

For Mac users:

Ftp to: ftp.classroom.net

Go to the *Wentworth/Classroom-Connect/Teacher-Aids* subdirectory and retrieve the *KIDPIX* file in the binary mode.

EXTENSION:

Access these Bionet newsgroups and post the text of the students' analogies. Invite readers to respond with feedback or to contribute their own analogies. If students have trouble composing their analogies, they can post requests for assistance here.

sci.bio	biology and related sciences
bionet.cellbiol	general discussions about cell biology
bionet.plants	discussions about all aspects of plant biology

Notes:

Seasons

Students are expected to use gopher to find weather information, to compare and contrast information, to draw pictures, and to exchange data via email with another class.

GRADE LEVELS: 3–5

OBJECTIVES:
• Find weather information on the Internet.
• Learn how the seasons differ in the northern and southern hemispheres.

MATERIALS:
• Personal computer with an Internet connection and gopher software
• Globe
• Graphical World Wide Web browser and graphic viewer (optional)

PROCEDURE:
1. Have students use gopher to connect to the University of Illinois Weather Machine. Track your local high and low temperatures for three to five consecutive days.
   Gopher to: wx.atmos.uiuc.edu
   Look in *States,* select your state, and then select the closest city
2. For the same period of time, gopher to Australian Weather Forecasts and record the daily highs and lows for Melbourne.
   Gopher to: gopher.austin.unimelb.edu.au
   Look in *Australian Bureau of Meteorology*
3. Compare the temperatures and talk about the differences.
4. Subscribe to the International Email Classroom Connections list to find an Australian class to communicate with.
   Email to: iecc-request@stolaf.edu
   Type subscribe **iecc<your name>** in the body of your message.
   When you subscribe you'll receive instructions on how to find a partner class.
5. Ask the Australian students how their local plants and temperatures have changed in the past few months. Tell them how they've changed in your area. Discuss the differences, and draw pictures to illustrate them.
6. What do those differences suggest about the seasons? Find Melbourne on a globe. Show that it is in the southern hemisphere, while your class is (probably) in the northern hemisphere.

EXTENSIONS:
1. Exchange email with the Australian class about the seasonal activities they enjoy, such as making snowballs or playing in leaves.
2. Access the Current Weather Maps and Movies page on the World Wide Web. Have students click on different parts of the U.S. map to get up-to-date weather reports for those areas. Talk about how those seasonal conditions differ from where you live even though you live in the same hemisphere.
   URL: http://rs560.cl.msu.edu/weather
   Select the *Interactive Weather Browser* (See Figure 1.22)

**FIGURE
1.22**

Notes:

Social Studies and English

Students are required to discuss and analyze journalism topics, to work in teams, to use the Internet to follow news on a specific topic over time, to write a class newspaper, and to cite sources.

GRADE LEVELS: 4-12

OBJECTIVES:
• Keep up with and discuss current events, using the Internet or commercial online services as news sources.
• Practice scanning news items to find the most important information.
• Learn about journalism topics such as the pyramid/inverted pyramid technique, "new journalism," tabloid journalism, ethics, print vs. electronic, hard news vs. feature, and follow trends, controversies, and styles in news coverage.
• Produce and distribute a two-page class news bulletin or newspaper based on your findings.
• Learn the proper techniques for paraphrasing, using quotes, and writing citations or bibliographic references.

MATERIALS:
• Personal computer with an Internet connection, including gopher, Usenet newsgroups, email, and World Wide Web access
• Word processor and printer

PROCEDURE:
1. Discuss the journalistic pyramid/inverted pyramid approach to writing and the "who, what, where, when, why, and how" elements usually found in news stories. Have students compare this approach to the essay style of writing.
2. Discuss the principle of "newsworthiness." Have students analyze the front page of a newspaper story by story, explaining why editors may have considered each story newsworthy.
For discussions of current journalism topics, subscribe to the following mailing lists or read these newsgroups.

Mailing Lists	
HSJOURN	High School Scholastic Journalism
HUMPHREY	UMCP College of Journalism
JOURNET	Journalism education
JRNTUT-L	Online journalism seminar
PHOTOTUJ	Photojournalism seminar

To subscribe to any of these mailing lists:
Email to: listserv@listserv.net
Type anything in the subject line or leave it blank. In the body of the message, type **subscribe <the name of the list> <your name>**

Newsgroups
  alt.internet.media_coverage
  alt.journalism
  alt.journalism.criticism

(These "alt" newsgroups contain valuable information but are unmoderated or loosely moderated. Teachers may want to scan the discussions first and print only appropriate discussion entries.)

If the school's newsgroup listing includes the clari. newsgroups it will feature many business-related and area specific groups, including news from commercial newswire services.

For a comprehensive guide to online journalism educational resources, including academic texts, mailing lists, and electronic publications, access *The Daily News Service* at The University of Michigan's Clearinghouse for Subject-Oriented Resource Guides.

Gopher to: una.hh.lib.umich.edu

Look in *inetdirs, News*

3. Divide the class into workable teams and give each a "beat," a topic to follow on a regular basis. Categories can include U.S. government and politics, health, international news, technology, business, the environment, entertainment, sports, and so on.

4. The Television News Archive provides abstracts from the big four news broadcasts and their evening news programs, as well as links to other valuable gopher news resources. On commercial services such as Prodigy or America Online, refer to electronic versions of *Time, The New York Times, Newsweek, Business Week*, and others. Also use whatever print news resources your school receives.

Gopher to: tvnews.vanderbilt.edu

Look in *Network Television Evening News Abstracts*

Voice of America

Gopher to: gopher.micro.umn.edu

Look in *News, Voice of America, News, an*d *English Broadcast*

NetManage WWW Starting Points

URL: http://www.netmanage.com/netmanage./nm11.html

Use the World Wide Web to find news via The Pathfinder, *Time* magazine's Web site.

URL: http://www.pathfinder.com (See Figure 1.23)

5. Collect printouts of news items and organize them into the different beats for a week. At the end of the week, have the group work together as editors to decide which items should be included in their reports. Remind them that each report can only be one page, front and back.

6. Instruct students to review the articles they select and compose condensed versions. If necessary, teach them how to paraphrase and the difference between it and plagiarism. Create handouts or use a text to provide guidelines for citations or bibliographies for the information in the paper.

7. Distribute copies of each group's report to other groups and other classes, and make them available at various locations throughout school. The report could also "piggyback" and be included in the school newspaper. Or the class could, via the Internet, exchange its work with another class. Post a query to education mailing lists to find partner classes.

**FIGURE
1.23**

Notes:

Sociology (Native Americans)

Students are expected to use the Internet to discuss Native American history and culture and misconceptions about Native Americans, to do research, to organize information into categories, and to write and illustrate a report using a word processor.

GRADE LEVELS: 7-12

OBJECTIVES:
- Discuss Native American history, culture, and contributions to North American culture.
- Use new vocabulary words.
- Practice using the Internet to find information.

MATERIALS:
- Personal computer with an Internet connection, including gopher, email, and World Wide Web access
- Folders or binders
- Word processor and printer
- Art supplies

PROCEDURE:
1. Midway through a unit on Native Americans, have students use the Internet to find materials to supplement their current studies. First, provide an overview of media portrayal of Native Americans. Discuss issues such as the stereotyping of Native Americans in the movies and on television.

2. Then, assign students the task of finding a wide variety of information about Native American tribes, including Indian nations and their relationship with the American government. They should also find material on cultural topics such as food, language, and clothing. Give students folders for their information, and have them access these World Wide Web and gopher resources.

Native American Home Page
   URL: http://galaxy.einet.net/galaxy/Community/Culture/Native-American.html (See Figure 1.24)
Native American Society and Culture
   URL: http://www.yahoo.com/Society_and_Culture/Cultures/Native_American_Indians/
NativeNet
   URL: http://kuhttp.cc.ukans.edu/~marc/native_main.html
National Museum of the American Indian Home Page
   URL: http://www.si.edu/nmai
University of Massachusetts
   Gopher to: k12.ucs.umass.edu
   Look in *basic, Government-History-UN-Social Studies-Women's Studies, Unbiased Teaching About Native Americans*
   Rice University
   Gopher to: riceinfo.rice.edu
   Look in *Information by Subject Area, Anthropology and Culture, Indigenous Peoples, Fourth World Center for Indigenous Studies*

3. Help students organize their information into categories. Possible categories include Native American Misconceptions; New Vocabulary Words; Native American Innovations; and Art, Music, and Food. Or, students can choose a specific tribe and concentrate on the details of its particular culture.

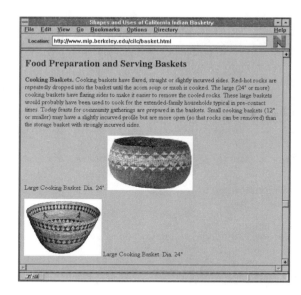

**FIGURE
1.24**

4. Have students pick a category and use a word processor to write a brief report, including illustrations or graphics they may have downloaded from the Internet. They can use computer software, clip art, or traditional art supplies to create illustrations.

5. Discuss the students' findings as a class. What misconceptions or myths did the research clarify or dispel? How will the students' new knowledge and awareness affect what they think about Native Americans? What movies, television shows, or toys do they now recognize as misrepresentative? What contributions have Native Americans made to society that we often overlook?

EXTENSION:

Have students subscribe to, follow, and participate in various Native American online discussion groups. Have them try to find a Native American with whom they can chat and share their research findings.

Mailing Lists

TRIBALLAW Laws and policies affecting Native Americans in North America
   Email to: listserv@thecity.sfsu.edu
   In the body of the message type **subscribe triballaw**

NATIVELIT-L Native American Literature
   Email to: listserv@cornell.edu
   In the message body type **subscribe NativeLit-L <your name>**

MINN-IND Midwest and northern plains Indian affairs and concerns
   Email to: dborn@maroon.tc.umn.edu
   Ask for information about MINN-IND and how to subscribe

INDKNOW Indigenous peoples' knowledge systems
   Email to: indknow@u.washington.edu
   In the message body type **subscribe indknow**

Students can also access these newsgroups.

alt.native	Indigenous people around the world
soc.culture.native	Aboriginal people around the world
sci.anthropology	Anthropology
sci.archaeology	Archaeology
sci.archaeology.mesoamerican	Archaeology of Mesoamerica
soc.religion.shamanism	Shamanism

Notes:

Solar System

Students are required to use telnet and other Internet tools to find information, to draw, and to use proportions to make a model.

GRADE LEVELS: 4–7

OBJECTIVES:
• Use the Internet to find information about the solar system.
• Make a scale model of the solar system, including the planets and their relative sizes and distances from the sun.
• Practice using telnet, ftp, and World Wide Web browser Internet tools.

MATERIALS:
• Personal computer with an Internet connection, including telnet, ftp, and Web access
• Graphics-capable printer
• Paper, string, tape, and a tape measure or yard stick

PROCEDURE:
1. Prepare a chart listing the planets and their diameters and mean distances from the sun. Telnet to NASA's SpaceLink for the information to complete the chart.
   Telnet to: spacelink.msfc.nasa.gov
   Login: **guest**
   Select the *Instructional Materials* menu
2. Record the diameter of each planet and the sun, and decide on a suitable scale for making a model of the solar system. Use proportions to determine the diameter of the model of each planet according to this scale.
3. Have students make a scale drawing of each planet, including a label with its name and diameter. Cut out each drawing.
4. Using the drawings, make a scale model of the solar system showing how far each planet is from the sun. Set the distance from the sun to Earth as one meter, then use proportions to figure out the distances of the other planets from the sun.
5. On a large bulletin board or empty wall, position the sun model on the far left. Cut a piece of string to scale so it represents the distance between the sun and Pluto, the planet farthest from the sun. Place the model for Pluto at the end of the string, then place the other planets in their respective positions along that string. Or, cut separate strings representing the distance to each of the other planets. (Depending on the scale you use, you may have to go outdoors to set up your model.)

EXTENSIONS:
1. Find images of the planets on ftp sites and the World Wide Web. Download and print the images. Place the actual images next to their respective planets on your model.
   Ftp to: iris1.ucis.dal.ca
   Look in the *pub/gif* subdirectories
   URL: http://www.w3.org/hypertext/DataSources/bySubject/astro/Overview.html
   Click on *Databases, Images and Surveys*. One great link at this site is *The Nine Planets: A Multimedia Tour of the Solar System by Bill Arnett.*

2. Check out Cornell University's Planetary Information Web server to find other online information about the planets.

URL: http://astrosun.tn.cornell.edu/Home.html (See Figure 1.25)

FIGURE 1.25

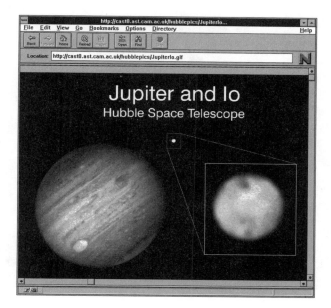

Notes:

Time

Students are expected to use the Internet to find the time for cities around the world, to read time, and to use a map.

GRADE LEVELS: K–3

OBJECTIVES:
• Read time from a clock.
• Discover that time varies from place to place around the world.
• Discover how night and day are related to the rotation of the Earth.
• Use the Internet to access worldwide time data.
• Increase global awareness by communicating with students in distant classes.

MATERIALS:
• Personal computer with an Internet connection, including gopher or World Wide Web access and email access
• Clock, globe, and flashlight

PROCEDURE:
1. Students will use the Internet to learn about time. To find up-to-date times for cities in Europe, Africa, Asia, and Australia, have students use these sites. Pick several cities from each continent and record the current time (hour only) for those cities.

University of Melbourne, Australia
Gopher to: gopher.austin.unimelb.edu.au (See Figure 1.26)
Look in *General Information, Local Times Around the World*

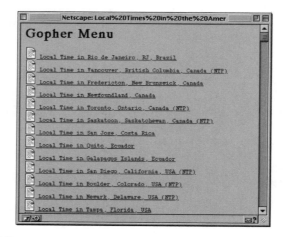

**FIGURE
1.26**

Washington and Lee Law Library
Gopher to: liberty.uc.wlu.edu
Look in *Netlink Server, Local Times Around the World*
HiLink Communications Guide to Times Around the World
URL: http://www.hilink.com.au/

2. Read your local time from an analog and a digital clock, then put up a large world map. Mark each city's location with a pin and write the time beside it.

3. Compare the various times. Put them in order from latest to earliest. Do students see a pattern to the times and the way cities are arranged on the map?

4. Discuss why time is different in various locations around the world. Use a flashlight and a globe to model the rotation of the Earth and to demonstrate day and night.

EXTENSIONS:

1. Have students write short stories describing what children their age in one of the selected cities might be doing while they are eating breakfast. Or students might write about what they are usually doing when it's bedtime for children in one of the cities.

2. Coordinate a real-time Internet Relay Chat with a class in a different time zone through the Cleveland Freenet. Or, arrange an ongoing discussion with another class via email to compare current time and activities.
Cleveland Freenet
    Telnet to: freenet-in-a.cwru.edu

If you haven't done so already, register as a new user and follow the online instructions for beginning an IRC session in the Cleveland Freenet Communications Center.

Notes:

U.S. Government (Nation's Capital)

Students are expected to use printed materials to do research, to work in teams, to use the Internet to do research, and to produce a report using word processors.

GRADE LEVELS: 4–6

OBJECTIVES:
• Use maps to locate important institutions in the nation's capital.
• Learn more about the functions of various governmental organizations and the buildings that house them, including the White House, Justice Department, and Department of Commerce.
• Practice using the World Wide Web to take virtual tours.

MATERIALS:
• Personal computer with an Internet connection, including Web access
• Word processor and printer

PROCEDURE:
1. Using the text and library reference works, briefly review the history of the nation's capital, including a survey of other American cities that served as the capital and details on how Washington, D.C. was planned and designed.
2. Access the online guide to Washington, D.C. Divide the class into seven teams and have each team pick a quadrant to explore (the White House counts as a quadrant).
   White House
   URL: http://ww.whitehouse.gov/wh/eop/html/dc_ma.html (See Figure 1.27)

**FIGURE
1.27**

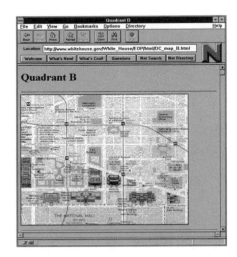

3. Have the teams draft reports on word processors about what they discovered on their tours. Have each team list the governmental bodies found in their quadrant and divide them into the branches they represent—legislative, executive, and judiciary. Ask them to describe the roles of each branch and how they interrelate.

4. Discuss the potential the Internet offers for providing a direct link to governmental representatives. Compare how information from the government's three branches is disseminated now to how it was conveyed in the past. Discuss the benefits of citizens having regular, free access to government information (via the Internet and otherwise) and its ramifications for democracy.

EXTENSIONS:

1. If the printer can handle transparencies, print out graphics and text documents found online and have the class present an "offline" tour to other classes. Use library resources to augment the presentation.

2. If time permits, have each student register in the White House Guest Book. Have them create the bulk of their messages offline on a word processor, then enter the information into the interactive Web form.

3. Using information gathered from the Web tour, each student should pick one governmental body he or she would like to work in and explain why.

Notes:

U.S. Government (Supreme Court)

Students are expected to use gopher to retrieve information from the Internet, to write essays, to discuss various issues as a class, and to use a word processor to write a report.

GRADE LEVELS: 10-12

OBJECTIVES:
• Learn how the Supreme Court reaches decisions, and how those decisions affect society and individuals.
• Identify individuals' constitutional rights that came from various court decisions.
• Locate and download via ftp the electronic text of the U.S. Constitution.
• Use the Internet to locate and study recent court decisions.

MATERIALS:
• Personal computer with an Internet connection, including gopher and ftp access
• Word processor and printer

PROCEDURE:
1. Travel to the court's Project Hermes gopher or ftp site to find and download the collection of recent Supreme Court decisions.
   Gopher to: info.umd.edu
   Look in *Educational Resources/Library Information and Resources(including Victor)/Reference Room/ A Wide Variety of Subject Guides/Browse for Information By Subject/Law/Supreme Court Decisions*
   Ftp to: ftp.cwru.edu
   Select the *hermes* subdirectory
2. Have each student or small groups of students browse the decisions and select one to print out and evaluate. It may be helpful first to download and scan the index of all the decisions. Give them ample time to evaluate the rulings and take notes. Instruct them to write brief essays, due for the next class meeting, explaining why they believe the decision is particularly important.
3. As a class, compare the decisions to see if any groups or individual students selected the same ones. Point out that each citizen may feel differently about which decisions are important. Remind students that they should be able to freely state their ideas and opinions without being unjustly criticized. Discuss the concepts of majority versus minority rule, and individual rights versus the greater good of society. Talk about how the court balances these concepts.
4. Use ftp to download an electronic version of the U.S. Constitution.
   Ftp to: ftp.spies.com
   Select the *Gov/US-History* subdirectory
5. Have each group read the Constitution to identify the constitutional rights affected by the decisions they evaluated. Teach them to use the copy-and-paste or append features of a word processor to prepare reports containing key sections of the decision. The report should also include their essays on why those decisions are significant to them as individuals, and related excerpts of the Constitution.

EXTENSIONS:
1. Return to the Project Hermes site and find biographies of Supreme Court justices. Discuss as a class their diverse backgrounds and philosophies and how they may or may not have shaped court rulings. Also discuss the nomination system and how presidential appointments can lead to a balanced, conservative, or liberal court.

2. Invite a district or county court judge to speak to the class. Or, take a field trip to observe a trial involving Supreme Court decisions or constitutional rights.

3. Investigate how Supreme Court decisions have affected the rights of students or minors. Access via gopher the Yale Teachers' Institute text of seminars discussing how the courts have adjudicated the constitutional rights of students over the past 50 years. How did the court handle race segregation, exclusion of students with mental or physical disabilities, or the special needs of students whose principal language was not English?

Gopher to: yaleinfo.yale.edu:7700

Look in *Yale-New Haven Teachers Institute, Curricular Resources, Teaching Units, 1992, Vol.1:The Constitution, Courts, and Public Schools*

Notes:

Writing (Autobiographical)

Students are expected to use the Internet to find grammar information, to write an autobiographical poem, and to email the poems to a partner class.

GRADE LEVELS: 3-12

OBJECTIVES:
• Write autobiographical poems to help students get to know each other.
• Practice writing with concrete and abstract nouns, adjectives, and adverbs.
• Communicate with and get to know a distant class via email.

MATERIALS:
• Personal computer with an Internet connection, including email and World Wide Web access
• Simple word processor and printer, or pencils and paper

PROCEDURE:
1. Before beginning the project, find a class to communicate with via email. It can be a class you're doing other projects with or, to find a partner class, post queries to the appropriate education newsgroups or mailing lists. (See Chapter 3, Educational Resources, for an extensive list of mailing lists.)

2. Review the differences between concrete and abstract nouns, adjectives, and adverbs. Students can use gopher or the World Wide Web to access the grammar tips and other usage documents at the University of Purdue Online Writing Lab (OWL).
   Gopher to: owl.trc.purdue.edu
   URL: http://owl.trc.purdue.edu/

3. Prepare your autobiographical poem in advance and write it on a chalkboard or post it on a bulletin board in the classroom for students to read. Here's an example:

Line 1	Your first name	Vince
Line 2	Son or daughter of...	Vince and Georgette
Line 3	Four traits (adjectives)	curious, ambitious, funny, talkative
Line 4	Lover of (concrete nouns)	pizza, doughnuts, cats, bikes
Line 5	Who acts (adverbs)	cautiously
Line 6	Who needs (abstract nouns)	companionship
Line 7	Who fears (concrete nouns)	lightning
Line 8	Who hopes for (abstract nouns)	peace
Line 9	Resident of	Lancaster
Line 10	Your last name	DiStefano

4. Have students write their autobiographical poems, then exchange them with a remote partner class via email. This is a great way to match students with similar interests for further correspondence.

EXTENSIONS:
1. For a fun class period, distribute the students' poems randomly among the class. Have each student read the poem but omit the names. See if other students can guess the author.

2. Have each student use a computer illustration program to do a self-portrait. If the school has an image scanner, they can scan in a photo of themselves. Teach them how to attach graphics files to email or to encode non-text files, and send the drawings with the corresponding autobiographical poems to the partner class.

Writing (Creative)

Students are expected to discuss the fundamental elements of fiction, access Internet writing resources and clip art, write the beginning of a short story, proofread, and send the story via email to a partner class for continuation.

GRADE LEVELS: 2-12

OBJECTIVES:
• Work in teams to produce a fictional short story.
• Find information about writing and proofreading on the Internet.
• Constructively evaluate other students' work.
• Communicate via email with a distant class.

MATERIALS:
• Personal computer with an Internet connection, including email, World Wide Web, and gopher access
• Word processor, graphics viewer (such as MacPaint, Paintbrush, or Lview) and printer

PROCEDURE:
1. The teacher will coordinate this lesson with a partner class. The two classes will cooperate in writing a short story, each taking a turn and using email to send completed sections back and forth. One class (Class A) will initiate the project by writing the beginning of a story and sending it to the partner class (Class B). For instructional materials and ideas for teaching creative writing, access the YaleInfo gopher server.
   Gopher to: yaleinfo.yale.edu
   Go to the *Browse YaleInfo (Yale and Internet Information)* menu, and select *YaleInfo Index (search YaleInfo by keyword)*. Enter **creative writing** as the keywords.
2. One or more weeks before starting the project, both classes should subscribe to the Creative Writing in Education for Teachers and Students mailing list. Print out discussions and have students contribute where appropriate.
   Email to: listserv@listserv.net
   Type **subscribe CREWRT-L <your name>** in the body.
   If you have access to newsgroups and newsreader software, you can also access the **rec.arts prose** discussion group.
3. After students have studied and discussed the fundamental elements of fiction, such as character, voice, and plot, inform them that they'll work together in groups and with a distant class to write their own stories. To make the project more challenging, have Class A find photographs or images of people, landscapes, or objects on the Internet to base their stories upon or to incorporate in some way.
   Fine art can be found at this newsgroup:
   alt.binaries.pictures.fine-art.graphics
   Ftp to: haskell.systemsz.cs.yale.edu
   Select the *pub/sjl/www/clipart* subdirectory
   Ftp to: ftp.classroom.net
   Select the *wentworth/clipart* subdirectory
   URL: http://www.acy.digex.net/~informart/clipart/

4. If the groups in Class A have trouble getting their stories started, have them visit OWL, the Purdue Online Writing Lab, and look for documents called "Coping with Writing Anxiety" and "Overcoming Writer's Block."
   URL: http://owl.trc.purdue.edu/by-topic.html

5. Once they've completed the beginning of their stories, teach the groups how to compose email offline and to attach graphics. Have them carefully proofread their work, and all subsequent parts in later steps, for spelling and grammatical errors. If time permits, have them go back to the OWL site to find documents on proofreading. When the proofing is complete, send the email to Class B.

6. Students in the groups in Class B should download, print, and carefully read the story beginning from Class A. Have them analyze the characters, setting, and basic plot elements started by the first class. Guide them through developing the action for the story. Instruct students to access the same online resources for clip art, idea generation, and proofreading. Have the students email the body of the story back to Class A.

7. If time permits, students from both classes can use email or Internet Relay Chat (IRC) to talk about the story, ask questions, or brainstorm ideas while the story is in progress.

8. Class A should further develop the story, then email the text back for Class B to write a conclusion.

9. When the short story is complete, print out a copy for each student in Class A and Class B. Read the book aloud. Students enjoy listening for parts they wrote and changes the other class made in the plot or character development.

EXTENSIONS:

1. Find a third class and send those students the story to read, edit, and illustrate. Distribute copies of the completed short story to all students in all three classes. Classes can meet in a predesignated IRC channel to discuss the writing process during the project, problems they faced while working in group fashion, and surprises they encountered.

2. At the end of the school year, have students read the book again and write short essays explaining how their writing skills have improved.

Notes:

Writing (Research)

Students are expected to research, write, and source a report, to use traditional and online resources for research, and to compare and contrast.

GRADE LEVELS: 5-12

OBJECTIVES:
• Discuss the fundamentals of report or essay researching and writing, and write a report on a given topic.
• Practice locating information in the school library.
• Practice finding information on the Internet.
• Compare and contrast traditional research approaches with electronic information gathering.

MATERIALS:
• Personal computer with an Internet connection, including World Wide Web, gopher, and email access
• Library resources, including magazines and newspapers, encyclopedias, and reference books

PROCEDURE:
1. Discuss as a class the fundamentals of report writing, including selecting a topic, elements of a report (thesis, introduction, body, conclusion, bibliography), conducting library research (using card catalogs and reference materials), primary vs. secondary research, paraphrasing and copyright issues, methods for note-taking, and so forth. Students can tap these Internet resources for additional information.

University of Texas Writing Centers
URL: http://www.en.utexas.edu/ (See Figure 1.28)
URL: http://www.utexas.edu/depts/uwc/.html/main.html

FIGURE 1.28

Online Writer
URL: http://www.missouri.edu/~wleric/writery.html

An accepted style for citing Internet resources is evolving. Discuss this issue with students. For background, try the book *Electronic Style: A Guide to Citing Electronic Information* by Xia Li and Nancy B. Crane (Mecklermedia, 1993). The new APA Publication Manual (4th edition) also has a section on how to cite online media and sources.

2. Assign students a report on a topic of their choosing. The length of the report and the deadline depends on how much time you have for this project and students' current abilities. Give them some general categories, such as the environment, music, art, biology, law, health and medicine, government, or technology.

3. Have students conduct their research in the school library, in a city or county library, and on the Internet. Structure the assignment to allow ample time for students to select a topic, conduct preliminary research to narrow it down, further research their topics, write rough drafts, get teacher feedback, and revise the reports. They should split their time equally between using traditional research methods and doing online research. Have them keep a log of the information they find via traditional sources and what information they find on the Internet, and how much time it took.

4. Give students some starting points for conducting online topical research, but let them explore the Net on their own to track down the information they need. (Make sure they're under close supervision during their "explorations." They can work in pairs or in groups so they can police each other. Or, have adult volunteers who can look over their shoulders as they wander online.) To do a focused search of the Internet, students can use Veronica or WAIS. (See Appendix B, Internet Tutorials, for Internet Navigation Tools.) They can also use these World Wide Web resources.

Alta Vista Home Page
URL: http://altavista.digital.com/
WebCrawler Searching
URL: http://www.webcrawler.com
University of Purdue Research Starting Points
URL: http://owl.trc.purdue.edu/research.html
ElNet Galaxy
URL: http://galaxy.einet.net/galaxy.html
Yahoo Index
URL: http://www.yahoo.com/
NetManage WWW Starting Points
URL: http://www.netmanage.com/netmanage/nm11.html

Students can use other online tools. For example, students writing papers on the future of virtual reality might want to look for information in the various computer newsgroups. (See Chapter 3, Educational Resources.) Students could also join relevant mailing lists to send email queries to experts in the field—a great way to conduct primary research.

5. After students have completed their papers, have the class discuss the differences between traditional research and online research. Which did they enjoy more? Which approach yielded the most information or the best information? Discuss the benefits and drawbacks of each approach. For example, most people have free access to libraries, but the information there might not be as up to date as that found online. Or, a specific resource might be unavailable because it's being used by someone else. Also, doing research online allows you to search for information quickly from your workstation or to download auxiliary materials such as graphics, but you need to have access to adequate computer equipment.

*"We want to see the child in pursuit of knowledge—
not knowledge in pursuit of the child."*
George Bernard Shaw

V I R T U A L   T O U R S

A walk through eight rich Internet sites for educators

Nothing beats actually visiting a place you've read or heard about. After all, while you may have seen plenty of commercials about Jamaica, you haven't experienced the island until you've strolled its lily-white beaches or caught a wave off the coast.

The same holds true for Internet sites. Several books have been published listing great educational sites and their Internet addresses, but they don't actually take you inside to explore them, understand how teachers can use the information, and learn how to get around. These virtual tours do just that.

In this chapter of *The Educator's Internet Companion,* we'll take you on a guided tour of some of the biggest and best educational sites on the Internet. At the same time, we'll show you how to gopher, telnet, ftp, and ride the World Wide Web. We've used a combination of text-only and graphical software and noted which was used for the tour of each site. We've also included information about the specific software and computers used, but these sites are accessible to users of many types of software and computers. Many of these sites are accessible by using several Internet navigational tools, so we've included other access addresses as well.

Where will we take you during these virtual tours? To ERIC, NYSERNet, and Scholastic via gopher. We'll telnet to CARL to visit libraries and then ftp to Oakland University to download software. We'll ride the World Wide Web to the Froggy Page, FedWorld, and then back to ERIC.

TOUR I

ERIC, the Educational Resource and Information Center

Operated from Syracuse University, ERIC is a public resource focusing mainly on K–12 education. It features more than 950,000 documents, including more than 1,000 lesson plans, thousands of education-related articles, bibliographies, resource pointers, and research papers. It is all searchable by keyword. A special feature is a free question and answer service for educators, students, and parents.

Navigation tool: Gopher
Site address: ericir.syr.edu
Type of Internet account used: Graphical SLIP/PPP
Navigation software used: TurboGopher 1.0.7 on a Macintosh PowerBook 520c

After logging into your graphical (SLIP or PPP) Internet account, click your mouse twice on the TurboGopher software icon. Once it's loaded, look under the File menu and select *Another Gopher*. Enter **ericir.syr.edu** as the Server Name, then click OK.

After a few seconds, this main menu appears. You're now in ERIC! Take a moment to read through the menu to see what's available. A good place to start is the *News and Information about ERIC and AskERIC* folder, at the top of the menu. Double click on those words with your mouse.

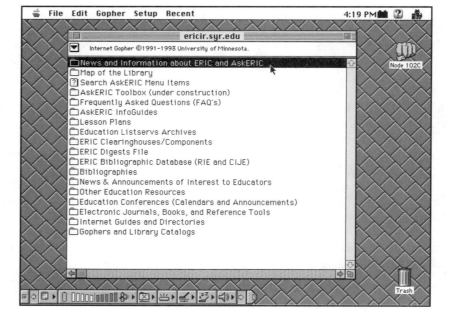

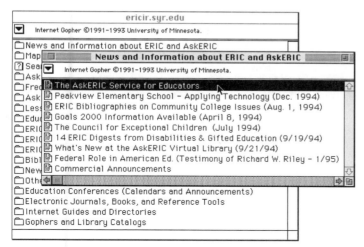

This is a long list of informational files about this Internet site. Notice that the new window simply opened on top of the old one. Double click on *The AskERIC Service for Educators* document to view it.

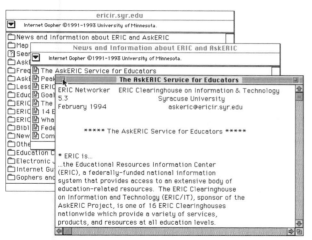

This document will appear. Use the scroll bars to the right to move up and down and read the file. When finished reading, click once on the button in the upper left-hand corner of the window and the document will disappear. The *News and Information about ERIC and AskERIC* window will reappear. You can close this window as well by clicking on the button in the upper left-hand corner.

The main menu reappears. Let's continue the journey and tap into ERIC's huge database of lesson plans. Click twice on the *Lesson Plans* menu item.

Impressive. ERIC's Lesson Plan database contains more than 1,000 individual plans on any curriculum topic. To speed up your search for an individual lesson plan, you can double click on *Search AskERIC Lesson Plans* and enter the word or words that most describe the plan you need. The results of your search will appear in a new window, which you can click through and read.

For the purpose of this tour, however, double click on the *Social Studies* folder to move on. (Make sure to return to this area to browse every menu item! The variety and quality of the material is amazing, and it's all free.)

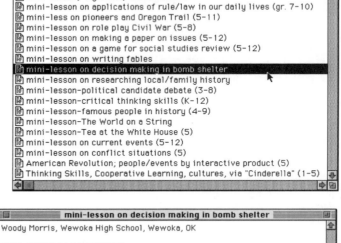

A list of more than 150 plans concerning Social Studies will scroll onto your screen. Near the top of the list is an item marked *mini-lesson on decision making in bomb shelter.* Double click on the plan to bring it up on your screen.

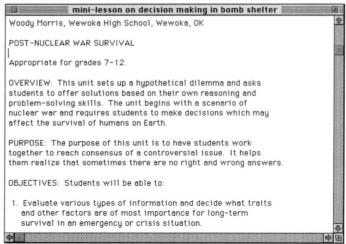

This lesson would stimulate grades 7–12. Select *Print* under the File menu to print a copy on your printer. You can also save a copy to your hard disk by selecting Save under the File menu.

Now, let's return to the main menu. This time, we'll do it differently. At the top of your screen, you'll see a menu item marked *Recent.*

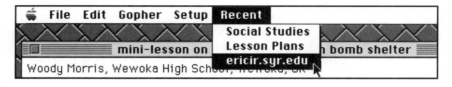

Click on that menu item, and drag down to the *ericir.syr.edu* listing. The main menu will reappear on your screen. Double click on *Gophers and Library Catalogs* to continue the tour.

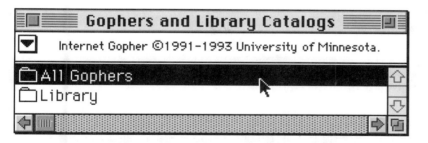

This menu is your jumping-off point to all of the gophers in the world. Double click on *All Gophers*.

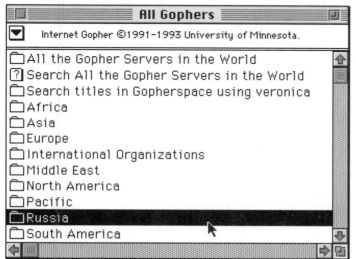

Here are links to all the Internet-connected gopher databases on the planet. Double click on *Russia* to move on.

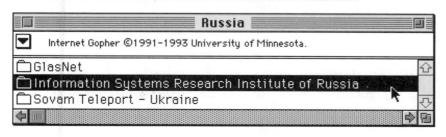

Click on *Information Systems Research Institute of Russia* to instantly connect with the institute's computer.

Welcome to Moscow! Double click on *Association for International Education* to learn more about special foreign exchange programs with Russia.

The Association offers all kinds of information about education in Russia and around the world.

Hope you've enjoyed your brief tour of ERIC's gopher site. Be sure to visit again and browse the wealth of information here for K–12 educators.

Association for International Education

Internet Gopher ©1991–1993 University of Minnesota.

- About Association for International Education (AIE)
- News and Information about AIE
- Educational System in Russia
- Distance Education throughout the World
- Educational and Other Information Resources in Internet
- Global Electronic Library
- Financial support for educational programms

How to access ERIC

Phone: (800) USE-ERIC
Email to: askeric@ericir.syr.edu
Gopher to: ericir.syr.edu
Ftp to: ericir.syr.edu
  Go to the *ael* subdirectory
Telnet to: ericir.syr.edu
  Login: **gopher**
URL: http://ericir.syr.edu

TOUR II

NYSERNet, The New York State Education and Research Network

One of the country's largest online systems connecting dozens of schools and thousands of K–12 educators, NYSERNet offers teachers telecomputing tools for the classroom and for their professional development. The network researches new uses of online resources and computer technology.

Internet navigation tool: Gopher

Site address: nysernet.org

Type of Internet account used: UNIX shell account

Navigation software used: Text-based gopher software

After logging into your text-based, UNIX shell account, type **gopher nysernet.org** and then press return to access the main menu.

If that doesn't work, keep in mind that some UNIX shell accounts may require you to type **gopher** then return at the prompt. Then, a **gopher>** prompt usually appears. At that prompt, type **open nysernet.org**, then hit enter, and you'll be connected.

Welcome to NYSERnet! For our tour, cursor down to item *18* on the menu, *Special Collections: K–12,* and hit return.

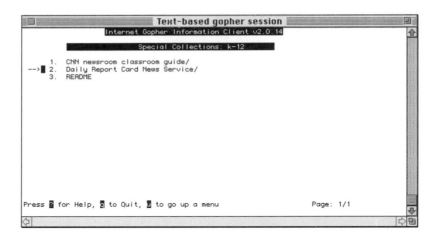

Let's check out the *Daily Report Card News Service*. It provides education-oriented news and information on the Internet. Cursor down to item *2* and hit return.

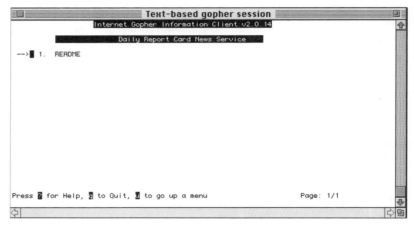

Uh oh. Looks like all that's here is a README file. Hit return to read it.

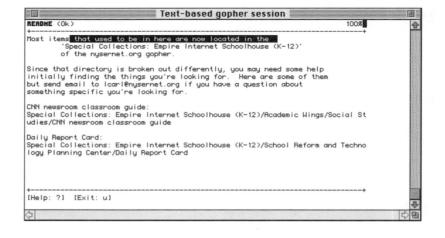

They've moved the Daily Report Card to a new place on the site. Let's find it. Hit **u** to exit the README file, then **u** again to back up one menu, then **u** yet again to jump back to the main menu.

According to the instructions, Daily Report Card is in the *Special Collections: Empire Internet Schoolhouse* area. That's item *11* on the menu. Cursor up and hit return.

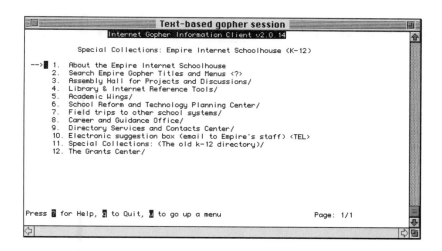

```
Text-based gopher session
Internet Gopher Information Client v2.0.14

      Special Collections: Empire Internet Schoolhouse (K-12)

--> 1.  About the Empire Internet Schoolhouse
     2.  Search Empire Gopher Titles and Menus <?>
     3.  Assembly Hall for Projects and Discussions/
     4.  Library & Internet Reference Tools/
     5.  Academic Wings/
     6.  School Reform and Technology Planning Center/
     7.  Field trips to other school systems/
     8.  Career and Guidance Office/
     9.  Directory Services and Contacts Center/
    10.  Electronic suggestion box (email to Empire's staff) <TEL>
    11.  Special Collections: (The old k-12 directory)/
    12.  The Grants Center/


Press ? for Help, q to Quit, u to go up a menu         Page: 1/1
```

Note all the wonderful things accessible through this menu. Before diving into each area, let's cursor down to item *6*, *School Reform and Technology Planning Center*, and hit return.

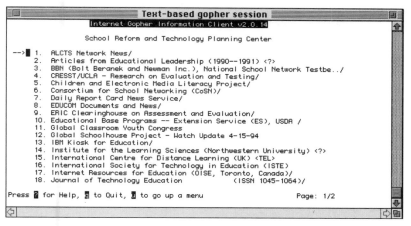

```
Text-based gopher session
Internet Gopher Information Client v2.0.14

        School Reform and Technology Planning Center

--> 1.  ALCTS Network News/
     2.  Articles from Educational Leadership (1990--1991) <?>
     3.  BBN (Bolt Beranek and Newman Inc.), National School Network Testbe../
     4.  CRESST/UCLA - Research on Evaluation and Testing/
     5.  Children and Electronic Media Literacy Project/
     6.  Consortium for School Networking (CoSN)/
     7.  Daily Report Card News Service/
     8.  EDUCOM Documents and News/
     9.  ERIC Clearinghouse on Assessment and Evaluation/
    10.  Educational Base Programs -- Extension Service (ES), USDA /
    11.  Global Classroom Youth Congress
    12.  Global Schoolhouse Project - Watch Update 4-15-94
    13.  IBM Kiosk for Education/
    14.  Institute for the Learning Sciences (Northwestern University) <?>
    15.  International Centre for Distance Learning (UK) <TEL>
    16.  International Society for Technology in Education (ISTE)
    17.  Internet Resources for Education (OISE, Toronto, Canada)/
    18.  Journal of Technology Education          (ISSN 1045-1064)/

Press ? for Help, q to Quit, u to go up a menu         Page: 1/2
```

Again, notice all the valuable material here. Item *7* is *Daily Report Card News Service*. Cursor down there and hit return.

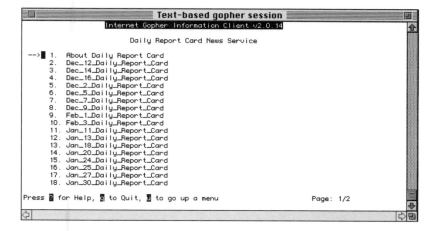

```
Text-based gopher session
Internet Gopher Information Client v2.0.14

              Daily Report Card News Service

--> 1.  About Daily Report Card
     2.  Dec_12_Daily_Report_Card
     3.  Dec_14_Daily_Report_Card
     4.  Dec_16_Daily_Report_Card
     5.  Dec_2_Daily_Report_Card
     6.  Dec_5_Daily_Report_Card
     7.  Dec_7_Daily_Report_Card
     8.  Dec_9_Daily_Report_Card
     9.  Feb_1_Daily_Report_Card
    10.  Feb_3_Daily_Report_Card
    11.  Jan_11_Daily_Report_Card
    12.  Jan_13_Daily_Report_Card
    13.  Jan_18_Daily_Report_Card
    14.  Jan_20_Daily_Report_Card
    15.  Jan_24_Daily_Report_Card
    16.  Jan_25_Daily_Report_Card
    17.  Jan_27_Daily_Report_Card
    18.  Jan_30_Daily_Report_Card

Press ? for Help, q to Quit, u to go up a menu         Page: 1/2
```

Pick the most current date from the list, cursor down to it, and hit return.

Check the contents of that week's Report Card. Be sure to return here and print a copy for yourself and your colleagues every week to take advantage of the valuable, interesting information here.

To continue the tour, hit **u** until you return to the main menu again. Then, cursor down to item *14*, or *Special Collections: Internet Help*.

```
═══════════════════ Text-based gopher session ═══════════════════
Feb_3_Daily_Report_Card (20k)                                  24% █
+--------------------------------------------------------------------+
  CHICAGO:  On the voucher trail. (#6)

TAKING STOCK
  NEW YORK CITY:  Parents rate school conditions. (#7)
  VALUES & QUALITY:  Reasons to go private says Mich. (#8)

CHARTING A NEW COURSE
  AN "UNCEREMONIOUS DEATH:"  Charter schools in Virginia. (#9)


       ==== GOAL EIGHT:  PARENTAL PARTICIPATION ====

*1   ADDRESSING DISPARITY:  IS THERE A ROLE FOR THE PTA?
       Parent Teacher Associations nationwide are redefining their
traditional role as school cheerleader.  In an era of trimmed
public school budgets, many PTAs are beginning to subsidize
essential classroom activities (Stecklow, THE WALL STREET
JOURNAL, 1/26).  Parents in some wealthy schools reportedly
sponsor high-scale fund-raising events to pay for teachers'
+--------------------------------------------------------------------+
[Help: ?]  [Exit: u]  [PageDown: Space]  [PageUp: b]
```

Here is a goldmine of Internet guidebooks and reference works. One of the best is menu *17, Gopher-Jewels.* Cursor down to it and hit return.

```
═══════════════════ Text-based gopher session ═══════════════════
▒▒▒▒ Internet Gopher Information Client v2.0.14 ▒▒▒▒
                 Special Collections: Internet Help

-->█ 1.  ASCII Clipart Collection (Texas Tech)/
     2.  Arts Resources
     3.  Big Dummy's Guide by Adam Gaffin (searchable, chapter version)/
     4.  Big Dummys Guide to the Internet, V 1.04
     5.  CWIS list
     6.  Clearinghouse for Subject-Oriented Internet Resource Guides (UMich../
     7.  Directory services/
     8.  Distance Learning Resources
     9.  FAQ About Anonymous FTP
    10.  FARNET 51 Reasons to Build the National Information Infrastructure/
    11.  FTP Gophers (Popular FTP Sites via Gopher)/
    12.  FTP list
    13.  Free On-Line Gopher Course/
    14.  Good Books About the Internet, by Jean Armour Polly, rev. 2-94
    15.  Gopher Information from U Minnesota/
    16.  Gopher Maintainer's Manual (from USCgopher)/
    17.  Gopher-Jewels/
    18.  Growth information about the Internet/

Press ? for Help, q to Quit, u to go up a menu      Page: 1/3
```

Under each menu item lie thousands of pointers to information in 13 subject areas on gopher servers around the world. Of most interest is item *14, Research, Technology Transfer and Grants Opportunities.* Cursor there and hit return.

```
═══════════════════ Text-based gopher session ═══════════════════
▒▒▒▒ Internet Gopher Information Client v2.0.14 ▒▒▒▒
                        Gopher-Jewels

-->█ 1.  GOPHER JEWELS Information and Help/
     2.  Community, Global and Environmental/
     3.  Education, Social Sciences, Arts & Humanities/
     4.  Economics, Business and Store Fronts/
     5.  Engineering and Industrial Applications/
     6.  Government/
     7.  Health, Medical, and Disability/
     8.  Internet and Computer Related Resources/
     9.  Law/
    10.  Library, Reference, and News/
    11.  Miscellaneous Items/
    12.  Natural Sciences including Mathematics/
    13.  Personal Development and Recreation/
    14.  Research, Technology Transfer and Grants Opportunities/
    15.  Search Gopher Jewels Menus by Key Word(s) <?>


Press ? for Help, q to Quit, u to go up a menu      Page: 1/1
```

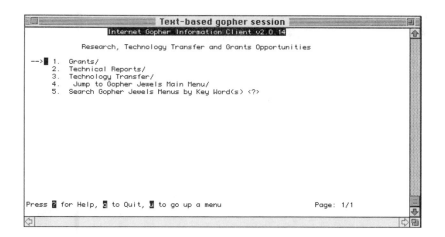

To look at grant information, hit return to access item *1, Grants*.

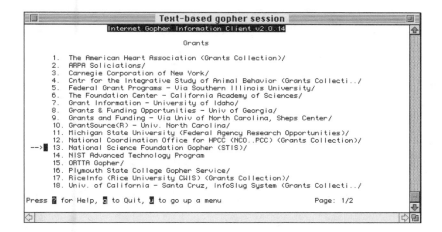

Here are two pages of links to grant information of all kinds to help bring the Internet and the online world into your K–12 classroom. Look through each menu item thoroughly, printing or saving the information to disk.

When finished here, press **u** until you return to the main menu. Then, take some time to explore on your own.

How to access NYSERNet

Email to: info@nysernet.org
Gopher to: nysernet.org
URL: http://nysernet.org

TOUR III

Scholastic Network

The Scholastic Internet Center is Scholastic's extension into the electronic world. Scholastic Inc. is one of the nation's leading publishers and distributors of children's books, classroom and professional magazines, professional books, technology products, and other educational materials.

Internet navigation tool: Gopher
Site address: scholastic.com 2003
Type of Internet account used: Graphical SLIP/PPP
Navigation software used: TurboGopher 2.0.1 on a Macintosh Performa 636CD

This time, we'll use the newest TurboGopher software on the Internet to navigate. Logon to the Internet and double click on the TurboGopher icon. After it's loaded, look under the Gopher menu and select *Another Gopher*.

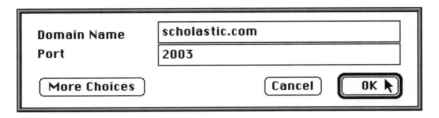

Enter **scholastic.com** as the Domain Name, and **2003** as the Port. Click OK to access the site.

This main menu window will appear. To start our tour, select the *Welcome to Scholastic!* document at the top of the menu by clicking on it twice.

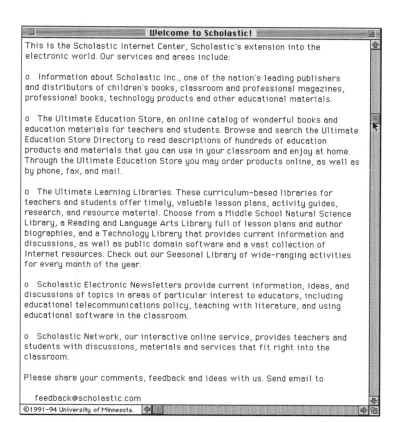

Read through Scholastic's online offerings, then click the box in the upper left-hand corner to erase that document. The main menu will reappear on the screen. Next, click on *Scholastic Internet Libraries*.

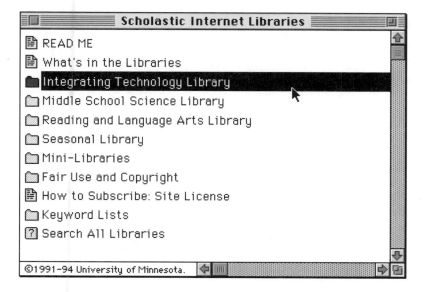

The Libraries are a content-rich, easy to use, valuable information resource targeted toward K–12 teachers and their students and designed to meet the needs of specific education audiences. Click twice on *Integrating Technology Library* to move on.

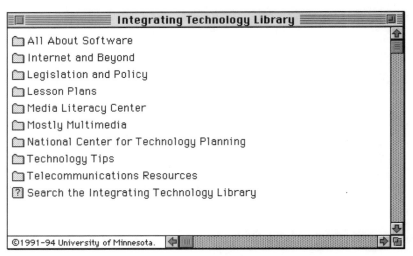

To find out more about integrating the Internet into your curriculum, click twice on *Internet and Beyond,* then *Articles,* then the *Internet Access for Educators* document.

This document is a great hands-on guide to the Internet and its education resources. Select Print under the File menu to save a copy for yourself.

Now, turn off all of the windows by clicking in the box in the upper left-hand corner of each until you reach the main menu again. Click twice on *Press Return: Online Magazine*.

This area contains the premier issue of *PRESS RETURN*, Scholastic Network's online multimedia magazine written by and for middle and high school students. This first issue is organized around the theme MY TOWN. Students were asked to consider the varied stories that make up the communities in which they live. Click twice on *Vol. 1, #1: MY TOWN*, then *MY TOWN Full Text* to view the first issue.

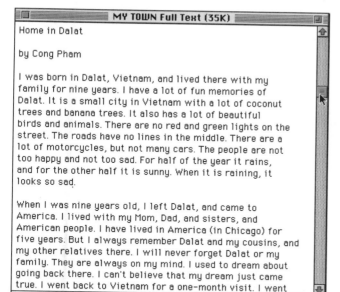

MY TOWN Full Text (35K)

Home in Dalat

by Cong Pham

I was born in Dalat, Vietnam, and lived there with my family for nine years. I have a lot of fun memories of Dalat. It is a small city in Vietnam with a lot of coconut trees and banana trees. It also has a lot of beautiful birds and animals. There are no red and green lights on the street. The roads have no lines in the middle. There are a lot of motorcycles, but not many cars. The people are not too happy and not too sad. For half of the year it rains, and for the other half it is sunny. When it is raining, it looks so sad.

When I was nine years old, I left Dalat, and came to America. I lived with my Mom, Dad, and sisters, and American people. I have lived in America (in Chicago) for five years. But I always remember Dalat and my cousins, and my other relatives there. I will never forget Dalat or my family. They are always on my mind. I used to dream about going back there. I can't believe that my dream just came true. I went back to Vietnam for a one-month visit. I went

©1991-94 University of Minnesota.

This is just one example of the hands-on projects offered through the Scholastic gopher site. Wander around the site a bit before you leave. You're sure to find reasons to return again and again.

How to access Scholastic

Gopher to: scholastic.com 2003
URL: http://scholastic.com:2005
America Online: Keyword **SCHOLASTIC**

TOUR IV

Colorado Alliance of Research Libraries (CARL)

A computer interface to thousands of local and national libraries around the world.

Internet navigation tool: Telnet (the only way to access this site)

Site address: pac.carl.org

Type of Internet account used: UNIX Account

Navigation software used: Standard, text-based telnet software

Logon to the Internet, and type **telnet pac.carl.org** at the prompt, then return. After logging into CARL, type **PAC** then return. Some systems may require that you type **telnet**, then press return. Then, a **telnet>** prompt usually appears. At that prompt, type **open pac.carl.org** then hit return to connect.

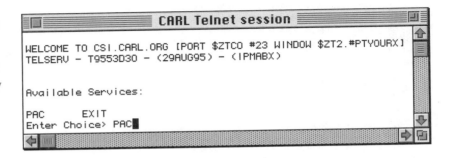

```
                CARL Telnet session
WELCOME TO CSI.CARL.ORG [PORT $ZTCO #23 WINDOW $ZT2.#PTYOURX]
TELSERV - T9553D30 - (29AUG95) - (IPMABX)


Available Services:

PAC      EXIT
Enter Choice> PAC█
```

Next, enter **5** as your terminal type. Most text-based Internet accounts use the VT100 type of terminal. If you know you're using a terminal other than VT100, select one of the other menu options, then hit return.

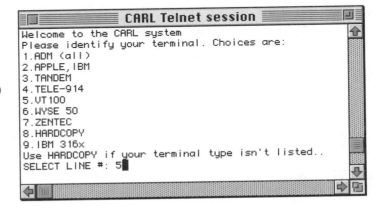

```
                CARL Telnet session
Welcome to the CARL system
Please identify your terminal. Choices are:
1.ADM (all)
2.APPLE,IBM
3.TANDEM
4.TELE-914
5.VT100
6.WYSE 50
7.ZENTEC
8.HARDCOPY
9.IBM 316x
Use HARDCOPY if your terminal type isn't listed..
SELECT LINE #: 5█
```

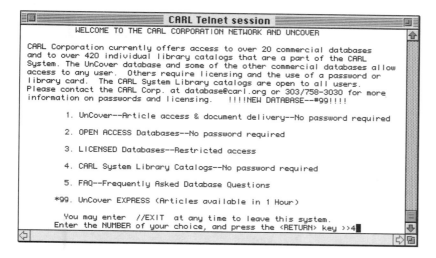

The main menu will appear seconds later. Type 4, for the *CARL System Library Catalogs,* and hit return.

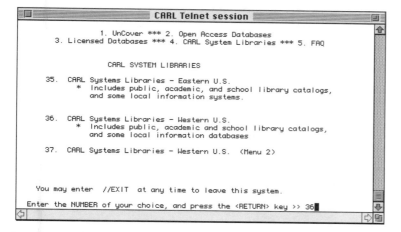

Lots of choices here. This menu is your jumping-off point to more than a hundred of the largest library catalogs in the United States. Select 36, for the *CARL Systems Libraries - Western U.S.,* and hit return.

Now we're getting somewhere! Select 83, for the *Boulder Public Library*, and hit return.

This welcome screen will appear. Press return to enter the system.

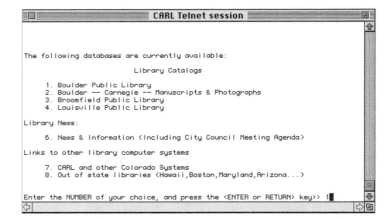

Press 1 to access the *Boulder Public Library* holdings.

Welcome to the Boulder Public Library! Let's do a quick search. Type **N Mark Twain** and hit return.

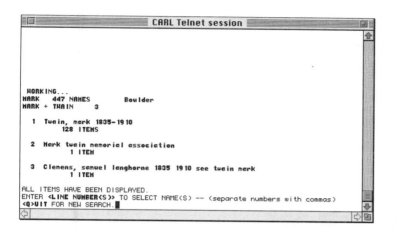

The system has found 130 items related to Mark Twain and Samuel Langhorne Clemens. Type **1** and return to select the main Mark Twain results.

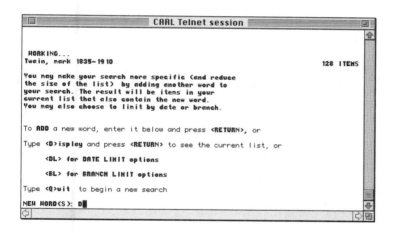

Our search was specific enough for this virtual tour, so type **D** and return to begin listing the search results.

Looks like we've found what we were looking for! To display a brief about item 7 from the list, type **7 B** and press return.

Looks like this is a two volume set, and they're both available to be checked out from the library. To get a full record listing, type **F** and return.

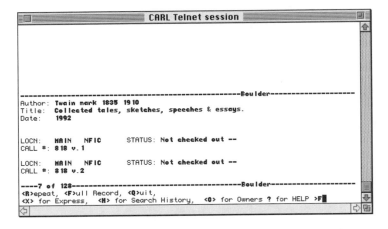

Looks great! Take the time to explore everything CARL has to offer. You'll be surprised at the diversity of the information available, most of it for free.

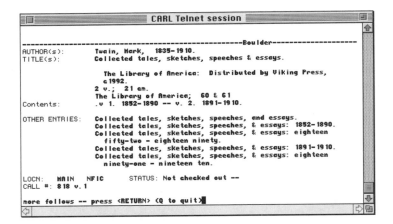

How to access CARL

Telnet to: pac.carl.org
Login: PAC

TOUR V

Oakland University FTP Archive

Perhaps the largest archive of free software and documents on the Internet for IBM and Mac computers.

Internet navigation tool: (ftp) file transfer protocol (the only way to access this site)

Site address: oak.oakland.edu

Type of Internet account used: UNIX Account

Navigation software used: Standard text-based ftp software

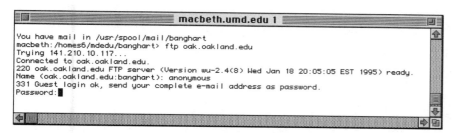

After logging into your text-based, UNIX shell account, type **ftp oak.oakland.edu** and then press return to access the main menu.

If that doesn't work, keep in mind that some UNIX shell accounts may require you to type **ftp** then return at the prompt. Then, a **ftp>** prompt usually appears. Here, type **open oak.oakland.edu** and you'll be connected. After you connect to the site, enter **anonymous** as your username, then your complete email address as your password.

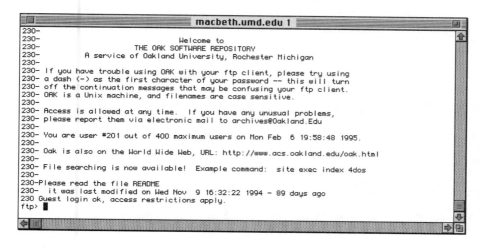

This Welcome message will scroll across your screen. We're user item *201* currently logged into the site! Finally, an **ftp>** prompt appears. Type **dir** to view the contents of the main-level directory. (Users navigate ftp sites with commands very similar to DOS operating systems.)

This is the site's main directory. Look at each directory item. The filename or directory name is the word on the far right. The numbers in the center tell you the size of the file or directory. Then, to the far left you'll see strange -rw-r—r— and drwxrwx-xr-x things. If the line starts with a hyphen (-), it's a file you can retrieve. If it starts with a d, it's a directory you can navigate through.

```
                                       macbeth.umd.edu 1
ftp> dir
200 PORT command successful.
150 Opening ASCII mode data connection for /bin/ls.
total 1026
-rw-r--r--    1 w8sdz     OAK           0 Nov 13 14:41 .notar
drwxr-x---    2 root      operator   8192 Dec 31 16:44 .quotas
drwx------    2 root      system     8192 Dec 30 19:16 .tags
-rw-r--r--    1 jeff      OAK      926582 Feb  6 03:19 Index-byname
-r--r--r--    1 w8sdz     OAK        1255 Nov  9 16:32 README
drwxr-xr-x    3 w8sdz     OAK        8192 Feb  6 19:52 SimTel
d--x--x--x    3 root      system     8192 Jan 19 20:26 bin
d--x--x--x    2 root      system     8192 Jul 30  1994 core
drwxr-x---    2 cpm       OAK        8192 Nov 21 16:41 cpm-incoming
d--x--x--x    5 root      system     8192 Dec 30 05:15 etc
drwxrwx---    2 incoming  OAK        8192 Feb  6 17:47 incoming
drwxr-xr-x    3 w8sdz     OAK        8192 Jan 30 17:37 pub
drwxr-xr-x   14 w8sdz     OAK        8192 Jan 30 17:35 pub2
drwxr-xr-x    6 w8sdz     OAK        8192 Jan 30 17:37 pub3
drwxr-xr-x    3 w8sdz     OAK        8192 Feb  6 19:52 simtel
drwxr-xr-x    2 jeff      OAK        8192 Apr 17  1994 siteinfo
drwx------   41 w8sdz     OAK        8192 Feb  5 17:38 w8sdz
226 Transfer complete.
1066 bytes received in 0.019 seconds (54 Kbytes/s)
ftp>
```

Type **cd simtel** to change to the simtel directory. You should get a message that the command was successful. Type **dir** to list the directory.

```
                                       macbeth.umd.edu 1
ftp> cd simtel
250-The files in this directory tree are a mirror of SimTel, the Coast to
250-Coast Software Repository (tm).  Please read README.COPYRIGHT for
250-information on distribution rights.
250-
250-Please read the file README.COPYRIGHT
250-  it was last modified on Sat Jan 28 14:52:09 1995 - 9 days ago
250-Please read the file README.MIRRORING
250-  it was last modified on Sat Jan 28 14:50:23 1995 - 9 days ago
250 CWD command successful.
ftp>
```

Now, let's take a look at the Windows programs and documents the site offers. Type **cd win3** to move into the Windows subdirectory, then type **dir** to list the contents of the directory.

```
                                       macbeth.umd.edu 1
ftp> dir
200 PORT command successful.
150 Opening ASCII mode data connection for /bin/ls.
total 24
-rw-r--r--    1 w8sdz     OAK         172 Jan 28 15:05 .message
-rw-r--r--    1 w8sdz     OAK           0 Jan 28 15:05 .notar
-rw-r--r--    3 w8sdz     OAK        4591 Jan 28 14:52 README.COPYRIGHT
-rw-r--r--    3 w8sdz     OAK        1573 Jan 28 14:50 README.MIRRORING
drwxr-xr-x  218 w8sdz     OAK        8192 Feb  6 20:02 msdos
drwxr-xr-x   80 w8sdz     OAK        8192 Feb  6 20:04 win3
226 Transfer complete.
401 bytes received in 0.023 seconds (17 Kbytes/s)
ftp>
```

```
┌─────────────────────────────────────────────────────────────────────┐
│ ■□▓▓▓▓▓▓▓▓▓▓▓▓▓▓▓▓      macbeth.umd.edu 1      ▓▓▓▓▓▓▓▓▓▓▓▓▓▓      ▣ │
├─────────────────────────────────────────────────────────────────────┤
│ ftp> dir                                                          ⬆  │
│ 200 PORT command successful.                                         │
│ 150 Opening ASCII mode data connection for /bin/ls.                  │
│ total 861                                                            │
│ -rw-r--r--   1 w8sdz     OAK           188 Jan 28 15:07 .message     │
│ -rw-r--r--   1 w8sdz     OAK             0 Jan 28 15:07 .notar       │
│ -rw-r--r--   3 w8sdz     OAK          4188 Jan 28 22:39 DIRLIST.TXT  │
│ -rw-r--r--   1 w8sdz     OAK         79202 Feb  6 20:04 FILES.IDX    │
│ -rw-r--r--   2 w8sdz     OAK          4591 Jan 28 14:52 README.COPYRIGHT │
│ -rw-r--r--   2 w8sdz     OAK          1573 Jan 28 14:50 README.MIRRORING │
│ -rw-r--r--   1 w8sdz     OAK          7423 Feb  6 20:02 README.descriptions │
│ -rw-r--r--   3 w8sdz     OAK          4188 Jan 28 22:39 README.dir-list │
│ -rw-r--r--   1 w8sdz     OAK          9293 Dec 23 19:29 README.file-formats │
│ -rw-r--r--   2 w8sdz     OAK          2982 Jan 29 22:59 README.how-to-upload │
│ -rw-r--r--   1 w8sdz     OAK          2363 Feb  4 11:07 README.simtel-cdrom │
│ -rw-r--r--   2 w8sdz     OAK         58657 Feb  5 17:40 SIMWNDEX.ZIP │
│ -rw-r--r--   2 w8sdz     OAK         57972 Feb  5 17:40 SIMWNLIS.ZIP │
│ drwxr-xr-x   2 w8sdz     OAK          8192 Dec 12 01:42 amipro       │
│ drwxr-xr-x   2 w8sdz     OAK          8192 Dec 12 01:42 animate      │
│ drwxr-xr-x   2 w8sdz     OAK          8192 Feb  5 22:27 archiver     │
│ drwxr-xr-x   2 w8sdz     OAK          8192 Feb  5 17:41 astronmy     │
│ drwxr-xr-x   2 w8sdz     OAK          8192 Jan 15 19:18 bakernws     │
│ drwxr-xr-x   2 w8sdz     OAK          8192 Dec 12 01:42 barcode      │
│ drwxr-xr-x   2 w8sdz     OAK          8192 Dec 31 23:57 batch        │
│ drwxr-xr-x   2 w8sdz     OAK          8192 Feb  5 17:41 bible        │
│ drwxr-xr-x   2 w8sdz     OAK          8192 Feb  5 17:41 biology      │
│ drwxr-xr-x   2 w8sdz     OAK          8192 Dec 31 23:57 cad          │
│ drwxr-xr-x   2 w8sdz     OAK          8192 Feb  5 17:41 calc         │
│ drwxr-xr-x   2 w8sdz     OAK          8192 Feb  5 17:41 calendar     │
│ drwxr-xr-x   2 w8sdz     OAK          8192 Jan 15 19:18 capture      │
│ drwxr-xr-x   2 w8sdz     OAK          8192 Jan 27 03:57 cdrom        │
│ drwxr-xr-x   2 w8sdz     OAK          8192 Jan 17 01:33 chem         │
│ drwxr-xr-x   2 w8sdz     OAK          8192 Jan 15 19:18 clipbrd      │
│ drwxr-xr-x   2 w8sdz     OAK          8192 Feb  5 17:41 clock        │
│ drwxr-xr-x   2 w8sdz     OAK          8192 Jan 10 15:40 commprog     │
│ drwxr-xr-x   2 w8sdz     OAK          8192 Feb  5 17:41 convert      │
│ drwxr-xr-x   2 w8sdz     OAK          8192 Feb  5 17:41 database     │
│ drwxr-xr-x   2 w8sdz     OAK          8192 Feb  5 17:41 desktop      │
│ drwxr-xr-x   2 w8sdz     OAK          8192 Dec 17 13:28 diskutil     │
│ drwxr-xr-x   2 w8sdz     OAK          8192 Feb  5 17:41 dll          │
│ drwxr-xr-x   2 w8sdz     OAK          8192 Feb  5 17:41 editor       │
│ drwxr-xr-x   2 w8sdz     OAK          8192 Feb  5 17:55 educate      │
│ drwxr-xr-x   2 w8sdz     OAK          8192 Jan 17 01:33 encode       │
│ drwxr-xr-x   2 w8sdz     OAK          8192 Feb  5 17:41 entertn      │
│ drwxr-xr-x   2 w8sdz     OAK          8192 Dec 12 01:42 eudora       │
│ drwxr-xr-x   2 w8sdz     OAK          8192 Feb  5 17:41 fax          │
│ drwxr-xr-x   2 w8sdz     OAK          8192 Feb  5 20:04 filedocs     │
│ drwxr-xr-x   2 w8sdz     OAK          8192 Feb  5 17:41 fileman      │
│ drwxr-xr-x   2 w8sdz     OAK          8192 Feb  5 17:41 fileutil     │
│ drwxr-xr-x   2 w8sdz     OAK          8192 Feb  5 17:41 finance      │
│ drwxr-xr-x   2 w8sdz     OAK          8192 Jan 27 03:57 font         │
│ drwxr-xr-x   2 w8sdz     OAK          8192 Feb  5 17:41 food         │
│ drwxr-xr-x   2 w8sdz     OAK          8192 Jan  6 05:49 gis          │
│ drwxr-xr-x   2 w8sdz     OAK          8192 Feb  5 17:41 graphics     │
│ drwxr-xr-x   2 w8sdz     OAK          8192 Dec 19 01:21 hamradio     │
│ drwxr-xr-x   2 w8sdz     OAK          8192 Dec 19 01:21 handicap     │
│ drwxr-xr-x   2 w8sdz     OAK          8192 Jan 27 03:57 icon         │
│ drwxr-xr-x   2 w8sdz     OAK          8192 Feb  5 17:41 info         │
│ drwxr-xr-x   2 w8sdz     OAK          8192 Jan 22 16:28 install      │
│ drwxr-xr-x   2 w8sdz     OAK          8192 Dec 12 01:42 internet  ⬇  │
└─────────────────────────────────────────────────────────────────────┘
```

There are more than 30 individual directories of files here! The directory names will give you a hint of the types of programs and files available in each directory.

Let's move into the education files. Type **cd educate** then **dir** to list the contents of the directory.

Look at all the free education software for Windows users! A flashcard program is listed as *flash_30.zip*. The .zip on the end means it's a zip file, one whose data has been compressed for easy storage. To uncompress a .zip file you need an unzip program. The most popular one is *pkunzip.exe* or *unzip.exe*. These two programs are available on most ftp sites, including *Classroom Connect's* ftp site. **Ftp to: ftp.classroom.net** and go to the *wentworth/Internet-Software* subdirectory.

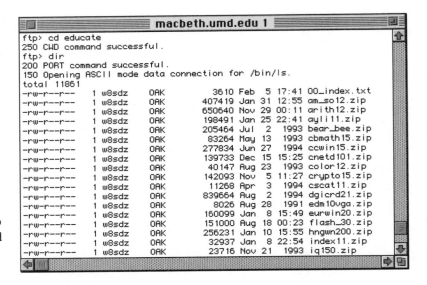

Let's get the file. First, because the file is zipped, we know it's a binary file. Type **binary** at the prompt, then type **get flash_30.zip** to retrieve the file. In our example, we're using a Unix shell account, so the file will be transferred to the Internet provider's computer.

To bring it from your provider's computer to *your* computer, type **sz -b flash_30.zip.** This means: "send the file using Z Modem in binary mode." Don't worry about the technical aspects—this command will work with

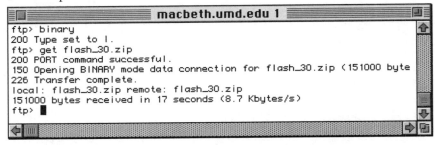

most ftp software. If it doesn't, consult your school's technical coordinator or your Internet service provider.

The file will be sent directly to your hard drive. Find it, use unzip software to uncompress it, and then load the software.

How to access Oakland FTP Archive

Ftp to: oak.oakland.edu

TOUR VI

The Froggy Page

A fun yet educational World Wide Web site that links students to all things froggy on the Web.

Internet navigation tool: World Wide Web (the only way to access this site)

Site address: http://www.cs.yale.edu/HTML/YALE/CS/HyPlans/loosemore-sandra/froggy.html

Type of Internet account used: Graphical SLIP/PPP

Navigation software used: Netscape 2.0 Web browser on a Macintosh PPC 6100

First, logon to your SLIP or PPP graphical account, then double click on the Netscape icon to load the browser software. After it's loaded, click on the Open button in the button bar at the top of the screen, then enter the above address (starting with **http://**) in the Open Location box that appears.

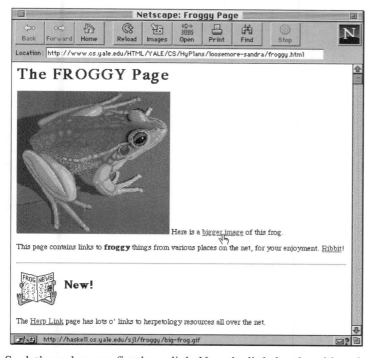

Welcome to the Froggy Page! After you type in the address of a Web site, a home page (or main menu) like this appears. Use the scroll bar on the right side of the window to move up and down so you can see everything on the page.

Note that some words are highlighted and underlined in blue. That means they're hyperlinks, or jumping-off points to more information pertaining to the word or picture that's highlighted. Click on a hyperlink once with a mouse, and you'll be automatically connected to a new page of information, no matter where it's stored on the Internet.

So, let's explore our first hyperlink. Note the little hand positioned over the words "bigger image" in the first sentence of this page, "Here is a <u>bigger image</u> of this frog." Click once on these words to see the larger picture.

After a few seconds, this frog will scroll onto your screen. You've followed your first link! Now, click once on the *Back* icon at the top of the screen to step back one page, and return to the main menu.

Once you return to the home page, Scroll down to the Froggy Sounds area and click on *Blurp*.

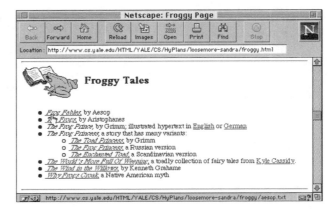

The sound will be sent to your computer and played for you. *Blurp!* Now, scroll even further down the page and click on the *Frog Fables* link under the *Froggy Tales*.

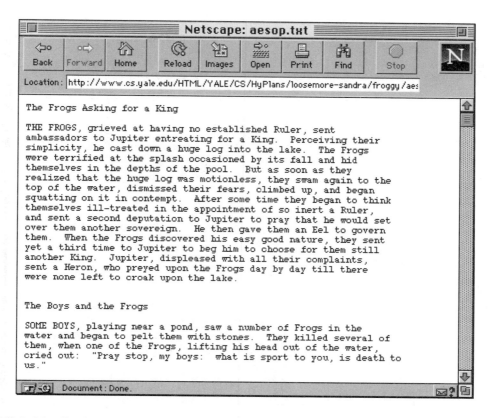

Here's a delightful collection of frog stories and fables from Aesop. Be sure to select *print* under the File menu to save a copy for yourself.

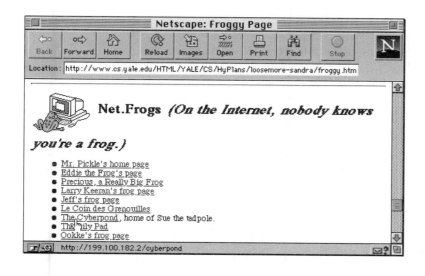

Let's link to other Web sites on other Internet computers. Press the Back button at the top of the screen to step back to the home page, then scroll down to the bottom and select *The CyberPond* from the *Net.Frogs* menu.

This is the home page of a completely
new Web site called CyberPond.
You've, um, leapfrogged, from one
computer to another with the click of
a mouse.

How to access The Froggy Page

URL: http://www.cs.yale.edu/HTML/
YALE/cs/HyPlans/loosemore-sandra/froggy.html

TOUR VII

FedWorld

The U.S. government's home page on the World Wide Web has links to more than 1,000 individual databases maintained by various government agencies and departments.

Internet navigation tool: World Wide Web

Site address: http://www.fedworld.gov

Type of Internet account used: Graphical SLIP/PPP

Navigation software used: MacWeb Web browser on a Power Macintosh 8100

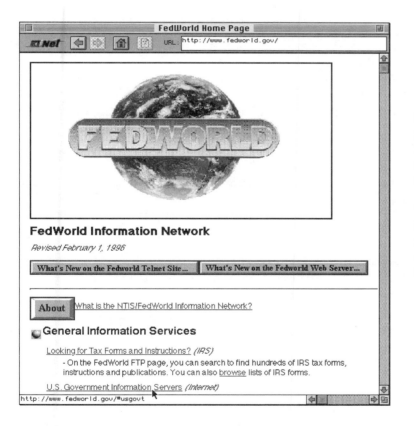

Sign on to the Internet and load your MacWeb software. Select *Open URL* under the File menu, and enter **http://www.fedworld.gov** as your destination.

Welcome to the U.S. government's home page! To get started, click on the *U.S. Government Information Servers* hyperlink located directly below the About button.

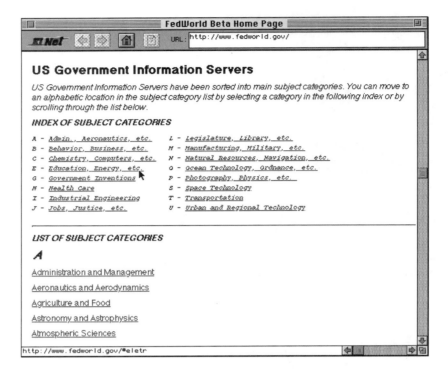

This index appears. Click on *Education, Energy, etc.* under the *Index of Subject Categories*.

Click on *Education and Humanities* under the big E to continue.

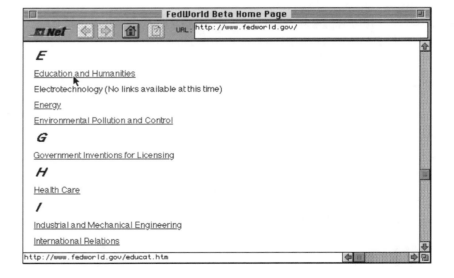

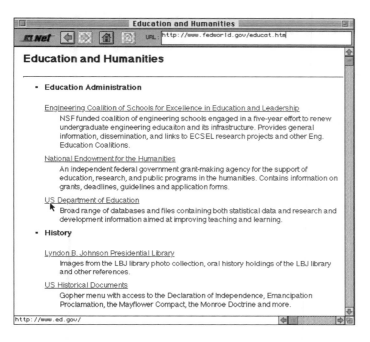

Finally, this index of indexes appears. Click on *U.S. Department of Education* to go to that Web site.

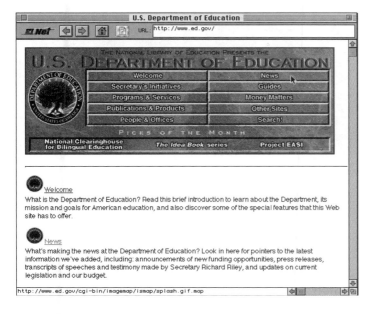

A real find. This area has more than 20 separate links to education information, from a list of National Education Goals to selected congressional testimony and speeches for the Secretary of Education. At the top of the screen, press the *News* button.

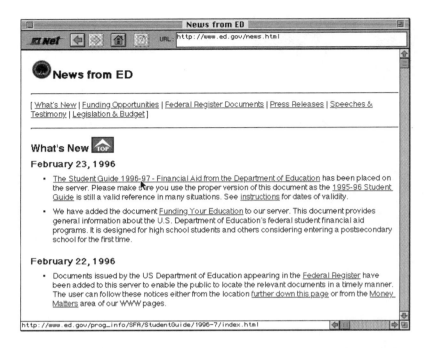

Here's the latest news from the Department of Education! Let's browse the new 1996–97 Student Guide to Financial Aid. Click on those words to continue.

Scroll down to the item called *Federal Stafford Loans,* and click it to continue.

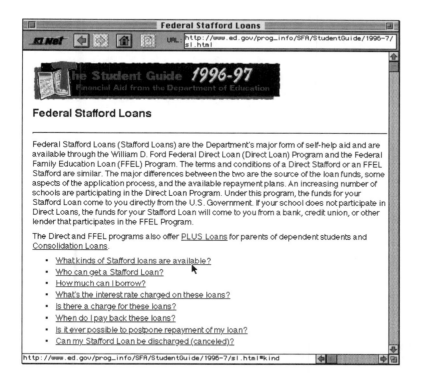

Here's complete information about Stafford Loans available from the federal government. Read through to get a feel for what's here. The information maybe of use to some of your high school students.

Did you know we can visit the Department of Education gopher site using our Web software? MacWeb, like all Web software, can access gopher sites as well as World Wide Web pages. So, look under File, select *Open URL*, and enter **gopher://gopher.ed.gov** as your destination. (Note that we just tacked **gopher://** on the front of the gopher address. Use this method with all gopher addresses to do the same thing with any Web browser.)

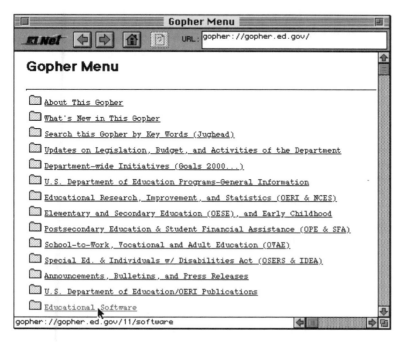

ERIC's gopher menu appears. Click on *Educational Software* to continue.

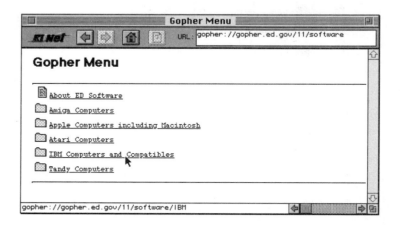

Here's a huge collection of free educational software for five popular computer platforms, including IBM PC's running Windows and Macintosh computers. Enjoy!

How to access FedWorld

Modem: (703) 321-8020
Ftp to: ftp.fedworld.gov
Telnet to: fedworld.gov
URL: http://www.fedworld.gov

TOUR VIII

ERIC

The AskERIC Virtual Library gives visitors graphical access to everything the Educational Resource and Information Center (ERIC) offers.

Internet navigation tool: World Wide Web

Site address: http://ericir.syr.edu

Type of Internet account used: Graphical SLIP/PPP

Navigation software used: Netscape 2.0 Web browser on a Macintosh Quadra 650

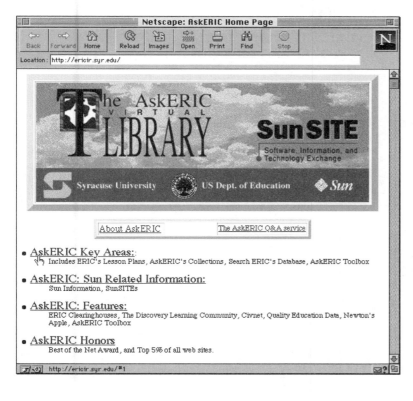

Sign on to the Internet and load your Netscape software. Then, select *Open location* under the File menu, and enter **http://ericir.syr.edu** as your destination.

You've arrived at the AskERIC Virtual Library. Click once on the words *AskERIC Key Areas*, then *AskERIC Virtual Library* icon to begin your tour.

The entire site is broken down into a single main menu. Take a look at each item, then select *AskERIC InfoGuides* near the center of the document.

Here are more than 200 individual indexes to information ranging from the latest Library Technology and African History entries, to Vocational Education and Whole Language. As you scroll through the list, note the functional toolbar at the bottom of the document. You can use it to quickly move to each of the site's main areas. Click on *Astronomy Sec.* located in the list of InfoGuides.

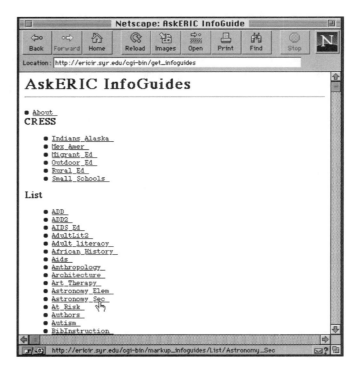

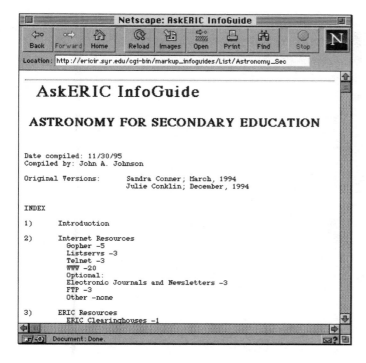

Here's an excellent document you can use to track down Astronomy resources on the Internet for use in a secondary school environment. Print a copy for yourself or a colleague! Be sure to check out the InfoGuides that are of interest to you as well.

Click on the little left arrow button at the top of your screen two times to step backwards until you return to the main menu, or home page. Then, click on the *AskERIC Slide Shows,* near the top of the page, to let the site take you on a tour.

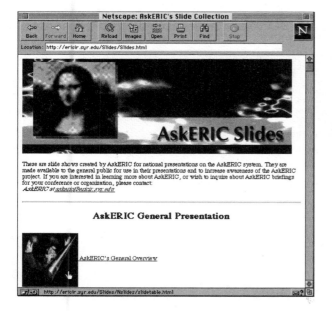

Now, click on *AskERIC's General Overview* icon to begin the tour.

```
┌─────────────────────────────────────────────────────────┐
│ ▦         Netscape: slidetable.html                    ▦ │
├─────────────────────────────────────────────────────────┤
│  ⇦o    o⇨    🏠    🔄    🖼    ⇉o    🖨    🔍    ⊗       │
│  Back Forward Home Reload Images Open Print Find  Stop  N │
├─────────────────────────────────────────────────────────┤
│ Location: http://ericir.syr.edu/Slides/Nslides/slidetable.html │
├─────────────────────────────────────────────────────────┤
│            The AskERIC Slide Show                        │
│                                                          │
│              Enter Slide Show                            │
│                                                          │
│   [slide]    [slide]    [slide]    [slide]               │
│   AskERIC     ERIC     ERIC Clearinghouse A User-based   │
│                          Locations       Approach        │
│                                                          │
│   [slide]    [slide]    [slide]    [slide]               │
│ AskERIC Goals AskERIC  AskERIC Service AskERIC Questions │
│              Components  Components     and Answers       │
│                                                          │
│   [slide]    [slide]    [slide]    [slide]               │
├─────────────────────────────────────────────────────────┤
│ 🔲 http://ericir.syr.edu/Slides/Nslides/slide1.html  ✉? │
└─────────────────────────────────────────────────────────┘
```

After you read each slide, click on word *Next* to move forward. Enjoy the tour!

We hope you've enjoyed the tours. These sites give only a hint of the valuable resources the Internet offers K–12 educators. Now that you know more about navigating the Net, go to Chapter 3, Educational Resources, pick a few sites, and take a few self-guided tours!

How to access ERIC

Phone: (800) USE-ERIC
Email to: askeric@ericir.syr.edu
Ftp to: ericir.syr.edu
 Go to the *ael* subdirectory
Telnet to: ericir.syr.edu
 Login: **gopher**
URL: http://ericir.syr.edu

"The Internet is our tool against ignorance in a rapidly changing world. It empowers people to reach out and make a difference."

David Barzilai
Lexington Public High School

EDUCATIONAL RESOURCES

An extensive list of Internet sites, mailing lists, and newsgroups for educators

The number of resources on the Internet is exploding. According to one estimate, more than 40,000 new Internet services and information locations come online *every month*. Hundreds of them are related to education.

Many Internet sites are valuable to educators—even those that don't seem so at first glance. The staff of *Classroom Connect* constantly searches for sites with lesson plans, text documents, software, anything that will enrich the classroom experience for students.

This chapter is a compilation of resources found after more than 1,000 hours of Net surfing. It includes the addresses and brief descriptions of gopher, telnet, and ftp sites and extensive lists of mailing lists and newsgroups covering topics of interest to educators and students.

Remember, the Internet is an evolving community. Addresses and list names, up to date when printed, are subject to change at any time. Patience and persistence count when you're on the Internet!

Gopher sites

Gopher sites often include pages and pages of menus and directories. After the address of each of the following gopher sites, follow the directions to "look in," or select, the menus we name. Then we'll show you a sample menu from the site.

Anthropology Corner at Yale

Gopher to: rsl.ox.ac.uk

Look in *Anthropology and Archaeology Corner*

Any K–12 educator or student doing a unit on anthropology will find useful information here. Includes links to dozens of documents and Internet sites with anthropology and archaeology areas.

Main menu
1. Search an Index of this Directory
2. Read Me!
3. Mambila Transcripts
4. Oxford University Union List of Anthropological Periodicals
5. Interactive Multimedia and Anthropology
6. Anthropology & Archaeology Archives Gopher at Yale
7. Anthropology (WAIS)
8. Anthropology in Education
9. Anthropology and Culture
10. Applied Anthropology Computer Network (Oakland)
11. Classicists & Mediterranean Archaeologists Gopher
12. FAQ: Internet Resources of Interest to Anthropologists
13. Internet Guide to Anthropology in Education
14. More Anthropology-related Gopher Servers
15. Prehistoric Archaeology of the Northeast United States
16. Social Science Information Gateway
17. Summer Institute of Linguistics (World languages)
18. The Electric Mystic's Guide to the Internet
19. World Email Directory of Anthropologists

Armadillo: The Texas Studies Gopher

Gopher to: chico.rice.edu 1170

Designed specifically for middle school educators and students interested in Texan natural and cultural history.

Main Menu
1. About Armadillo (The Texas Studies Gopher from HISD)
2. Better Version of Armadillo for Windows Users
3. More About Armadillo and Other Gophers
4. Developmental History of Texas Studies Project
5. Fact and Fiction about Armadillos
6. Human Resource Development Opportunities
7. Library Resources and Services
8. Other Gophers and Information Servers with a Texas Twist
9. Super Projects!
10. Technology Help and Multimedia Software and Lessons
11. Texas Studies Instructional Information and Resources
12. Weather Information
13. What's Happening
14. Search Armadillo by Title (Jughead)
15. Work in Progress

EDITOR'S
CHOICE

AskERIC

Gopher to: ericir.syr.edu

A public, educational resource concerning K–12 education. Features educational documents and more than 1,000 lesson plans for every conceivable curriculum area—all free. ERIC also operates AskERIC, a free, email question and answer service for educators, students, and parents.

Email to: askeric@ericir.syr.edu

Main Menu
1. News and Information about ERIC and AskERIC
2. Map of the ERIC Library
3. Search AskERIC Menu Items
4. AskERIC Toolbox
5. Frequently Asked Questions (FAQs) about ERIC
6. AskERIC InfoGuides
7. Lesson Plans
8. Education Listservs Archives
9. ERIC Clearinghouses/Components
10. ERIC Digests File
11. ERIC Bibliographic Database (RIE and CIJE)
12. Bibliographies
13. News & Announcements: Professional & Commercial Organizations
14. Other Education Resources
15. Education Conferences (Calendars and Announcements)

Best of K–12 Internet Resources via TIES

Gopher to: tiesnet.ties.k12.mn.us

Includes a vast array of K–12 educational information, including news, online guides, books, and access to other educational gopher sites. Technology and Information Educational Services (TIES) is owned and operated by eight greater-Minnesota school districts and 41 Twin Cities metropolitan area school districts.

Main Menu
1. Technology and Information Educational Services (TIES) Information
2. Workshops, Seminars and Training
3. Internet, Connectivity, & Associated Services
4. Applicant Search [Online Educator Search]
5. Student Services
6. Teaching and Learning Department
7. Special Interest Groups [SIGS]
8. EIS Coordinators
9. UNIX Help and Manual Pages
10. TIES Organizational PhoneBook
11. Veronica Searches (Keyword Search for Gopher Items)
12. InforMNs Gopher Server (Direct Link)

Daily Report Card

Gopher to: nysernet.org

Look in *Special Collections:Empire Internet Schoolhouse (K-12), Special Collections (The Old K–12 Directory)*

Special Collections (The Old K-12 Directory)
1. AskERIC - (Educational Resources Information Center)
2. CNN Newsroom Classroom Guide
3. Center for Talented Youth (CTY) - Johns Hopkins University
4. Classroom Earth BBS
5. CoSN.bylaws.draft
6. CoSN.charter.draft
7. Consortium for School Networking (CoSN)
8. Daily Report Card News Service
9. Distance Learning Resources
10. ERIC Clearinghouse on Assessment and Evaluation
11. K–12 Keypals list
12. Keypals Wanted
13. Keypals Wanted - Readme
14. Math & Science Education Guide; T.C. O'Haver; v1.2; 10/29/93
15. More Education Gophers (Rice)
16. Newton Educational BBS
17. Telnet to K-12 Libraries
18. US Dept. of Education and OERI Gopher
19. infrastructures.ps

 **EDITOR'S CHOICE**

Gopher Jewels

Gopher to: cwis.usc.edu
Look in *Other Gophers and Information Resources, Gophers by Subject, Gopher Jewels*

A jam-packed site full of pointers to thousands of gopher sites on any subject level. A great place to start a gopher journey.

Main Menu
1. GOPHER JEWELS Information and Help
2. Community, Global and Environmental
3. Education, Social Sciences, Arts & Humanities
4. Economics, Business and Store Fronts
5. Engineering and Industrial Applications
6. Government
7. Health, Medical, and Disability
8. Internet and Computer Related Resources
9. Law
10. Library, Reference, and News
11. Miscellaneous Items
12. Natural Sciences including Mathematics
13. Personal Development and Recreation
14. Research, Technology Transfer and Grants Opportunities
15. Search Gopher Jewels Menus by Key Word(s)

Home Economics

Gopher to: calypso.oit.unc.edu
Look in *Worlds of SunSITE—by Subject, Browse all Sunsite Archives, Docs, Recipes, Fatfree,* or *Usenet-Recipes*

More than 1,000 recipes—from desserts to main dishes. A rich resource for home economics teachers with access to the Internet.

FatFree menu
1. Beans (61 items)
2. Breads (103)
3. Breakfast (35)
4. Chili (22)
5. Condiments (107)
6. Desserts (145)
7. Dips (42)
8. General (470)
9. Indian (50)
10. Japanese (75)

Internet Business Resources

Gopher to: cob.fsu.edu:4070

Look in *Internet Business Resources*

High school business teachers integrating the Internet into their curriculum will find hundreds of pointers to online business information here—economic statistics, links to business schools worldwide, and Internet mailing lists and Usenet groups devoted to business.

Main menu
1. About Internet Business Resources
2. Business School Gophers
3. Business and Economic Data
4. Business and Economics Compilations
5. Commercial Services
6. Electronic Serials, Mailing Lists, Newsgroups
7. Governmental Bodies Affecting Business
8. Organizations Related to Business
9. Various Topics Related to Business

 EDITOR'S CHOICE

Lesson Plans

Gopher to: ericir.syr.edu

Look in *Lesson Plans*

Gopher to: copernicus.bbn.com

Look in *National Network Testbed, UCSD InterNet Lesson Plans*

The first site is at ERIC and the second is at Bolt, Beranek, and Newman (BBN), a company that offers Internet servers designed for education. Together, the two sites contain more than 3,000 free lesson plans on topics ranging from anatomy to zoology.

Lesson Plans menu from ERIC
1. Search AskERIC Lesson Plans
2. Astronomy: Curriculum Unit for Intermediate Elementary Students
3. CNN Newsroom Daily Lesson Plans
4. The Discovery Channel/The Learning Channel
5. Language Arts
6. Liquid Crystal
7. Mathematics
8. Miscellaneous
9. NASA's SIR-CED Education Program
10. Newton's Apple Educational Materials
11. School Library Media Activities Monthly
12. Science

UCSD InterNet Lesson Plans Menu from Copernicus
1. About this Collection
2. Biology
3. Earth Science
4. English
5. Lessons in Spanish
6. Mathematics
7. Physical Science and Chemistry
8. Physics

Mathematics Archives Gopher

Gopher to: archives.math.utk.edu

The primary goal of the Mathematics Archives Gopher is to provide educators with access to most public domain and shareware software and many other materials for the teaching of mathematics in high schools, community colleges, and colleges and universities. The site also includes a database with information about the free software and about commercial packages used to teach mathematics.

Main Menu
1. About the Mathematics Archives Gopher
2. Organization of the Mathematics Archives
3. Software (Packages, Abstracts, Reviews)
4. Teaching Materials
5. Other Mathematics Gophers
6. Submitting Materials to the Archive
7. Other Ways of Accessing the Archive
8. Other Math Archives Information (Newsletters)
9. What is Gopher?
10. Information about Gophers
11. Announcing our WWW Server
12. World Wide Web FAQ
13. Search the Archive using Jughead

Museum of Natural History

Gopher to: gopher.peabody.yale.edu
Look in *Search Peabody Collections*

The Yale Peabody Museum of Natural History (YPM) has long been a center for education and research in the natural sciences and anthropology. Through a major public education effort, the museum emphasizes the importance of studying the Earth's history and the diversity of its inhabitants. More than 11 million specimens are held by the museum's ten curatorial divisions, less than one percent of which can be publicly displayed at any given time.

Search Peabody Collections Menu
1. Anthropology
2. Entomology
3. Herpetology
4. Historical Scientific Instruments
5. Ichthyology
6. Invertebrate Paleontology
7. Invertebrate Zoology
8. Mammalogy
9. Mineralogy
10. Ornithology
11. Paleobotany
12. Vertebrate Paleontology

NASA Space Shuttle Small Payloads Program

Gopher to: sspp.gsfc.nasa.gov

Features information for prospective users and others interested in the U.S. Shuttle Small Payloads Program. Of interest to shuttle enthusiasts are a program overview, user documents, general shuttle pictures in GIF format, small payload pictures and illustrations, newsletters, information on conferences, education initiatives and symposia, and more.

Main Menu
1. NASA Shuttle Small Payloads Overview
2. NASA Shuttle Payload Information
3. Shuttle Small Payload Documents
4. NASA Shuttle Small Payload Images
5. General Shuttle Images
6. SSPP Software
7. Hitchhiker and GAS Capabilities
8. NASA Shuttle Small Payloads Flight Schedules
9. Small Payloads Education Initiatives
10. Small Payloads News Update
11. Educational Space Experiments

NYSERNet

Gopher to: nysernet.org

The New York Educational Network's headquarters on the Internet, offering online resources for K–12 teachers using telecomputing tools in the classroom and for their professional development. NYSERNet is part of a national Internet testbed researching new uses of online resources and computer technology in the nation's classrooms.

Main Menu
1. Disclaimer
2. NYSERNet Related Information (Includes Information about this Gopher)
3. Index for the NYSERNet Gopher
4. Newsletters (NYSERNet User)
5. Reference Desk
6. Search the Internet
7. NYSERNet Internet Training & Education Center (NITEC)
8. Special Collections: Breast Cancer Information Clearinghouse
9. Special Collections: Business and Economic Development
10. Special Collections: Community Networks
11. Special Collections: Empire Internet Schoolhouse (K-12)
12. Special Collections: High Bandwidth Testbeds (NYSERNet and Others)
13. Special Collections: Higher Education
14. Special Collections: Internet Help
15. Special Collections: Libraries
16. Special Collections: New York State and Federal Info
17. Special Collections: Software
18. Special Collections: K-12
19. Weather
20. What's NEW in Gopher Space
21. FTP Archives

Shadowy Science Projects

Gopher to: ralphbunche.rbs.edu

Look in *Shadows Science Projects*

An online database of discussions, articles, and projects featuring the sun, shadows, the Earth's rotation, and more.

Shadowy Science Projects Menu
1. Measuring Shadows
2. Drawing Of Students Measuring Shadows
3. Winter By Ana Martinez
4. My Favorite Season Is .....
5. The Change of Seasons by David Crowell
6. Thoughts about the seasons
7. The Change of Seasons
8. Nature and Her Seasons
9. Shorts in the Summer
10. Seasons Are Like Boomerangs
11. Changing of Seasons
12. About Seasons
13. My Favorite Season
14. The Changing of Seasons
15. Winter by Shameka Day
16. Summertime

Teacher Education Internet Server

Gopher to: state.virginia.edu

Look in *Teacher Education Internet Server (TEIS)*

The Society for Information Technology and Teacher Education (SITE), the University of Virginia, and the University of Houston have collaborated to establish a Teacher Education Server on the Internet. The Teacher Education Internet Server (TEIS) was established to explore the ways in which the Internet could benefit teacher education programs around the world. It's full of great ideas for all K–12 teachers integrating the Internet into the classroom.

Main Menu
1. About SITE
2. Electronic_Publications
3. Mathematics Education
4. Research
5. Social Studies
6. Special Education
7. Educational Technology
8. Teach-IT Modules
9. International Education
10. Software_Archives
11. Telecommunications and Networking
12. Interactive Resources
13. Other Internet Resources
14. Grants, Development Opportunities

 EDITOR'S CHOICE

U.S. Government Gophers

Gopher to: stis.nsf.gov

Look in *Other US. Government Gopher Servers*

This site is a jumping-off point to an abundance U.S. government gopher systems.

Telnet access to Gopher

This is a list of telnet sites which offer free remote access to gopher. If a school or Internet account doesn't offer direct access to gopher, telnet to one of these sites and use that computer's gopher program.

Telnet to: gopher.msu.edu
Login: **gopher**

Telnet to: consultant.micro.umn.edu
Login: **gopher**

Telnet to: nicol.jvnc.net
Login: **nicol**

Telnet to: cat.ohiolink.edu
Login: **gopher**

Telnet to: solar.rtd.utk.edu
Login: **gopher**

Telnet to: gopher.virginia.edu
Login: **gwis**

Telnet to: ecosys.drdr.virginia.edu
Login: **gopher**

Telnet to: telnet.wiscinfo.wisc.edu
Login: **gopher**

Telnet to: ux1.cso.uiuc.edu
Login: **gopher**

Telnet to: panda.uiowa.edu
Look in *Online Information Services, Other Gopher Servers*

The Chronicle of Higher Education

Gopher to: chronicle.merit.edu

"Academe This Week" is an online supplement to *The Chronicle of Higher Education,* a weekly printed magazine. A new edition is on the Internet beginning every Tuesday at noon, eastern time. It's a timely, in-depth look at issues and breaking news affecting the higher education community.

Also available via the World Wide Web.

URL: http://chronicle.merit.edu

Comments about the service are welcome.

Email to: editor@chronicle.merit.edu

Main Menu
1. New in "Academe This Week"
2. A Guide to The Chronicle of Higher Education
3. Organizations in Academe
4. — News of Organizations
5. — Information Provided by Annenberg/CPB Project
6. Information Technology in Higher Education
7. — News of Information Technology
8. — Information Provided by Lotus Development
9. Finances and Personal Planning in Academe
10. — News of Finances and Personal Planning
11. — Information provided by Fidelity Investments
12. Best-Selling Books in Academe
13. Events and Deadlines in Academe
14. Facts and Figures on U.S. Higher Education
15. Jobs in and out of Academe
16. Information about The Chronicle's Publications
17. About "Academe This Week": Search Tips and More

U.S. National K–12 Gopher

Gopher to: copernicus.bbn.com

This is a national educational research and development resource which schools, administrators, and parents use to experiment with online applications.

Main Menu
1. Welcome to BBN's National School Network Testbed
2. BBN Internet Server (Specializing in K-12 School Internet Connectivity)
3. National School Network Testbed
4. BBN - Educational Technologies Dept.
5. K-12 on the Internet (Resources)
6. Software Libraries
7. AskERIC
8. General Information Resources
9. Internet Information
10. State Resources
11. Federal Resources
12. Other Gopher and Information Servers
13. Search Titles in Gopherspace using Veronica
14. People at BBN

Telnet sites

Internauts who use telnet can actually logon to a computer system at another location. For example, the first site on this list is at California State University in Fresno, California. You can logon to it from any Internet-connected computer in the world. Each telnet site on our list includes the telnet address, the login command, the password (if necessary), and commands visitors use to exit or take other actions.

Advanced Technology Information Network (ATINet)

Telnet to: caticsuf.csufresno.edu
Login: **super** or **public**
Exit command: **0** (zero) at the main menu

ATINet provides information for the agricultural and biotechnology markets in California. It includes national and worldwide agricultural news, exporter information, a publications index, and biotechnological research information. Vocational agricultural classes or science classes interested in biotechnology will find value here.

Big Sky Telegraph

Telnet to: bigsky.bigsky.dillon.mt.us
Login: **bbs** or **visitor**
Exit command: At the main menu, **G**. From any other prompt, **bye**.

Big Sky Telegraph offers access to a wealth of educational resources and a multitude of ideas for use in the classroom. From lesson plans to science labs, the site has something for every K–12 teacher, including library resources, bulletin boards, and community networks. Only $50 buys subscriber privileges for a year. Online training sessions are available. Director Frank Odasz invites teachers to contact him at Western Montana College of the University of Montana, (406) 683-7338, with questions or problems.

Bulletin Board for Libraries

Telnet to: sun.nsf.ac.uk or **128.86.8.7**
Login: **janet**
Password: **guest**
Hostname: **uk.ac.glasgow.bubl**
Exit command: **quit** or **q**

This site is devoted to information for and about libraries with an emphasis on those in the United Kingdom but is of interest to people in the library field in any country. Includes reviews of library journals and their most recent contents, a review of library-related online mailing lists, and software used to manage a library.

Canada Institute for Scientific and Technical Information (CISTI)

Telnet to: cat.cisti.nrc.ca
or **132.246.80.250**
login: **cat**

The Canada Institute for Scientific and Technical Information (CISTI) is Canada's national service for worldwide information in science, technology and medicine. They also have one of the world's largest collections of scientific and technical information, including 55,000 journals, and worldwide conference proceedings and technical reports. This telnet site allows users to order documents, view the latest news, or do general searches.

Cleveland Free-Net

Telnet to: freenet-in-a.cwru.edu
or **freenet-in-b.cwru.edu**
or **freenet-in-c.cwru.edu**
Login: Type **2** to enter as a visitor
Exit command: **x**

The Cleveland Free-Net is the flagship telnet site for the National Public Telecommunications Network, which provides free, unlimited, and easy access to online resources of all kinds. It contains an enormous number of historical documents, including the Magna Carta, the U.S. Constitution, and the Declaration of Independence. It also includes a vast amount of information about the arts, science and technology, medicine, education, and business and provides an up-to-date news service. Of particular interest to educators is Academy One, an experimental NPTN program designed to meet the information and communication needs of students and educators.

Cookie Server

Telnet to: astro.temple.edu 12345

Every time a user logs into this server, a humorous saying or story is returned. No login or exit command is required, as users are automatically disconnected as soon as the saying is printed.
Sample responses:
- "Innovation is hard to schedule."—Dan Fylstra
- Katz' Law: Man and nations will act rationally when all other possibilities have been exhausted.
- "I'd love to go out with you, but I'm converting my calendar watch from Julian to Gregorian."
- Hindsight is an exact science.

Cornell Extension Network (CENet)

Telnet to: empire.cce.cornell.edu
Login: **guest**
Exit command: **bye**

A wealth of agricultural and environmental information, the site's main menu leads to agricultural production and management information, community education and resources, field crops and agronomy, food and nutrition, fruit and vegetable production and management, forestry, wildlife, and marine science, and integrated pest management and pesticide information.

Conversational Hypertext Access Technology (CHAT)

Telnet to: debra.dgbt.doc.ca 3000
Login: **chat**
Exit command: **goodbye**

CHAT is a research project examining the nature of human-computer interactions. Users access a natural language program that allows them to ask questions in plain English of an Internet computer and receive answers. (The software can also be adapted to other languages.) History of the development of the project is available. Be sure to fill out the questionnaire before leaving.

Dartmouth College Library Online System (DCLOS)

Telnet to: lib.dartmouth.edu
Exit command: **bye** or **quit**

A list of information about nearly all items owned by the library in its nine locations, including the CIA World Factbook, MLA biography, full text of 33 Shakespeare plays, electronic dictionary, encyclopedia, the *Bible*, a portion of the MEDLINE Medical Database, and much more.

Diversity University

Telnet to: moo.du.org 8888

This online university is specifically designed for teachers to bring their classes of students to do work. Visitors can take a tour of the human brain, perform science experiments, travel through Dante's Inferno or T.S. Eliot's Wasteland, or just hang out in the student lounge and chat with other teachers.

Educational Technology Network (Medical)

Telnet to: etnet.nlm.nih.gov
or **130.14.10.123**
Login: **etnet**
Exit command: **0**

The Educational Technology Network (ETNET) has a series of online conferences for professionals and students interested in learning or sharing information about the use of technology in medical education. Although the conferences focus on medical education, the ideas discussed in some groups have wide application to instructional technology students as well as K–12 teachers.

E-Math

Telnet to: e-math.ams.org
Login: **e-math**
Password: **e-math**
Exit command: Press **0** (zero) to exit

Primarily for math educators and professionals, the site provides online access to employment opportunities, software, and a variety of math publications. The American Mathematical Society (AMS) maintains and supports this site.

Environmental Protection Agency (EPA) Libraries

Telnet to: epaibm.rtpnc.epa.gov
Login: Select **4** (Public Access Applications Menu), then **1** (EPA National Online Library System)

Provides citations and abstracts of articles and reports pertaining to environmental issues to make bibliographic information available to the public. Citations include topics from other countries (e.g., depletion of rain forests in Brazil, acid rain in Eastern Europe, etc.). Science educators can find citations for technical reports on the effects of various pollutants, field studies of endangered organisms, reports on the status of rain forests, procedures for water testing, and general information about ecosystems. Social studies teachers could find information on public policy and resources in other countries.

 EDITOR'S CHOICE

FedWorld

Telnet to: fedworld.gov
A gateway to more than 150 government-operated Internet databases.

FDA Electronic Bulletin Board

Telnet to: fdabbs.fda.gov
Login: **bbs**
Exit command: **quit**
   Access to information regarding the Food and Drug Administration, including its actions, congressional testimony, news releases, consumer information, material on AIDS, and information on veterinary medicine.

Free-Nets

   Free-Nets are free, online bulletin board systems offering access to Internet resources for educators. Use the modem number listed to dial directly into the system nearest you. Users with Internet access will find telnet addresses for each system.

United States

ALABAMA
Mobile Area Free-Net
Telnet to: ns1.maf.mobile.al.us
Modem: (334) 405-4636

ARIZONA
Arizona Telecommunication Company
Telnet to: aztec.asu.edu
Login: **guest**
Password: **visitor**
Modem: (602) 965-6699
Modem: (602) 965-4151

CALIFORNIA
Los Angeles Free-Net
Telnet to: lafn.org
Login: **2**
Modem: (818) 776-5000

SLONet
San Luis Obispo
Telnet to: 199.74.141.2
Login: **visitor**
Modem: (805) 781-3666

COLORADO
Denver Free-Net
Telnet to: freenet.hsc.colorado.edu
Login: **guest**
Modem: (303) 270-4865

Fort Collins Community Computer Network
Telnet to: www.fortnet.org
Login: **guest**
Modem: (303) 416-1446

FLORIDA
Alachua Free-Net
Telnet to: freenet.ufl.edu
Login: **visitor**
Modem: (904) 334-0200

Southeast Florida Library Information Network
Email to: infodesk@bcfreenet.seflin.lib.fl.us
Telnet to: bcfreenet.seflin.lib.fl.us
Login: **visitor**
Modem: (305) 735-4332

Tallahassee Free-Net
Telnet to: freenet.fsu.edu
Login: **visitor**
Modem: (904) 488-5056
Modem: (904) 488-6313

GEORGIA
Worth County Free-Net
Modem: (912) 776-1255

ILLINOIS
Heartland Regional Network
Telnet to: heartland.bradley.edu
Login: **bbguest**
Password: **Hit RETURN**
Modem: (309) 674-1100

PrairieNet
Telnet to: prairienet.org
Login: **visitor**
Modem: (217) 255-9033
Modem: (217) 255-9000

MARYLAND
Chesapeake Free-Net
Telnet to: cfn.bluecrab.org
Modem: (410) 819-6860

MASSACHUSETTS
UMassK12 Free-Net
Telnet to: k12.oit.umass.edu
Login: **guest**
Modem: (413) 572-5583
Modem: (413) 572-5268

MICHIGAN
Almont Expression Free-Net
Modem: (810) 798-8290

Educational Central Free-Net
Telnet to: edcen.ehhs.cmich.edu
Login: **visitor**
Modem: (517) 774-3790

Genesee Free-Net
Telnet to: genessee.freenet.org
Login: **guest**
Modem: (810) 232-9905

Grand Rapids Free-Net
Telnet to: grfn.org
Login: **visitor**
Modem: (616) 949-2111

Great Lakes Free-Net
Modem: (616) 969-4536

Greater Detroit Free-Net
Telnet to: detroit.freenet.org
Login: **visitor**
This system has dozens of modem numbers. Write
to the address below and request dial-in numbers
by region.
Greater Detroit Free-Net
User Registration
P.O. Box 5068
Warren, MI 48090-5068

MISSOURI
Columbia Online Information Network (COIN)
Telnet to: bigcat.missouri.edu
Login: **guest**
Modem: (314) 884-7000 (Main)
Modem: (816) 248-1670 (Fayette)
Modem: (314) 642-2398 (Fulton)

RAIN - Rural Area Information Network
Telnet to: rain.gen.mo.us
Login: **visitor**
Modem: (816) 834-2555

MONTANA
Big Sky Telegraph
Telnet to: bigsky.bigsky.dillon.mt.us
Login: **bbs**
Modem: (406) 683-7680

Ozarks Regional Information Online Network
(ORION)
Telnet to: ozarks.sgcl.lib.mo.us
Login: **guest**
Modem: (417) 864-6100

NEW YORK
Buffalo Free-Net
Telnet to: freenet.buffalo.edu
Login: **freeport**
Modem: (716) 645-3085

NORTH DAKOTA
SENDIT
Telnet to: sendit.nodak.edu
Login: **bbs**
Modem: (701) 237-3283

OHIO
Cleveland Free-Net
Telnet to: freenet-in-a.cwru.edu
Telnet to: freenet-in-b.cwru.edu
Telnet to: freenet-in-c.cwru.edu
Login: **visitor**
Modem: (216) 368-3888

Dayton Free-Net
Telnet to: 130.108.128.174
Login: **visitor**
Modem: (513) 229-4373

Greater Columbus Free-Net
Telnet to: Free-Net.columbus.oh.us
Login: **guest**
Modem: (614) 292-7501

Learning Village Cleveland
Telnet to: nptn.org
Login: **visitor**
Modem: (216) 247-6196

Lorain County Free-Net
Telnet to: freenet.lorain.oberlin.edu
Login: **guest**
Modem: (216) 277-2359
Modem: (216) 366-9753 (Elyria)

Medina Area Free-Net
Modem: (216) 723-6732

SouthEastern Ohio Regional Free-Net
Telnet to: seorf.ohiou.edu
Login: **guest**
Modem: (614) 593-1439

Talawanda Learning Community Network
Telnet to: tlcnet.muohio.edu
Login: **visitor**
Modem: (513) 529-4999

Tristate Online Free-Net
Telnet to: tso.uc.edu
Login: **visitor**
Modem: (513) 579-1990

Youngstown Free-Net
Telnet to: yfn2.ysu.edu
Login: **visitor**
Modem: (216) 742-3072

RHODE ISLAND
Ocean State Free-Net
Telnet to: 192.207.24.10
Login: **visitor**
Modem: (401) 831-4640

TENNESSEE
Jackson Area Free-Net
Telnet to: jackson.freenet.org
Login: **visitor**
Modem: (901) 427-4435

TEXAS
Rio Grande Free-Net
Telnet to: rgfn.epcc.edu
Login: **visitor**
Modem: (915) 775-5600

VIRGINIA
Central Virginia's Free-Net
Telnet to: freenet.vcu.edu
Login: **guest**
Password: **visitor**
Modem: (804) 828-8694

WASHINGTON D.C.
CapAccess
National Capital Area Public Access Network
Telnet to: capaccess.org
Login: **guest**
Password: **visitor**
Modem: (202) 785-1523

WASHINGTON
Kitsap Free-Net
Telnet to: 198.187.135.22
Login: **visitor**
Modem: (360) 698-4737

Seattle Community Network
Telnet to: scn.org
Login: **visitor**
Modem: (206) 386-4140
Email to: randy@cpsr.org

Canada

BRITISH COLUMBIA
CIAO! Free-Net
Telnet to: freenet.victoria.bc.ca
Login: **guest**
Modem: (604) 368-5764

Prince George Free-Net
Telnet to: freenet.unbc.edu
Login: **guest**
Modem: (604) 563-3977

Sea to Sky Free-Net
Telnet to: sea-to-sky-freenet.bc.ca
Login: **guest**
Modem: (604) 892-3500

Vancouver Regional Free-Net
Telnet to: freenet.vancouver.bc.ca
Login: **guest**
Modem: (604) 257-8778

Victoria Free-Net
Telnet to: freenet.victoria.bc.ca
Login: **guest**
Modem: (604) 595-2300

MANITOBA
Blue Sky Free-Net
Telnet to: winnie.freenet.mb.ca
Login: **guest**
Password: **guest**
Modem: (204) 987-1234

NOVA SCOTIA
Chebucto Free-Net
Telnet to: cfn.cs.dal.ca
Login: **guest**
Modem: (902) 494-8006

ONTARIO
National Capital Free-Net
Telnet to: freenet.carleton.ca
Login: **guest**
Modem: (613) 564-3600
Modem: (613) 564-0808

Toronto Free-Net
Telnet to: freenet.toronto.on.ca
Login: **guest**
Modem: (416) 780-2010

Germany

Free-Net Erlangen-Nuernberg
Telnet to: freenet-a.fim.uni-erlangen.de
Login: **gast**
Modem: +49 9131 21916

New Zealand

Wellington CityNet
Telnet to: kosmos.wcc.govt.nz
Modem: +64 4801 3060

Gabriel's Horn

Telnet to: 138.26.65.78 7777

This site automatically returns a random verse from either the New or the Old Testament. Here is a sample result: *"For I know that my redeemer liveth, and that he shall stand at the latter day upon the earth."*— Job 19:25 [KJV]

Georgia College EduNet

Telnet to: gcedunet.peachnet.edu
Exit command: **L** to logout

A large collection of resources for K–12 educators, including Internet directories and online texts, CNN and Newsweek curriculum guides, a software evaluation library, Georgia's Quality Core Curriculum, a multimedia file exchange for Macintosh, Apple II, Apple IIgs, IBM, and Amiga platforms, and more.

Geographic Name Server

Telnet to: martini.eecs.umich.edu 3000
Exit command: **exit**

Gives geographic information for U.S. cities, counties, and North American places by name, state/province, or zip code.

Ham Radio Callbook

Telnet to: callsign.cs.buffalo.edu 2000
Exit command: **quit**

Primarily for ham operators, this national directory is useful to anyone seeking the address or callsign of a ham operator. Provides the callsign and address of individual operators or a list of operators at a particular location. The service will search for a name and return the address and callsign if the person is a registered ham operator.

Internic Directory and Database Services

Telnet to: ds.internic.net
or: **198.49.45.10**
Login: **guest**
Exit command: **6** from the main menu

Access basic Internet information and a keyword-searchable database of Internet and online-related documents. A tutorial for using the system can be retrieved by using ftp.

Ftp to: ds.internic.net

Go to the *ftp/internic.info* subdirectory. Retrieve the *guest.tutorial* file.

International Education Bulletin Board

Telnet to: nis.calstate.edu
Login: **intl**
Exit command: Type **q** to quit

Established by the California State University System's Study Abroad Programs, this site is valuable for educators associated with international education programs, students who are going to study aboard, or anyone interested in international education as well as overseas travel. Menu listings include Study Abroad Programs, Campus Exchange Agreement, Campus International Directory, and the Listing of Overseas U.S. educational advising centers.

Internet Relay Chat (IRC)

Public sites offering access to online rooms full of Internauts chatting with each other. The sites listed contain many rooms concerning education-related subjects safe for students and educators. Login as **IRC**.
Telnet to: ara.kaist.ac.kr
Telnet to: santafe.santafe.edu

IPAC Extragalactic Database

Telnet to: ned.ipac.caltech.edu
or: **134.4.10.118**
Login: **ned**
Exit command: **Control-X**

The NASA/IPAC Extragalactic Database (NED) is a research-supported program at the Infrared Processing and Analysis Center (IPAC), Jet Propulsion Laboratory, and California Institute of Technology, under contract with the National Aeronautics and Space Administration. NED is open to the astronomical community worldwide. Funded by NASA, it is an effort to make available over computer networks the rapidly accumulating literature on extragalactic objects.

Knowbot Information Service

Telnet to: info.cnri.reston.va.us 185
or **regulus.cs.bucknell.edu 185**
Exit command: **quit**

A service useful for locating someone with an Internet address. Knowbot does not have its own telephone "white pages" listing of Internet users, but it can access information services that have "white pages" and do a search. However, the Internet is growing so rapidly and adding so many different systems that a "white pages" is becoming less useful. It is therefore less likely that you will locate a user with the Knowbot.
Sample search: **query Mary Jane Landis**

Library of Congress Information System (LOCIS)

Telnet to: locis.loc.gov and **dra.com**
Exit command: Type **12** at the prompt
   More than 15 million catalog records and 10 million records of federal legislation, copyright registrations, Braille and audio materials, organizations, and foreign law are available. Two searching manuals are available on the Internet for users of LOCIS. Each can be retrieved through a single ftp site.
Ftp to: seq1.loc.gov
Go to the *pub/LC.Online* subdirectory

Lunar-Planetary Institute

Telnet to: lpi.jsc.nasa.gov
Login: **lpi**
Exit command: Select **exit** from the main menu
   Offers online resources related to geology, geophysics, astrophysics, and astronomy.

Martin Luther King, Jr., Online Library

Telnet to: forsythetn.stanford.edu
       or: **36.172.0.41**
Account: **socrates**
Your Response: **select mlk**
Exit command: Type **end** to quit
   The library contains approximately 2,700 bibliographic references pertaining to Martin Luther King, Jr., and the civil rights movement, especially the Black freedom struggle. References include works and speeches about and by Dr. King. Verification of citations and updates on included works are continually refined by the Martin Luther King, Jr., Papers Project.

MediaMOO

Telnet to: purple-crayon.media.mit.edu
Login: **connect guest**
   MediaMOO provides a place for those who are interested in integrating technology, education, and writing. Every Tuesday, users gather informally in the Netoric cafe to talk about these issues and other writing-related topics. This site is aimed more at teachers and researchers than students.

MicroMUSE: A Virtual Reality Adventure Game

Telnet to: michael.ai.mit.edu
Login: **guest**
Program: **tt**
Command: **connect visitor**
Exit command: **QUIT**

A combination of a real-time "chat" group and a role-playing science fiction game. The user enters the twenty-fourth century world of MicroMUSE and meets characters who inhabit the space colony. MicroMUSE may acquaint a student with computer networking as well as provide an exercise in creativity because students communicate, explore, and design their own corner of this cyberspace microworld. A similar game called BattleTech 3056 is available at the following site.
Telnet to: btech.netaxs.com 3056

National Distance Learning Center

Telnet to: ndlc.occ.uky.edu
Login: **ndlc**
Password: **Your phone number**
Exit command: Type **Ctrl-]** to quit

A database for distance learning appropriate for K–12 adult basic skills, post-secondary courses, and continuing education programs. The service offers an excellent opportunity for homebound disabled students or students unable to access coursework locally. The site can be searched by subject areas, date, audience, and media.

Newton Bulletin Board System

Telnet to: newton.dep.anl.gov
Login: **bbs**
Exit command: Type **5** at the main menu

An educational BBS sponsored by the Argonne National Laboratory Division of Educational Programs and intended primarily for math and science teachers. Its purpose is to promote the networking of teachers and students and to exchange ideas.

Oceanic Network Information Center (OCEANIC)

Telnet to: delocn.udel.edu
Username: **INFO**
Exit command: **$**
Gopher to: gopher.cms.udel.edu

A source of information for the World Ocean Circulation Experiment (WOCE). Research programs collect data and provide summaries of projects, along with maps, resources, dataset directories, a searchable directory of oceanographers who have Internet addresses, and a searchable international database of oceanographic research ship schedules.

PENPages

Telnet to: psupen.psu.edu
Username: **Your two-letter state abbreviation, such as PA**
Exit command: Type **0** (zero) to quit

The College of Agriculture at Pennsylvania State University fills this site with information on local and national agriculture as well as current educational issues. Of interest to the educators are the MAPP and SENIORS SERIES databases. MAPP is the National Cooperative Extension family database, supporting family educators and extension professionals around the world. The SENIORS SERIES provides information on the concerns of the aging and the elderly. Research by Penn State professors and their colleagues across the country is published via this database.

Regional Educational Laboratory

Telnet to: r2d2.jvnc.net 4446
Exit command: **quit**

This site is sponsored by the Office of Educational Research and Improvement (OERI) of the U.S. Department of Education and by ten Regional Educational Laboratories across the United States. They have pooled their database resources into five interactively searchable databases of interest to educators.

 EDITOR'S CHOICE

SENDIT K12 Educational Telecommunications Network

Telnet to: sendit.nodak.edu
Login: **bbs**
Password: **sendit2me**
Exit command: Select **exit** from the main menu

An Internet-accessible BBS that offers more than a dozen online resources for K–12 educators, including links to Kidlink information and projects, Electronic Classroom forum, Academy One, and the SENDIT Users Directory.

 EDITOR'S
CHOICE

SERVICES Telnet Gateway to the World

Telnet to: library.wustl.edu
Login: **Hit return twice to get to the main menu**
  An excellent information gateway providing access to 153 telnet sites around the world. Users access the sites by menu selection; therefore, in most cases, the user can visit several sites without reconnecting through the telnet prompt. That feature eliminates the need to know hundreds of other site addresses. SERVICES also offers a brief description of each site, including its direct telnet address, login and exit information, and the email address of the contact person. This provides the user with a "mini resource guide" to many other telnet sites.

SpaceLINK NASA

Telnet to: spacelink.msfc.nasa.gov
or **128.158.13.250**
Userid: **guest**
Password: **guest**
Exit command: Type **1** from the main menu
Gopher to: spacelink.msfc.nasa.gov
  This database provides access to current and historical information on NASA aeronautics and space research. Also includes suggested classroom activities that incorporate information on NASA projects to teach scientific principles.

SpaceMet Internet

Telnet to: spacemet.phast.umass.edu
Login: **guest**
Exit command: **Control-]** or **G**
  A rich, easy-to-use service for educators and students interested in space and space related topics. Includes a large database of NASA news and information about current and past space shuttle missions.

Science & Technology Information System (STIS)

Telnet to: stis.nsf.gov
Modem: (703) 306-0212
Login: **public**
Exit command: **7** or **logout**
  An electronic dissemination system that provides fast, easy access to National Science Foundation (NSF)

publications, including the NSF Bulletin, Program announcements, NSF Directories, and award abstracts (1989–present). Easy to search using keywords.

Politics Databases

Telnet to: sunsite.unc.edu
Login: **politics**
Exit command: **q**

Seven different information servers provide 12 different sources of politically oriented information—all searchable by keyword. Search the president's speeches, news briefings, White House papers, and congressional documents. Educators will find great value in the numerous up-to-date, primary sources of current interest topics. Social studies, history, economics, and health students will find useful information.

TC Forum

Telnet to: tcforum.unl.edu
Exit command: **G** or **Q**

Designed to serve the educational needs in Nebraska, this site is operated by Teachers College, University of Nebraska. Its purpose is to encourage and promote the free exchange and discussion of educational information, ideas, and opinions.

Weather Underground: U.S. Weather Service

Telnet to: madlab.sprl.umich.edu 3000
Exit command: **X**

A complete weather service covering forecasts for U.S. regions and cities, including current weather observations, long-range forecasts, ski conditions, earthquake reports, hurricane advisories, marine forecasts, national weather summary, and severe weather advisories. Includes information about Canadian weather and some international data. Free for personal and educational use.

National Agricultural Library

Telnet to: opac.nal.usda.gov
or **192.54.138.20**
Login: **isis**

This is an agricultural union catalog that includes bibliographic citations for materials from the U.S. National Arboretum Library and the five USDA, Agricultural Research Service (ARS) Regional Libraries: Eastern Regional Research Center, National Center for Agricultural Utilization Research, Russell Research Center, Southern Regional Research Center, and Western Regional Research Center.

ResourceNet

Telnet to: resnet.fmhi.usf.edu
or **131.247.74.80**
   ResourceNet is a bulletin board service for those interested in child and family issues, policy, and systems of care, providing a place where parents, youth, researchers, educators, policy makers, service providers and others can share and exchange information about issues facing children and their families.

Substance Abuse Network of Ontario

Telnet to: sano.arf.org
Login: **guest**
   This bulletin board focuses on drug and alcohol abuse, including tobacco research. There are public forums and discussions, the latest publications and articles, job postings, and a lengthy section on addiction information and drug therapy.

Anonymous ftp sites

   By using file transfer protocol (ftp), Internauts can visit sites to transfer text documents, computer software, or graphics to their computers.
   When accessing the following anonymous ftp sites, be sure to type **anonymous** as the username and **your complete email address** as the password. The review of each site includes names of the directories and subdirectories with the most valuable material and a brief description of their content.

AskERIC

Ftp to: ericir.syr.edu
Go to the *ael* subdirectory
   AskERIC has a wealth of information for K–12 educators. Teachers can access material ranging from complete lesson plans to mini-searches on a wide range of subjects.

•••••••••••••••••••••••••••••••••••••••

Material in the *ael* **subdirectory**

Clearinghouses	Information on contacting and getting the most out of ERIC's 13 educational clearinghouses in the U.S.
Digests	ERIC Digests on thousands of education-related topics.

| **InfoGuides** | Education information on various subjects, including grants and teaching methods. |
| **Lesson** | Complete lesson plans for any subject. Most include goals and objectives, and detailed information for achieving those goals. |

....

Center for Electronic Records—U.S. National Archives

Ftp to: ftp.cu.nih.gov
or **128.231.64.7**

The Center for Electronic Records of the U.S. National Archives and Records Administration.

Center for Innovative Computer Applications (CICA)

Ftp to: ftp.cica.indiana.edu
or **ftp.monash.edu.au**
Go to the *pub/win3* subdirectory

The anonymous ftp clearinghouse for Microsoft Windows (version 3.0 and up) software applications, tips, utilities, drivers, and more. CICA provides access to more than 300 megabytes of public domain and shareware files. The files are **not** virus checked, and by retrieving software from CICA, users assume full responsibility for its use on their computers. Make sure you scan downloaded files for viruses with virus-checking software, which is available at this site.

....

Material in the *win3* **subdirectory**

demo	Various Windows Demo Programs
desktop	Desktop Image Utilities
printer	Software and Printer Drivers
video	Software Drivers for video applications
fonts	WindowsSoft Fonts
atm	Adobe Type Manager (ATM) Fonts
truetype	TrueType Fonts
games	Windows Games and Diversions
icons	Windows Icons and Icon Editors
nt	Windows NT Files
programmer	Windows Programming
programr/bcpp	Borland C++ Windows Programs
sounds	Windows Sounds and Utility Files
util	General Windows Utilities
winword	Word for Windows Utilities and Files
wrk	Windows Resource Kit Files
wpwin	WordPerfect for Windows Utilities

....

Computers and Academic Freedom Archive

Ftp to: ftp.eff.org

Go to the *pub* subdirectory

Access the latest education-oriented materials concerning computer freedom, freedom of expression, and copyright issues and computers.

•••••••••••••••••••••••••••••••••••

Material in the *pub* subdirectory

Alerts	Calls to arms for protectors of electronic freedom
EFF	Electronic Frontier Foundation information
publications	Various electronic journals and publications related to computer freedom
legal	Legal issues of computer-mediated communication

•••••••••••••••••••••••••••••••••••

December's Archive

Ftp to: ftp.rpi.edu

Go to the *pub* subdirectory

A rich resource for people interested in developing their Internet skills *on* the Internet, and who have access to and are familiar with anonymous ftp. Named after John December, compiler of the two files we refer you to later in this paragraph, the archive is a wealth of information on all aspects of the Internet, including descriptive information regarding the Internet and computer-mediated communication (CMC). Resources exploring the technical, cognitive, social, and psychological aspects of CMC are also available. The following two files are essentially compilations of other ftp sources, organized and listed according to topic with addresses, directory, and subdirectory information. Look in the *pub/communications* subdirectory and retrieve the *internet-cmc* and *internet-tools* files.

•••••••••••••••••••••••••••••••••••

Material in the *pub* subdirectory

anti-virus	The latest anti-virus software and information
communications	Computer Mediated Communications files
consulting	Archive of computer consultants and information about consulting
resources	Internet resource guides of interest to educators
www	World Wide Web information and overview

•••••••••••••••••••••••••••••••••••

Equal Access to Software and Information (EASI) Archive

Ftp to: ftp.isc.rit.edu
Go to the *pub/vms_served/easi* subdirectory

This site is a project of the EDUCOM Educational Uses of Information Technology (EUIT) Program. EASI intends to reduce barriers to education for people with disabilities and offers an archive of text files about disabilities. All files are available via the top-level directory after logging in.

Free University of Berlin

Ftp to: ftp.fu-berlin.de
Go to the *pub* subdirectory

Files are available concerning physics, mathematics, chemistry, meteorology, geography, computer science, games, German, and medicine. Look in the *science, mac, doc,* and *pc* subdirectory.

Gatekeeper Archive

Ftp to: gatekeeper.dec.com

Numerous shareware and freeware programs are available here. The *pub* directory has more than 30 subdirectories, and almost all of them have additional subdirectories. Individual README files are in most, but not all, of the subdirectories.

· ·

Material in the *pub* subdirectory

comm	Kermit, Zmodem, and modem programs
data/Gutenberg	Project Gutenberg's electronic texts of classic literature
data/Shakespeare	Texts of Shakespeare's works
doc/telecom.glossary.text	Glossary of 330 telecommunication terms
doc/telecom.glossary.acronyms	More than 150 common and unusual telecommunication acronyms
doc/security	Virus protection programs
maps	City, state, and world maps
recipes	More than 500 recipes

· ·

History Archive

Ftp to: ftp.msstate.edu
Go to the *pub/docs/history* subdirectory

Many offerings for those interested in history and telecommunications. The site is menu-driven and most of the files are uncompressed and in ASCII text format. Novices can browse the site and read and retrieve files with ease.

· ·

Subdirectories

USA	Information about American history from colonial times
databases	Information about other Internet-based databases of history information
gifs	Classic art such as Vermeer.gif and Venus.gif, plus world maps
netuse	Introduction to the use of ftp sites, Internet accessible library catalogs and databases, and history listservs

· ·

Institute for Academic Technology Archive

Ftp to: gandalf.iat.unc.edu

A real find for anyone interested in technology in education. The site allows educators to share new methods of using and evaluating various media in their classrooms. Includes newsletters, articles, technical papers, primers, and conference and seminar information—all on the use of educational technology.

· ·

Subdirectories

guides	Extensive bibliography on educational technology issues
newslett	Covers technology topics relevant to education
technote	Other subdirectories, including a helpful consumer guide to educational technology products

· ·

Internet Hunts

Ftp to: ftp.cic.net

Go to the *pub/hunt/questions* subdirectory

Teach students to use the Internet by following these online scavenger hunts for the K–12 crowd. Hunts and their answers are available for every grade level and on several educational topics.

· ·

Sample of a hunt

THE INTERNET HUNT
October, 1994
Total points: 39
Answers due by midnight (GMT-07), Oct. 8, 1994

Hunting for rules, scoring, prizes, etc.?
Just finger **rgates@locust.cic.net** for the location of the Hunt files nearest you!

Question 1 (3 points)
(Question designed by Carole Leita, John Makulowich, Kimberley Robles)
I'm going to be visiting Berkeley, CA next month and am in a
wheelchair. I'd like a list of wheelchair-accessible bookstores
(including addresses, phone #'s, specialities, etc.)

Question 2 (5 points)
(Question designed by Alan Shapiro and Karen Schneider)
What airline flies between Chicago, Atlanta, Newark, and Florida
for one-way prices ranging from $69 to $149? The toll-free
number would also be helpful.

Question 3 (5 points)
(Question designed by Dan Marmion)
Miles Davis once recorded an album that contained the song
"Surrey with the Fringe on Top." How many stars did *Down Beat*
magazine give that album?

....

InterNIC Archive

Ftp to: ftp.sura.net
Go to the *pub* subdirectory
   A vast array of Internet "how-to" documents.

....

Subdirectories

archie	Learn to use Archie to search for files on ftp sites
mbone	Information about sending video and audio over the Net
security	Internet security information and pointers

....

Internet Statistics

Ftp to: nis.nsf.net
Go to the *statistics/nsfnet* subdirectory
   The latest information on Internet backbone (NSF) traffic and usage.

Internet Resource Directory
Ftp to: badger.state.wi.us
Go to the *agencies/dpi/other/ftp_site* subdirectory
Although not an exhaustive list by any means, there are enough educational Internet sites listed in this archive
to keep a net-savvy teacher busy for hours on end. Any important site dealing with technology and education
can be found here.

Logo Archive

Ftp to: cherupakha.media.mit.edu
Go to the *pub* subdirectory

Logo, a simple, yet extremely powerful computer language, has been successfully taught to elementary students beginning with second grade. Many educators believe it facilitates the development of higher order thinking skills and problem solving. This archive has several freeware versions of Logo for different computing environments, a complete archive of the UseNet discussion group **comp.lang.logo,** and several bibliographies of Logo articles and books.

....

Subdirectories

logo	Gateway to the various directories of the archive
logo/literature	Brief articles on simple Logo programming projects
logo/potluck	Submit Logo ideas and programs to this directory
logo/software	Freeware versions of Logo for Windows, DOS, and Macintosh

....

Lyrics & Discography

Ftp to: cs.uwp.edu
or **ftp.uwp.edu**

Archive of song lyrics and discographies of classical and popular artists. More than 225 discographies and 1,000 songs and albums are listed, including lyrics to popular songs and folk music. Lyrics are listed alphabetically under the artists' names and range from the Andrews Sisters to Frank Zappa. Look in the *artists, classical, discog, folk, guitar, interviews, lyrics, pictures,* and *sounds* subdirectories.

NASA Archives

Ftp to: ames.arc.nasa.gov
or **128.102.18.3**

The subdirectory *space* is the most relevant file for educators. Three files are worth downloading.

....

File name	Subsubdirectory
sc11.26.90	SPACE.CLASSROOM
hst09.91	HST (Hubble Space Telescope)
mr1026.90	MARS.ROVER

....

Project Hermes

Ftp to: ftp.cwru.edu

Up-to-the-minute Supreme Court documents are available in the *hermes/briefs* and *hermes/ascii* subdirectories. Initiated as an experiment in 1990, the project was deemed a success and since 1993 has been labeled "official" by the court. Information here is of interest to those studying law, government, and general current events. Includes court syllabi and opinions, concurring and dissenting. The immediacy and availability of full text are invaluable for anyone who wants to get right to the source.

Science Education Archive

Ftp to: ftp.bio.indiana.edu

A technical archive for molecular biology, and a private collection of public molecular biology software recently opened to Internet users. Look in the *chemistry, biology, molbio, util,* and *help* subdirectories.

Travel Information Archive

Ftp to: rtfm.mit.edu

Go to the *pub/usenet/rec.answers/travel/ftp-archive*

Archive of travel guides, travelogues, or trip reports, and a compilation of Usenet newsgroup postings about recreation and travel to almost any location in the world. Descriptions are of tourists' detailed, daily experiences including reactions to cultural differences and environmental factors.

University of Iowa Software Archive (UISA)

Ftp to: grind.isca.uiowa.edu

This archive holds an extensive set of software files for several computer systems, including Amiga, Apple 2, Macintosh, MS-DOS, and UNIX. Includes a variety of software, from word processing and graphics to spread sheets and network support. Look in the *amiga, apple2, mac, ms-dos, next, sound,* and *unix* subdirectories.

Washington University Public Domain Archives

Ftp to: wuarchive.wustl.edu

One of the biggest ftp sites in the world, this is known as a "mirror site," a site that copies other ftp sites. It's a very useful site for educators since most major ftp sites are archived here. Look in the *doc, edu, graphics, network_info, packages pub,* and *systems* subdirectories.

Word List Archive

Ftp to: ftp.uu.net

Go to the *pub/dictionary/DEC-collection* subdirectory

A collection of dictionaries in eight languages—Dutch, English, German, Italian, Norwegian, Swedish, Finnish, and Japanese. The French dictionary was removed because it was not in the public domain, but visitors are instructed how to access it elsewhere.

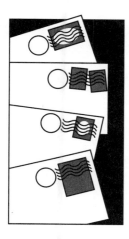

Mailing lists

Internet mailing lists are interactive, email-based discussion groups addressing specific topics. They are interactive because a subscriber anywhere in the world can read messages posted to them and can send a message to the list—all by Internet email.

Anyone with access to Internet email can subscribe to and participate in an Internet mailing list. Users of commercial online services such as America Online, Prodigy, CompuServe, Delphi, and Net-connected bulletin board services (BBSs) can subscribe. You can search for mailing lists by keyword.

Email to: listserv@cunyvm.cuny.edu

In the body, type **list global /<keyword>** and leave the subject line blank.

The search will return you a list of the active mailing lists that match your keyword.

Here are the most popular and heavily used mailing lists for K-12 education.

Children Accessing Controversial Information

Can children be prevented from accessing online materials which are controversial? Is preventing access desirable? This list seeks to discuss and resolve these issues. In its short life to date, hundreds of people have joined the list and contributed their thoughts. Hands-on suggestions for implementing filters and supervision methods are the main focus.

Email to: caci-request@media.mit.edu

Type **subscribe** in the body of the message, and type anything you wish in the subject line.

EduPage

A bi-weekly summary of recent news items on the educational use of computer technology. A very informative, useful resource.

Email to: listproc@educom.edu

Type **subscribe EDUPAGE <Your Name>** in the body of the message, and type anything you wish in the subject line.

Field Trips

This mailing list links K–12 classes to hundreds of other students in the U.S. and abroad. Each class posts detailed messages about its recent field trips and shares its experiences with an interested audience of the same age or grade level. Access to a broad audience of peers motivates students to observe and learn during their trips.

Email to: majordomo@acme.fred.org

Type **subscribe fieldtrips-L** in the body of the message, and type anything you wish in the subject line.

INCLASS

Sponsored by Canada's SchoolNet Project, INCLASS is a moderated mailing list offering information about using the Internet in the classroom from a Canadian perspective.

Email to: listproc@schoolnet.carleton.ca

Type **subscribe INCLASS <Your Name>** in the body of the message, and type anything you wish in the subject line.

International Email Classroom Connections (IECC)

The IECC list is a virtual meeting place for teachers seeking partner classes for international and cross-cultural electronic mail exchanges. This list is different in that subscribers and contributors are looking for an entire class of email partners rather than individuals.

Email to: iecc-request@stolaf.edu

Type **subscribe iecc <Your Name>** in the body of the message, and type anything you wish in the subject line.

Kidsphere

The most active K–12 mailing list on the Internet. Discussions about all aspects of bringing technology into the classroom.

Email to: kidsphere-request@vms.cis.pitt.edu

Type **subscribe kidsphere <Your Name>** in the body of the message, and type anything you wish in the subject line.

MIDDLE-L

Middle school educators will find the MIDDLE-L online mailing list to be an indispensable resource. Teachers, administrators, researchers, parents, and others interested in middle school education share ideas, projects, resources, problems, and solutions.

Email to: listserv@listserv.net

Type **subscribe middle-L <Your Name>** in the body of the message, and type anything you wish in the subject line.

World Wide Web in Education

More than 1,000 educators around the world use this list to discuss how to use the World Wide Web in the K–12 classroom. Recent topics include setting up Web pages at your school, creating Web sites, and more.
Email to: listserv@k12.cnidr.org
Type **subscribe wwwedu <Your Name>** in the body of the message, and type anything you wish in the subject line.

How to subscribe to a list

What follows is an extensive list of mailing lists for many interests and topics. Although some of the lists fall under the heading of Higher Education, most welcome and encourage participation by educators from the K–12 arena. Subscribe to the lists that look appealing and read the incoming posts for a week or two. If a list isn't what you expected, simply unsubscribe.

To join or subscribe to a list, follow these steps:
1. Pick a list, such as AEDNET listed below.
2. Create a new email message and address it to: **listserv@listserv.net**
3. Type anything you wish in the subject line or leave it blank.
4. In the body of the message, type: **subscribe AEDNET Lois Lane** (Instead of Lois Lane, type your name.)
5. Send the message. You will be automatically added to the AEDNET subscriber list and begin receiving posts in your email within a few hours. You will receive a welcome message. Keep this message because it contains important information, such as guidelines for subscribers, how to send messages to the list, and how to leave the list.
6. To subscribe to other lists, simply replace AEDNET with any of the mailing list names below.

Other mailing lists

Education—Adult

ADLTED-L	Canadian adult education network
AEDNET	Adult Education network
CAUCE-PP	Canadian University Continuing Education Policy
CREAD	Latin America and Caribbean distance education forum
DEOS-L	American Center for Study of Distance Education
DEOSNEWS	Distance Education Online Symposium
DISRES-L	Distance education research
DISTED	Journal of distance education and communication
NIATRN-L	National Institute of Aging Trainees
PRISON-L	Teachers in prison programs
TECHED-L	Employment training and literacy
TESLIT-L	Adult education and literacy test literature
TRDEV	Training and development of human resources

Education—Higher, Administrative

ADA-LAW	Americans with Disabilities Act Law discussion
AIR-L	Institutional Researchers/University Planners
AJCUASD	AJCU Arts and Science Deans
AJCUAVP	AJCU Academic Vice Presidents
AJCUCOMM	AJCU Communications Committee
AJCUPRES	AJCU Presidents
AMC	Administrative Management Council
ARCLIST	Administrative Resource Center participants
BANNER-L	Student Information Systems discussion
CAIRNET	California Association for Institutional Research
CAMPCLIM	Campus climate, physical environment on campus
CANDG-L	Contract and Grant representatives
CHAIRS-L	Academic chairpersons problems, issues
CIO-L	Higher education Chief Information Officer
COMP-CEN	Computer Center Managers
DASIG	Data Administrators
DSSHE-L	Disabled Student Services in Higher Education
EDAD-L	Educational Administration
ERECS-L	Management and preservation of electronic records
FINAID-L	Administration of Student Financial Aid
FISC-L	Fee-based information services in Academia
FUNDLIST	Computer support of fundraising programs
GRAD-L	German Graduate Students
GRADCOLL	Graduate College News
GRADREF	CAS Graduate reference information
HDESK-L	Help Desk list
JOBPLACE	Job, career advisors, educators
LONG	Long Term Planning
NAEB-L	National Association of Educational Buyers
POD-L	Professional Organizational Development
PUBPOL-L	Public policy, administration, planning students
PUBS-L	Publications Offices, educational and non-profit
RECMGMT	Education Records Management
RHA-L	Resident Hall Association

Education—Higher, General Academic

ABLE-L	Ability Journal discussion
ABILITY	The academically, artistically and athletically able
AFAM-L	African-American Research
AFAS-L	African American Studies and Librarianship
AFROAM-L	African American issues in higher education
HUMANIST	International discussion of computing issues in Humanities
INTERDIS	Discussion of Interdisciplinary Studies
KONFER-L	Conference Announcements

Education—Higher, Research

AFAM-L	African-American Research
ERL-L	Educational Research
FACINTL	International Funding Opportunities

GRANTS-L	NSF grants/contracts
REACH	Research and Educational Applications of Computers
RESEARCH	Extramural funding

Education—Higher, Student

ACMSTCHP	Association of Computing Machinery Student Chapters
ACTIVIST	Social goals through personal action
ACTNOW-L	College activism events database
ARTIST-L	Student artists
ASA-L	African Students Association discussion
BRAS-NET	Brazilian Students Communications Net
C-BOWL	College Bowl Teams and Officials
CAMPED-L	Campus Editors discussion
DJ-L	Campus radio disc jockeys
ECONET	Environmental preservation, ecology workers
FRANKLIN	Benjamin Franklin Scholars
GRDEMP-L	Graduate Student Employment issues
GREEN	Environmental movement information
GREENORG	Green movement study
GSO	Graduate Student Organization
INT-ED	Education International students
LAWSCH-L	Law students issues
MEDSTU-L	Medical Students worldwide
MSA-L	Muslim Student Association
MGSGRAD	Management Science Graduate Students
PEACE	Peace Studies
PHYS-STU	Physics Students discussion
PSYCGRAD	Psychology graduate student discussion
SBSWE-L	Society of Women Engineers—Student Section
SGANET-N	Student Government North American mail network
SGANET	Student Government Global mail network
SEDS-L	Students for exploration and development of space
T-ASSIST	College and University Teaching Assistants

Education—Higher, Teacher and Faculty Development, General

AAUFD-L	AAU Faculty Development Committee
AERAMC-L	American Educational Research Association
ALTLEARN	Alternative approaches to learning
ASSMNT-L	Assessment discussion
ASSESS	Assessment methods in higher education
BGEDU-L	Forum for the quality of education
CANDI-L	Curriculum And Instructional Department
CESNEWS	Coalition for Essential Schools
CREA-CPS	Creativity and Creative Problem Solving in Education
CURRICUL	Curriculum development issues, Higher Education to K–12
DTS-L	Dead teachers' society discussion
EDPOLYAN	Education Policy Analysis discussion
EDSTYLE	Learning Styles Theory and Research
ERL-L	Education Research
NEWEDU-L	Exploration of the way we educate, K through post-graduate
PBL-IIST	Problem Based Learning

PHILOSED	Students and teachers discussion of Educational Philosophy
PIAGET-L	Cognitive, structural development and knowledge
PSATC	Problem Solving Across the Curriculum
SIREN	Swedish Initiative for Research and Education
SPCEDS-L	Special education students
STLHE-L	Society of Teaching and Learning in Higher Education
T-ASSIST	College and University Teaching Assistants, International
TEACHEFT	Teaching Effectiveness

Education—Higher, Teacher and Faculty Development, Subject Area

ACSD-SCI	Alliance for Teaching of Science
ALLIANCE	North Carolina Science and Math Alliance
AATFREN	American Association of Teachers of French
AATG	American Association of Teachers of German
BIOCIS-L	Biology Curriculum Innovation Study
BIOPI-L	Secondary Biology teacher enhancement
CHEMED-L	Chemistry education discussion
CREWRT	Creative writing pedagogy for teachers, students
ECONED-L	Research in Economics education
ECONHIST	Teaching and Research in Economic History discussion
EDSTAT-L	Statistics education discussion
EDUMATE	Educacion Matematica en Chile
GENE-L	Genetics education
GEOGED	Education issues in Geography
H-TEACH	Teaching history
IDFORUM	Global industrial design education, research
ISPS	Teachers International Study Program in Statistics
JTE-L	Journal of Technology Education
MBA-L	MBA student curriculum issues, programs
MUSIC-ED	Music education
NBEA-L	National Business Education Association
NDDDESIGN	Graphic and industrial design education
OBTS-L	Organizational Behavior Teaching Society
PSRT-L	Political science research and teaching
SLART-L	Second Language Acquisition Research and Teaching
SPCEDS-L	Special education students
T321-L	Teaching Science in Elementary Schools
TESL-L	Teaching English as a second language
TESLFF-L	Fluency First and Whole Language
TIPS	Teaching in the psychological sciences
WAC-L	Writing Across the Curriculum, Center for Writing

Education—Higher, Teacher and Faculty Development, Media

ADVISE-L	User services staff, advisors, consultants
AESRG-L	Applied Expert Systems Research Group
AILIST	Artificial Intelligence discussion
AHC-L	Association for history and computing
CALLCD	Computer assisted language learning
CBEHIGH	Computer Based Education in Higher Education
CDROM-L	CD-ROM discussion
CDROMLAN	Use of CD-ROM in LAN environment
CETH	Center for Electronic Texts in the Humanities

CGE	Computer Graphics Education
CNEDUC-L	Computer Networking Education discussion
COMPUMED	Computers in Medicine and Medicine Curriculum
COSNDISC	Consortium for School Networking (COSN)
CTI-COMPLIT	Computer literacy in Higher Education
CTI-L	Issues in Teaching using computers
CUPLE-L	Physics learning environment software
DEOS-L	American Center for Study of Distance Education
DEOSNEWS	Distance Education Online Symposium
DISRES-L	Distance education research
DISTED	Online journal of distance education
E-COURSE	E-Mail Course Planning Conference
EDNET	University-K–12 educators exploring the Internet
EDTECH	Educational Technology
EDUCOM-W	Technology and education issues of interest to women
EDUPAGE	Information technology newsletter
EDUTEL	Education and information technologies
EJVC-L	Electronic Journal of Virtual Culture in Higher Education for K–12
ERUDITIO	Knowledge through electronic communication
ETDIR-L	Educational Technology Research and Development
EUITLIST	Educational uses of information technology
GTRTI-L	Research and Teaching in Global Information Technology
HCFNET	Humanities Computer Facilities Network
HYPERCRD	Hypercard discussion
I-VIDTEK	Video technology discussion
IAAMEDIA	Compatibility of multimedia applications
INFED-L	Uses of computers in education
INSTEC-L	Instructional Technology Advisory Committee
INTECH-L	Instructional Technology discussion
IPCT-L	Interpersonal Computing and Technology forum
JTIT-L	Japanese Teachers and Instructional Technology
LABMGR	Academic microcomputing lab management
LIBER	Library/media services
LLTI	Language learning and technology
LM_NET	School library/media services
MMEDIA	Discussion of all types of multimedia
MMOS2-L	Multimedia aspects in OS/2 programming
NET-HAPPENINGS	Useful announcements gathered from all over the Internet by Net scout and educator, Gleason Sackmann
NET-RESOURCES	InterNIC Information Services—new resources
NETTRAIN	For trainers in network access
NIS	Net Information Services announcements digest
PAGEMAKR	Pagemaker Desktop publishing
PERSEUS	Multimedia resource of art, text, and archaeological materials from ancient Greek world for teaching and research
PHOTO-L	All aspects of photography
PUBRADIO	Public Radio discussion
EACH	Research and Educational Applications of Computers
SATEDU-L	Using satellite images in teaching
SIMEDU-L	Simulated applications in business education
TECHNET	Technical Support for education, research staff
TESLCA-L	Computer assisted language learning
TRAIN-L	College and University Computer Trainers
TYPO-L	Discussion of typography
US-WG	User Services Network Training Materials
VIDPRO-L	Professional video production, all aspects

Education—International

AFRICA-L	Forum Pan-Africa
AFRICANA	Information Technologies Activities in Africa
AJBS-L	Association of Japanese Business Studies
ARAB-PRESS	Unedited quotes from the Arab/Muslim world
ARGENTINA	General discussion and information about Argentina
BALT-L	Lithuania, Latvia and Estonia information
BALZAC-L	French culture
BERITA-L	Malaysia, Singapore, Islam-related news
BORIKEN	Cultura y sociedad de Puerto Rico
BRDOMAIN	Brazil network
BRAS-NET	Brazilian Students Communications Net
BUDDHIST	Forum on Indian and Buddhist studies
CANALC	Latin America and Caribbean digest from Canada
CASID-L	Canadian Association for Study of International Development
CASTOR	American Schools of Oriental Research in Canada
CCMAN-L	Canadian Chinese Magazine
CENTAM-L	Central America discussion
CH-LADB	Latin America Database
CHICLE	Chicano literature and discussion
CHILE-L	Chile discussion
CHINA	China Studies
CHINA-N	China News Network
CHINANET	Networking in China
COLUMBIA	News and information about Columbia
COMDEV	Communication and International Development
CNDPSU-L	China News Digest
CREAD	Latin America and Caribbean distance education forum
DEUTSCHE-LISTE	German literature and culture
DEVEL-L	Technology transfer in international development
E-EUROPE	Central, Eastern Europe and CIS
EC	European Community
ECONOMY	Analysis of less developed countries' economies
ECUADOR	General discussion and information about Ecuador
ERMIS	Greek discussion
ESPORA-L	Spain/Portugal history
EUEARN-L	Discussion of Eastern European topics
FULBNEWS	Fulbright Education Advisory Newsletter
GC-L	Internationalization of business curriculum
GEOGRAPHY	Geographic information and issues
GER-RUS	Germans from Russia
GIS-L	Geographic information systems
H-LATAM	Latin American history
H-NET	Discussion of Hungarian Academic Research
HEBREW-L	Jewish and Near Eastern Studies
HOSPEX-L	Hospitality exchange discussion
HRD-L	Human Resources Development
HRIS-L	Human Resources Information (Canada)
HUNGARY	Scholars, students of Hungary
IBERIAN_ISSUES	Iberoamerica discussion
INDIA	India and regional issues
INDIA-L	Discussion of Indian sub-continent
INT-DEV-L	Educator's Forum on International Development
INT-ED	Education International students

INT-LAW	Foreign and International law issues
INTERCUL	Communication across cultures
JAPAN-L	Discussion of everything Japanese except language
JEP-BB	Networking for Universities in Central Slovakia
JPINFO-L	Information about Japan
JUDAICA	Jewish and Near Eastern Studies
L-CHA	Canadian Historical Association
LASNET	Latin America Studies Network
LITERA-L	Literatura en Ingles y Espano
MCLR-L	Latino research
MEXICO-L	Knowledge of Mexico: people, places, culture
MIDEUR-L	Discussion of Middle Europe topics
MISG-L	Malaysian Islamic Study Group
MSA-L	Muslim Student Association
MUSLIMS	The Islamic Information and News Network
PACIFIC	Pacific Ocean and Islands discussion
PAKISTAN	Pakistan News Service
PBDLIST	Indonesian Development Studies
PCBR-L	Pacific Business Researchers Forum
PCORPS-L	Discussion for International Volunteers
PERMIKA	Indonesian group—Montreal
POLAND	Polish news bulletins
REDALC	Latin America and Caribbean Networks
RURALDEV	Community and Rural Economic Development International
RUSSIA	Russia and her neighbors
SEANET=L	Southeast Asian Studies
SEASIA-L	South East Asia
SCS-L	Soc.culture.soviet (Usenet list via email)
SIIN-L	Small Islands Information International
SLOVAK-L	Discussion of Slovak issues
SM-LADB	Latin America database
TAMIL-L	Tamil Studies
TEL	Turkish electronic discussion
TRKNWS-L	Turkish cultural exchange program
TSA-L	Turkish Studies Association discussion
TUNISNET	The Tunisian Network
TWUNIV-L	Chinese Scholars and Students discussion
UN	United Nations
UP-LADB	Latin America database
USCINT-L	USC Office of International Student Services
VXLA-L	Information exchange on Venezuela
XCULT-L	International Intercultural Newsletter
XCULT-X	Intercultural Communications Student Practicum
XCULTINS	Effects of Culture on Instructional Design

Education—K–12

AACE-L	Association for the Advancement of Computing in Education
ABILITY	Study of the academically, artistically, athletically able
ACTIV-L	Civil and human rights, peace, non-violence, politics
ALTLEARN	Alternative learning strategies for physically handicapped
APPLE2-L	Exchange of Apple II and Apple IIGS educational software
BGEDU-L	Forum for the quality of education
BIOPI-L	Secondary Biology teacher enhancement
CESNEWS	Coalition for Essential Schools

CHATBACK	Planning forum for Chatback UK and International education nets for disabled children
CHEMED-L	Chemistry Teacher Discussion
COSNDISC	Consortium for School Networking (COSN) discussion
CPI-L	College Preparatory Initiative
CREAD	Latin America and Caribbean Electronic Distance Education
CREWRT-L	Creative Writing in Education for Teachers and Students
CSRNOT-L	Center for the Study of Reading
CTI-L	Computers in Teaching Initiative
CURRICUL	Curriculum development issues, Higher Education to K–12
CW-L	Teaching writing with word processors, telecommunications
DRUGABUS	Drug Abuse Education Information and Research
DTS-L	Dead teachers' society discussion
EAT-L	Cultural food history and international recipe exchange
ECENET	Early childhood education (0-8 years)
ECEOL-L	Early Childhood Education discussion, projects
EDUCAI-L	Educational Applications Of Artificial Intelligence
EDUCOM-W	Technology and Education Issues of Interest to Women
ELED-L	Elementary Education list
EJVC-L	Journal of Virtual Culture in Higher Education to K–12
EUITLIST	Educational Uses of Information Technology
GLITTER	Metacognition and teaching methodology
GRAVITY	Gravity topics for spacetime course
HYPERCRD	Discussions of Hypercard software for the Macintosh
INSTOOLS	Discussion of Technical Tools Used for Instruction
IPCT-L	Interpersonal Computing and Technology
JESSE	Open Library and Information Science Education Forum
K12ADMIN	K–12 Educators interested in educational administration
KIDCAFE	Youth dialog between students worldwide
KIDCAFEP	Portuguese youth dialog
KIDLINK	Kidlink Projects
KIDLIT-L	Children's Literature discussion
KIDPROJ	Special Kidlink projects
KIDS	Kidsphere for kids
KIDS-95	Global dialog between 10- to 15-year-olds
KIDZMALL	Kids exploring interests and issues
LIBER	Library/media services
LM_NET	School library/media services
MAC-L	Macintosh News and Information
MSPROJ	Annenberg/CPB Math-Science Project
MULTI-L	Language and education in multi-lingual settings
NCPRSE-L	Reform discussion for science education
NEWEDU-L	New Paradigms in Education
PENPAL-L	Pen pal/Keypal Discussion
PHYSHARE	Sharing resources for high school physics
PUBYAC	Children and young adult library services
SAIS-L	Science Awareness and Promotion
SCHOOL-L	Primary and post-primary schools
SUSIG	Discussion on teaching Math
T321-L	Teaching Science in Elementary Schools
TAG-L	Discussion about Education for talented and gifted children
TALKBACK	Kids forum for CHATBACK, disabled children
TESL-L	Teaching English as a second language
TESLEC-L	Electronic communication and pen pals
TESLFF-L	Fluency First and Whole Language
TFTD-L	Thought for the Day
TQMEDU-L	Total Quality Management in education

UKERA-L	Dialog on educational reform
VT-HSNET	Vermont K–12 School Network
WX-TALK	Weather phenomena discussion
Y-RIGHTS	Children's rights
YOUTHNET	YouthNet

Education—Multicultural and Related

AFROAM-L	Critical Issues in African American life and culture
AFAM-L	African-American Research
AFAS-L	African American Studies and Librarianship
ASA-L	African Students Association discussion
BUDDHA-L	Buddhism discussion
DTEAM-L	Diversity Team discussion
DIVERS-L	Diversity
DIVERSE	Diversity in development
H-ETHNIC	Ethnicity, immigration history
HRD-L	Human Resources Development
INTERCUL	Study of Intercultural Communication
JEM	Jewish electronic mail conference
MINCON	Minority Recruitment and Retention Conference
MULTI-L	Minority language and education in multi-lingual settings
NAT-CHAT	Issues pertaining to aboriginal people
NAT-EDU	Educational issues pertaining to aboriginal peoples
NAT-1492	Native-L Columbus Quincentenary
NATIVE-L	Issues pertaining to aboriginal peoples
NIPRI	National Indian Policy Research Institute
ORTRAD-L	Interdisciplinary studies of oral traditions, African, Hispanic, Native American
POLAND-L	Culture of Poland and Polish Americans
TESL-L	Teaching English as a second language
TESLIC-L	Intercultural communication
TESLIE-L	Intensive English program
WORLD-L	Teaching method and theory of a scientific and non-Eurocentric world history
XCULT-X	Intercultural Communications Practicum, global village

Education—Special

ADA-LAW	Americans with Disabilities Act Law discussion
ALTLEARN	Alternative approaches to learning for the handicapped
ASLING-L	American Sign Language
AUTISM	SJU autism and developmental disabilities
AXSLIB-L	Issues of disabled access to libraries
BEHAVIOR	Behavioral and Emotional disorders in children
BLIND-L	Computer use by and for the blind
BLINDNWS	Blind News Digest
BRAILLE	Discussion for the blind in Czechoslovakia and England
CDMAJOR	Communication Disorder discussion
CHATBACK	Planning forum for Chatback UK and International; educational network for disabled children
COMMDIS	Speech disorders
DDFIND-L	Forum for networking on disabilities
DEAF-L	Deaf
DISRES-L	Disability research
EYEMOV-L	Eye Movement network
L-HCAP	Handicapped people in education

MOBILITY   Mobility disabilities
SCR-L   Study of cognitive rehabilitation
SPCEDS-L   Special education students
STUT-HLP   Support list for stutterers and their families
STUTT-L   Stuttering Research and clinical practice

Arts

78-L   Music on 78-rpm records and phonographs
ACMR-L   Association for Chinese Music Research
ALLMUSIC   Discussion about all forms of music
ARTNET   Artists alliance
ARTIST-L   Student artists
BGRASS-L   International Bluegrass Music Association
BRASS   Brass musical instruments
CADLIST   Computer Aided Design general discussion
CHPOEM   Chinese poetry
CINEMA-L   Discussion of all forms of cinema
CLASSM-L   Classical music
CLAYART   Ceramic arts/pottery
COMEDIA   Discussion of Hispanic Classic Theater
CREA-CPS   Creativity and Problem Solving in education
DANCE-L   International folk and Traditional dance
DLDG-L   Dance Librarians Discussion Group
DESIGN-L   Basic and applied design in art and architecture
EARLYM-L   Early music discussion
EMUSIC-L   Electronic music
ETHMUS-L   EthnoForum—a global ethnomusicology forum
FACXCH-L   Forum for faculty in art, architecture and design
FILM-L   Film making and reviews
FINE-ART   Fine Art forum
FINEART   Artists, scientists on computer use
FRAC-L   Computer generation of fractal images as art
GEODESIC   Discussion of Buckminster Fuller's work and philosophy
GRAPHIX   Computer graphics hardware, software, files
IDFORUM   Global industrial design education, research
L-ARTECH   Les Artes et les nouvelles technologies
MUSIC-ED   Music education
NDDDESIGN   Graphic and industrial design education
OPERA-L   Opera discussion
PERFORM   Medieval performing arts
PERFORM-L   Modern performance
SAVOYNET   Gilbert and Sullivan works, productions, related discussion
SCREEN-L   Film and TV studies
TUXCH-L   Art, architecture, design
TML-L   Thesaurium Musicum Latinarium, Latin music theory debate
UPNEWS   Electronic music news

Computer

AHC-L   Association for History & Computing
AIL-L   Artificial Intelligence & Language
ANN-LOTS   Annotated Lists-of-Things, top-level guides
C+HEALTH   Health effects of computer use

CAF-talk	Computers and Academic Freedom
CCS	Center for Computational Science
CDPLUS-L	CDPlus software user group
CETH	Center for Electronic Texts in the Humanities
COGS	Computing on a Grand Scale
COMMUNET	Community, civic and Free-Net operation, planning
CONFER-L	Interactive conferencing online in academia
CPSR	Computer Professionals for Social Responsibility (CPSR)
CWIS-L	Campus-Wide Information Systems (CWIS)
CYBERLAW	The Law and Politics of Computer Networking
DECNEWS	Digital Equipment Corporation Education News
DOMAIN-L	Internet Domains discussion group
DTP-L	Desktop publishing digest
E-HUG	Electronic Hebrew Users Group
EDI-L	Electronic Data Interchange issues
ELLHNIKA	Greek TeX for anyone typesetting ancient Greek
EMAILMAN	Learning about accessing electronic information
ERUDITIO	Knowledge through electronic communication
ETHICS-L	Ethics in computing discussion
EUEARN-L	Computer networking in Eastern Europe
FUNDLIST	Computer support of fundraising programs
GTRTI-L	Research and Teaching with Global Information Technology
HOST	History of Science and Technology
HTECH-L	History of Technology
INFO-GCG	Genetics software discussion
INFONETS	Networks including questions about connections
ITSNEWS	Information Technology Services newsletter
L-VIRUS	Viruses
LICENSE	Software licensing
OHEUG-L	Oracle Higher Education Users Group
OPT-PROC	Optical computing, neural nets, holography processing
PC-EVAL	PC evaluation
PCBUILD	PC hardware, upgrades, building, low-cost sources
PCSERV-L	Public Domain software servers user
PCTECH-L	MS-DOS-compatibles support group
PCSUPT-L	Forum for discussion of PC user support
REACH	Research and Educational Applications of Computers
SCHOLAR	Natural language processing in editing of historical and literary texts
SHOTHC-L	Society for History of Technology—computing history list
THEORYNT	Computer Science theory network

Future Studies

21ST-C-L	Forum for 21st Century discussion
BEVPUB-L	Blacksburg, Virginia Electronic Village open discussion
FNORD-L	New ways of thinking discussion
HIT	Highly imaginative technology and science fiction
NSP-L	Noble Savage Philosophy
SMKCC-L	Subject Matter, Knowledge and Conceptual Change
SOCORG-K	Social Organization of Knowledge discussion
TNC	Technoculture discussion
XTROPY-L	Extropians, discussion and development

Help

ANN-LOTS	Annotated Lists-of-Things, indexed Internet guides
MAILMAN	Learning about accessing electronic information
HELP-NET	For solving user problems with utilities, software, on-the-net questions and answers
NET-HAPPENINGS	Useful announcements culled from the Internet by Net scout and educator, Gleason Sackmann
NET-RESOURCES	InterNIC Info. Services—new resources
NIS	Net Information Services announcements digest
SUEARN-L	Internet digest, news, how-to questions

History and Humanities

AGOR	Agora, an ejournal in classics
AHC-L	Association for History and Computing
AIBI-L	Computerized analysis of Biblical Texts
AMERCATH	History discussion on American Catholicism
AMERSTDY	American Studies
AMWEST-H	American West History Forum
ANCIEN-L	History of the ancient Mediterranean
ANSAX-L	Culture and history of England before 1100
ARCHIVES	Archives discussion
ASEH-L	American Society of Environmental Historian
ASTR-L	Theatre history, American Society of Theatre Research
BMCR-L	Bryn Mawr Classical Review, e-book review
BMMR-L	Bryn Mawr Medieval Review, ejournal
C18-L	Discussion of 18th century interests by scholars, students
CAMELOT	Arthurian legend and Grail lore
CELTIC-L	Celtic culture list
CLIOLOGY	Theories of History
COMHIST	History of Human Communication
CONTEX-L	Cross-disciplinary analysis of ancient texts
EARAM-L	Society of Early Americanists
ELENCHUS	Christianity in Late Antiquity discussion
EMEDCH-L	Chinese history between Han and Tang dynasties
EMHIST-L	Early modern history forum
ESPORA-L	History of Iberian Peninsula
ETHNOHIS	Ethnology and general history
FICINO	Renaissance and Reformation discussion
FRANCEHS	French history scholars
GAELIC-L	Gaelic language bulletin board
GERLING	Older Germanic languages (to 1500 AD)
GRMNHIST	German history forum
H-ALBION	British History
H-AMSTDY	American Studies
H-CIVWAR	U.S. Civil War history
H-DIPLO	Diplomatic history, U.S. foreign affairs
H-DURKHM	European social thought
H-ETHNIC	Ethnicity, immigration history
H-FILM	Film and History discussion
H-IDEAS	Intellectual history
H-LABOR	Labor history
H-LAW	U.S. legal and constitutional history
H-LATAM	Latin American history
H-POL	U.S. political history

H-RHETOR	History of rhetoric
H-RURAL	Rural, agricultural history
H-SOUTH	U.S. South history
H-TEACH	Teaching History
H-URBAN	Urban history
H-WOMEN	Women's History
HASTRO-L	History of Astronomy discussion
HAPSBURG	Austrian history since 1500
HISLAW-L	History of Law, (Feudal, Common, Canon)
HISTEC-L	History of Evangelical Christianity
HISTORY	History, generic
HOLOCAUS	Holocaust studies, anti-Semitism
HOPOS-L	Forum for discussing history of science & philosophy
HPSST-L	History and philosophy of Science
HTECH-L	History of Technology
HUMANIST	Uses of computer in Humanities
IBYCUS-L	Scholarly computer use in Ancient Greek History
IEAHCNET	Early American History and Culture
INDOLOGY	Academics interested in study of classical India
INTERSCRIPTA	Medieval Seminar Topics
IOUDAIOS	First century Judaism
ISLAM-L	History of Islam
JEWSTUDIES	Jewish Studies
JUDAICA	Judaic studies
KANSAS-L	Kansas history and life
L-CHA	Canadian Historical Association
LATIN-L	Latin and neo-Latin discussion
LASNET	Latin American Studies Network
MCLR-L	Latino Research
MEDIEV-L	History and issues of the Middle Ages
MEDTEXTL	Medieval Texts, Philology, Codicology
MILHST-L	Military History
NAHUAT-L	Aztec Studies and Language
NT-GREEK	Scholarly study of Greek New Testament
OHA-L	Oral History Association discussion
OT-HEBREW	Scholarly study of Hebrew Old Testament
PERSEUS	Multimedia resource of art, text and archaeological materials from ancient Greek world for teaching and research
PERSIA-L	Jewish history and literature in the Persian period
PREZHIST	Presidential History forum, lives, campaigns, tenure, politics
RENAIS-L	Early modern history—Renaissance
ROOTS-L	Genealogy
RUSHIST	Russian History Forum
SCHOLAR	Online newsletter about natural language processing and editing of historical and literary texts
SHAKER	Shaker studies
SHARP-L	History of authorship, reading, the printed word
SHOTHC-L	Society for the History of Technology—History of Computing
SOCHIST	Social history
STHCULT	Southern Cultures Journal, history, literature, folklore
VICTORIA	Victorian studies
VWAR-L	Vietnam War
WHIRL	Women's History in Rhetoric and Language
WORLD-L	World history, non-Eurocentric
WWII-L	World War II history

Language—Communications Studies

CCANET	Canadian Communications Association
CDMAJOR	Communication Disorder discussion
CMC	Computer mediated communications (CMC) discussion
CRTNET	Communications Studies announcements
COMDEV	Global interaction between people working in international and development communications
COMHIST	History of human communication
COMMDIS	Speech disorders
COMMED	Communications education
COMMJOBS	Communications Studies job listings
COMSERVE	Sponsor of numerous lists in communications
COPYEDITING-L	King's English, other editorial issues
DISPRAC	Disciplinary practices in communications studies
EDUTEL	Computer Mediated Communication in education contexts
EJCREC	Electronic Journal of Communications, scholarly online journal
ETHNO	Ethnomethodology/conversation analysis
FAMCOMM	Marital and Family communication issues
GENDER	Topics in Communications and Gender
INHEALTH	International health communication issues
INTERCUL	Communication across cultures
INTERPER	Interpersonal/small group communications
JDOCS-DB	Journalism/Mass Communications document database
JOURNET	Journalism education discussion
MAGAZINE	Communication Studies magazine publication issues
MASSCOMM	Mass Communications and new technologies
MCJRNL	Media Journal distribution
METHODS	Research methodology—qualitative and quantitative
NEWBOOKS	New book notices in Communications Studies
ORGCOMM	Communication in organizations
PHILCOMM	Philosophy of Communications, theory, epistemology
POLCOMM	Political Communications issues discussion
RHETORIC	Study of rhetoric, analysis, social movements, persuasion
SCIT-L	Studies in Communications and Information Technology
SNET-L	Human Communications, Social Networks

Language—International

AATFREN	American Association of Teachers of French
AATG	American Association of Teachers of German
BORIKEN	Cultura y sociedad de Puerto Rico
CAUSERIE	"Chat" in French
CCNET-L	Chinese Computing Network (in Chinese)
CHICLE	Chicano literature and discussion
ECP-PIF	Programme Int'l de Formation
EDISTA	Educacion a Distancia
EDUMATE	Educacion Matematica en Chile
ESPER-L	Esperanto
FLAC-L	Foreign Language Across the Curriculum
GAELIC-L	Gaelic language bulletin board
GER-RUS	Germans from Russia
HELLAS	Hellenic (Greek with Latin characters)
HIROKO	Taniyam Hiroko (Japanese)

INFORM-L	Cultura Informatica en Mexico y America Latina
IROQUOIS	Iroquois language discussion
JTEM-L	Japanese Thru Electronic Media
JTIT-L	Japanese Teachers and Instructional Technology
LANTRA-L	Interpreting and Translation
LLTI	Language learning and technology international information
LTEST-L	Language Testing Research and Practice
MENDELE	Yiddish literature and language
MEXICO	Lista di distribucion Mexico
MULTI-L	Language and Education in multi-lingual settings
NAHUAT-L	Aztec Studies and Nahuatl Language
NEDER-L	Elektronische distributieljst voor de Nederlandistit
PERU	Cultural exchange, news about Peru (in Spanish)
PIADAS	Humor distribution forum (in Portuguese)
RUSSIAN	Russian language issues
S-PRESS	German student press discussion
SDOMINGO	Culture y sociedad de la republica de Santo Domingo
SEELANGS	Slavic and Eastern European languages and literature
SLART-L	Second Language Acquisition Research and Teaching
TELUGU	Telugu language and culture
TESL-L	Teaching English as a Second Language
TESLFF-L	Fluency First and Whole Language
UNIANDES	Espacio Abierto para Uniandinos
WELSH-L	Welsh language bulletin board

Language—Linguistics

ABSTRACT	Linguistic abstract
ADS-L	American Dialect Society
FLN	Figurative Language Network
LANGIT	Discussione Centri Linguistici Italiani
LIBTHEA	Thesaurus Science
SCHOLAR	Newsletter about natural language processing and editing of historical and literary texts
SEMIOS-L	Semiotic critical studies
SLLING-L	Sign Language Linguistics
WORDS-L	A forum for the discussion of the English language

Language—Literature

AMLIT-L	American Literature Discussion Group
ASIMOV-L	Discussion of Isaac Asimov's works
ASTR-L	American Society of Theatre Research discussion list
AUSTEN-L	Readers of Jane Austen, Maria Edgeworth, etc.
AXE-LIST	Quebec Literature Studies
AXE-TALK	Quebec Literature Studies discussion
BALZAC-L	French literature, culture
C18	Discussion of 18th century interests by scholars, students
CAMELOT	Arthurian legend and Grail lore
CHAUCERNET	Discussion of Chaucer's literary work
CHICLE	Chicano literature discussion
CHPOEM-L	Sharing, discussion of Chinese poems
CLASSICS	Classics and Latin discussion
DEUTSCHE-LISTE	German literature and culture
FOLKLORE	Folklore discussion

FWAKE	Discussion of James Joyce's *Finnegan's Wake*
FWAKEN-L	Finnegan's Wake textual notes
GUTNBERG	Electronic texts—*Moby Dick*, other classics
H-AMSTDY	American studies
HIT	Highly imaginative technology and science fiction
HORROR	Horror stories
INTERTEXT	Electronic fiction digest
LITERA-L	Exchange of ideas on literature, language, philology
LITERARY	For any lover of literature
LITSCI-L	Society for literature and science
LORE	Folklore list
MEDEVLIT	Medieval English literature discussion
MEDTEXTL	Medieval textual studies
MENDELE	Yiddish literature and language
MILTON-L	Electronic digest for scholars, students of Milton
MODBRITS	Modern British and Irish literature 1895-present
NEDER-L	Dutch language and literature (in Dutch)
ORTRAD-L	Interdisciplinary studies of oral traditions, African, Hispanic, Native American
PERSIA-L	Jewish literature and history in the Persian period
PYNCHON-L	Thomas Pynchon's writings
RRA-L	Romance Readers Anonymous
REED-L	Records of Early English Drama
SCHOLAR	Natural language processing and editing of historical and literary texts
SEMIOS-L	Semiotic critical studies
SF-LIST	Science fiction author lists
SFLOVERS	Science Fiction
SHAKSPER	Shakespeare researchers, students in seven countries
SHARP-L	History of authorship, reading, the printed word
TNC	Technoculture discussion
TOLKIEN	J.R.R. Tolkien books, readers
TWAIN-L	Mark Twain forum
WORKS-L	Writers List Works

Language—Writing

COMICS-L	Comic Writer's Workshop
COMPOS	Study of computers and writing
COMPOS01	Composition digest
COPYEDITING-L	King's English, other editorial issues
CREWRT	Creative writing pedagogy for teachers, student
CW-L	Computers and writing
DARGON-L	Dargon Project Writers Forum
H-RHETOR	History of Rhetoric
JOURNET	Issues of interest to journalists, faculty
PURTOPOI	Scholarly forum for writing and language discussion
RHETORIC	Rhetoric, social movements, persuasion
SCRNWRIT	Screen writing discussion
SEDIT-L	Scholarly Editing Forum
WAC-L	Writing Across the Curriculum
WRITERS	Discussion for professional and aspiring writers
WWP-L	Brown University Women Writer's Project
ZINES-L	Writers, publishers, writing teachers, fans of zines

Library and Information Retrieval

AFAS-L	African American Studies and librarianship
AJCUILL	Law Librarians/Interlibrary Loan
ALA	ALA file
ALAcoun	ALA Council
ALF-L	Academic Librarians forum
ARCHIVES	Archives and archivists
ARLIS-L	Arts Libraries discussion
ARIZSLS	Library Science conference
ASIS-L	American Society for Information Science
BABL-L	Boston Area Business Libraries discussion
BI-L	Assisting library users with bibliographic instruction
BIBOSCAN	Bibliographical Society of Canada, International scope
BIBLIST	Topics in Research Library user services
BIBSOFT	Bibliographic database and formatting software
BLACKLIB	Conference of Black Librarians
BRS-L	Full text retrieval software discussion
BUSLIB-L	Business library issues
CIRCPLUS	Circulation department issues
CIRLNET	Community of Industrial Relations Librarians
COLLDV-L	Collection development
COMENIUS	Library and information services development through computer technology
CONSALD	Committee on South Asian libraries and documentation
CWIS-L	Campus Wide Information System—creation, implementation
DLDG-L	Dance Librarians discussion group
ELDNET-L	Engineering Libraries
ELEASAI	Open Library/Information Science Research forum
ELLASBIB	Library automation in Greece
ELN-L	Electronic Library Network project
EMAILMAN	Learning about accessing electronic information
EXLIBRIS	Rare Book and special collections forum
FEDSIG-L	Federal electronic data users
FISC-L	Fee-based Information Services in Academia
GLSWICHE	Library Science conference
GOVDOC-L	Federal deposit libraries
GTRTI-L	Research and Teaching in Global Information Technology
GUTNBERG	Electronic texts—*Moby Dick*, other classics
IIRS	Israeli Information Retrieval Specialists
ILL-L	Interlibrary Loan discussion group
INDEX-L	Indexers discussion group
INFO+REF	Discussion of interests in information and referral services
INFONETS	Info-Nets
INFOSYS	Information systems
IR-L	Information retrieval
INT-LAW	Foreign and international law librarians
IRLIST	Any topic information retrieval and computer use
JESSE	Open library/information sciences education forum
KATALIST	Discussion of Library systems and databases
LALA-L	Latin Americanists Librarians announcements
LAW-LIB	Law librarians
LIBADMIN	Issues of library administration and management
LIBER	Library/media services
LIBEVENT	Library Information Services
LIBINFO	Harvard Information Services discussion

LIBNET-L	Libraries and networks in North Carolina
LIBPER-L	Library personnel issues
LIBRARY	Libraries and librarians
LIBRES	Library and information science research
LM_NET	School library/media services
MAPS-L	Map librarians
MEDLIB-L	Medical and health science libraries
METALIB	Metal library
MITIRLIB	MIT Industrial Relations Library
MLA-L	Music Library Association e-conference
MLAVES-L	Music Library research support
MUSEUM-L	Museum administration
NAGARA-L	Association of Government Archivists
NASIG	North American Serials
NISO	National Information Standards Organization
NNEWS	Library and Information resources on the Net
NOTRBCAT	Rare book and special collection catalogers
OFFCAMP	Off-campus library services
PACS-L	Public Access Computer Systems forum
PUBLIB	Use of the Internet in Public Libraries
PUBYAC	Children and young adult library services
SERCITES	Citations for serial literature
SERIALST	Serials in Libraries—user discussion
SHARP-L	History of the Printed Word
SLAJOB	Job board international for Special Librarians
SPILIB-L	Spires library discussion
TESLA	Technical standards for library automation
TQMLIB	Total Quality Management for Libraries
VISIONS	Visions for Libraries of the future
VPIEJ-L	Scholarly Electronic Journals discussion

Philosophy

BIOMED-L	Biomedical Ethics
BRAIN-L	Mind-brain discussion group
CPAE	Center for Professional and Applied Ethics
FNORD-L	New ways of thinking discussion
HEGEL	Hegel Society
HPSST-L	History and philosophy of Science
HOPOS-L	Forum for discussing history of science and philosophy
HUMANIST	Humanist issues, lively discussion
HUME	Discussion list of Hume Society
INFOSTDY	Information studies philosophical discussion
LITSCI-L	Society for literature and science
PEIRCE-L	Discussion of philosophy of Charles S. Peirce
PHILCA	Canadian philosophy
PHILCOMM	Philosophy of communication
PHILOS-L	For philosophers in United Kingdom and elsewhere
PHILOSED	Students and teachers discussion of Educational Philosophy
PHILOSOP	Academic philosophy
SKEPTIC	Paranormal claim analysis
SOCETH-L	Interdisciplinary Social Ethics
SOCORG-K	Social Organization of Knowledge discussion
SOPHIA	Ancient Philosophy, Hesiod to Iamblichus
SWIP-L	Society for Women in Philosophy

Science

ACSD-SCI	Alliance for Teaching of Science
ALLIANCE	North Carolina Science and Math Alliance
AMATH-IL	Applied Mathematics in Israel
ASTR-O	Astronomy information exchange
AT-NET	Approximation Theory Network
BIOCIS-L	Biology Curriculum Innovation Study
BIOESR-L	Biological Applications of Electron Spin Research
BIOMCH-L	Biomechanics and Movement Science
C-ALERTL	Contents Alert by Elsevier Science Publishers
CHEMCONF	Conference on Chemistry research and education
CHEMCORD	General Chemistry coordinators discussion group
CHEME-L	Chemical engineering
CHEMED-L	Chemistry education discussion
CHEMIC-L	Chemistry in Israel
CHMINF-L	Chemical information sources
CLASS-L	Classification, taxonomy
CONFOCAL	Microscopy
CYAN-TOX	Cyanobacterial toxins discussion
CVNET	Color and vision research
CYBSYS-L	Cybernetics and systems
DIBUG	Biosyn technologies software users
ECIXFILES	Energy and climate information exchange
EDUMATE	Educacion Matematica en Chile
EMFLDS-L	Electromagnetics in Medicine, Science
ENTOMO-L	Entomology
EPP-L	Albert Einstein Papers Project discussion
FISICA-L	Information exchange in Physics
FORUMBIO	Molecular biology forum
FRAC-L	Fractal discussion
GENE-L	Genetics education
GENETICS	Clinical human genetics
GEOLOGY	Geology discussion
HCDB-L	Open forum on the Hadron Colorimeter Data Bank
HIRIS-L	High Resolution Infrared Spectroscopy
IAPCIRC	International Arctic Project Student Projects
IAPEXPD	International Arctic Project Expeditions
IAPWILD	International Arctic Project Wildlife
ICS-L	International Chemometrics Society
IFPHEN-L	Interfacial Phenomena
ILAS-NET	International Linear Algebra
INTERF-L	Interfacial Phenomena
ITRDBTOR	Dendrochronology—tree ring data bank
JCMST-L	Journal of Computers in Math and Science
JCMT-L	James C. Maxwell Telescope
KINST-L	Hand microsurgery research network
LASMED-L	Laser medicine
MEDNETS	Medical telecommunications nets
MEDNEWS	Health information-communications network newsletter
MEDPHY-L	EFOMP Medical Physics information services
MEDSEA-L	Marine Biology of the Adriatic Sea
MEDSTU-L	Medical Students worldwide
METHODS	Bioscience research methods
METHODS	Research Methodology, qualitative and quantitative

MATH-L	Math documents
MODAL	Modal Analysis
MOLLUSCA	Molluscan Phylogeny and Systematics
MOSSBA	Mossbauer spectroscopy, software and forum
NDRG-L	Non-linear Dynamics Research group
NIC-INFO	Numerically Intensive Computing general information
NMBRTHRY	Number Theory
NEURO1-L	Neuroscience Information Forum
NEUS582	Methods in modern neuro-science
OPTICS-L	Optics newsletter
ORGCHE-L	Organic Chemistry
OTS-L	Organization for Tropical Studies at Yale
PANET-L	Medical education and health information
PHOTOSYN	Photosynthesis Researchers
PHYS-L	For teachers of college and university physics
PHYSIC-L	Physics
PHYSICS	Physics discussion
PHYSJOB	Physics job discussion
PHYS-STU	Physics Students discussion
POLYMERP	Polymer physics
QMLIST	Researchers, clinicians Quantitative Morphology
QNTEVA-L	Quantitative methods, theory and design
QUAKE-L	Earthquake and seismology
SAIS-L	Promoting Science awareness
SAME	Symbolic and Algebraic Manipulation in Education
SCIFRAUD	Discussion of fraud in Science
SCIMAT-L	Arkansas Science and Math education
SEDS-L	Students for exploration and development of space
SISMD-L	Seismology
SPACE	Space topics discussion
SPACE-IL	Israeli Space and Remote Sensing
SUP-COND	Superconductivity
T321-L	Teaching Science in Elementary Schools
THPHYSIO	Thermal physiology
USTC84-L	University Science and Technology discussion
UCGIA-L	University Consortium for Geo. Information and Analysis
WKSPHYS	Workshop Physics, a constructivist approach

Science—Social

ABSLST-L	Association of Black Sociologists
ADDICT-L	Academic and scholarly discussion of addiction
ANTHRO-L	General Anthropology bulletin board
APASD-L	APA research psychology network
APASLN	APA Science Leaders Network
APASPAN	APA Grassroots Network
APB-L	Advancement of Paradigmatic Behaviorism
APSSCNET	American Psychological Society Student Caucus
AQUIFER	Pollution and ground water re-charge
ARCH-L	Archaeology
ASEH-L	American Society of Environmental Historians
AUDITORY	Research in auditory perception
CHAOPSYC	Society for Chaos Theory in Psychology

COGSCI-L	Cognitive Science Centre
CONSIM-L	Conflict Simulation games
ECOLOG-L	Ecological Society of America—discussion, grants, jobs
ECONED L	Research in Economics Education
ECONHIST	Teaching and Research in Economic History discussion
EJVC-L	Electronic Journal of Virtual Culture in K–12 education
ENVST-L	Environmental studies
ETHNO	Ethnomethodology/conversation analysis
ETHNOHIS	Ethnology and History general discussion
ETHOLOGY	Animal behavior and behavioral ecology
FAMCOMM	Marital and family communication
FAMLYSCI	For researchers, scholars on family
FEDSIG-L	Federal Electronic Data Special Interest Group
GEOGED	Education issues in Geography
GLOMOD-L	The Global Modeling forum
GLOSAS-L	Global Systems Analysis and Simulation
H-DURKHM	Durkheim; European social thought
H-US-POL	U.S. political history
HOLISTIC	Holistic discussion
HUMANETS	Human Nets digest
HUMBIO-L	Biological anthropology
HUMEVO	Human Evolution Research discussion
IAPSY-L	Interamerican Psychologists
LIVE-EYE	Color and Vision discussion forum
MEH2O-L	Middle East water discussion
MERTON-L	Scholarly inquiry into contemplative life
METHO	Methodologie quantitative sciences sociales
METHODS	Research Methodology, quantitative and qualitative
MPSYCH-L	Society for Mathematical Psychology
NIATRN-L	National Institute of Aging Population Research
NNSP-L	National Network of State Polls
OBTS-L	Organizational Behavior Teaching Society
ORTRAD-L	Interdisciplinary studies of oral traditions, African, Hispanic, Native American
PACARC-L	Pacific Rim archaeology
PEN-L	Progressive Economists Network
PLAY-L	Multi-disciplinary discussion of play, games, sport
POLCOMM	Study of Political Communication
POLI-SCI	Political Science Digest
POPCULT	Analytical discussion of all aspects of popular culture
POR	Public Opinion Research academic, professional discussion
PSRT-L	Political Science, with constitutional law book reviews
PSYC	Psycoloquy, e-journal of Psychology
QUALRS-L	Qualitative research in the human sciences
QUALRSED	Qualitative research in education
QNTEVA-L	Quantitative methods
SENIOR	Senior health and living
SMKCC-L	Subject Matter, Knowledge and Conceptual Change
SNET-L	Human Communications, Social Networks and simulations
SOCORG-K	Social organization of knowledge
SOCWORK	Social Work discussion
SOS-DATA	Social Science Data
TECGRP-L	Technology & Social Behavior discussion

Statistics

CSA-DATA	Chinese Statistical Archive
EDSTAT-L	Statistics education discussion
ISPS	Teachers International Study Program in Statistics
PSTAT-L	Discussion of statistics and programming
PSYSTS-L	Psychology statistics discussion
QNTEVA-L	Quantitative methods: theory and design
SOS-DATA	Social Science Data
STAT-GEO	Quantitative Method in Geosciences
VSTAT-L	Vital Statistics

Women's Studies

EDUCOM-W	Women and information technology
EWM	European Women in Mathematics
FEMAIL	Forum for discussion of women's interests
FEMINIST	Feminist Task Force discussion list
FIST-L	Feminism in/and Science and Technology
GENDER	Study of Communications and Gender
GEOFEM	Gender issues in Geography
H-WOMEN	Women's History
HELWA-L	Malaysian women in U.S. and Canada
MEDFEM-L	An open discussion forum for medievalist feminists
MENOPAUS	Informal discussion for women of all ages
SBSWE-L	Society of Women Engineers—Student Section
STOPRAPE	Sexual assault activist
WIP-L	Society for Women in Philosophy and Information Science
WHIRL	Women's History in Rhetoric and Language
WIML-L	Women's Issues in Music Librarianship
WISENET	Women in Science and Engineering Network
WMST-L	Women's Studies
WWP-L	Brown University Women Writers Project

Usenet newsgroups

Usenet newsgroups, or newsgroups, are like a giant bulletin board. Anyone can read or post an article to any of the more than 10,000 different groups. Unlike mailing lists, Net users don't have to subscribe to a newsgroup to read its posts, but their Internet service provider must allow them access to "read news."

The following list includes newsgroups of interest to educators of all kinds. If the school or Internet service provider's news server does not carry a group you are interested in, ask them to add it. These are publicly available, free newsgroups any Internet service provider can access. Some are moderated, meaning a person reads the posts before putting them on the network. However, most are not moderated, so choose newsgroups carefully if students will have access to them. While the newsgroups listed here are appropriate for schools, it's good practice to always scan news articles in a newsgroup before making it available to students. The most active general newsgroup for teachers is **k12.chat.teacher**.

Education—Adult

alt.education.distance	Distance learning via computers

Education—Higher, Academic

bit.listserv.ashe-l	Higher Education Policy and Research
bit.listserv.edpolyan	Professionals and Students Discuss Education
bit.listserv.erl-l	Educational Research
bit.listserv.lawsch-l	Law School Discussion
bit.listserv.mba-l	MBA Student curriculum Discussion
comp.edu	Computer science education
info.academic-freedom	Academic freedom in the computer age (Moderated)
info.nsf.grants	NSF grant notes (Moderated)
misc.int-property	Discussion of intellectual property rights
misc.legal	Legalities and the ethics of law
sci.edu	The science of education

Education—Higher, Administrative

bit.listserv.billing	Chargeback of computer resources
bit.listserv.cumrec-l	CUMREC-L Administrative computer use
comp.archives.admin	Issues in computer archive administration

Education—Higher, Student

alt.folklore.college	Collegiate humor
alt.save.the.earth	Environmentalist causes

bit.listserv.psycgrad	Psychology Graduate Student Discussions
bit.listserv.sganet	Student Government Global Mail Network
comp.org.issnnet	International Student Society for Neural Networks
soc.college	College, college activities, campus life
soc.college.grad	General issues related to graduate schools
soc.college.gradinfo	Information about graduate schools

Education—Instructional Media

alt.bbs	Computer BBS systems and software
alt.bbs.ads	Ads for various computer BBSs
alt.bbs.allsysop	SysOp concerns of ALL networks and technologies
alt.bbs.internet	BBS systems accessible via the Internet
alt.bbs.lists	Postings of regional BBS listings
alt.bbs.lists.d	Discussion about regional BBS listings
alt.binaries.multimedia	Sound, text and graphics data rolled in one
alt.binaries.sounds.d	Sounding off
alt.binaries.sounds.misc	Digitized audio adventures
alt.cable-tv	Discussion of cable television service
alt.cd-rom	Discussions of optical storage media
alt.culture.usenet	The USENET community
alt.dcom.telecom	Discussion of telecommunications technology
alt.education.distance	Learning over networks
alt.hypertext	Discussion of hypertext—uses, transport
alt.internet.access.wanted	Connecting to the Internet
alt.internet.services	Services available on the Internet
alt.irc	Internet Relay Chat Discussion
alt.sb.programmer	Programming of the Sound Blaster sound cards
alt.uu.tools	Tools useful in self-education, distance learning
bit.general	Discussions Relating to BitNet and Usenet
bit.listserv.cw-email	Campus-wide E-Mail Discussion
bit.listserv.edtech	EDTECH—Educational Technology (Moderated)
bit.listserv.lstsrv-l	Forum on listserv mailing lists
bit.listserv.nettrain	Internet Trainers
bit.listserv.new-list	NEW-LIST - New Mailing List Announcements (Moderated)
bit.listserv.pagemakr	PageMaker for Desktop Publishers
bit.listserv.vpiej-l	Electronic Publishing
comp.ai.edu	Artificial Intelligence Applications to Education
comp.bbs.misc	All aspects of computer bulletin board systems
comp.editors	Topics related to computerized text editing
comp.edu	Computer science education
comp.fonts	Typefonts—design, conversion, use
comp.graphics	Computer graphics, art, animation, processing

comp.graphics.apps.pagemaker	Discussion about the use of PageMaker
comp.graphics.misc	Miscellaneous information about computer graphics
comp.graphics.visualization	Information on scientific visualization
comp.groupware	Soft/hardware for shared interactive environments
comp.ivideodisc	Interactive videodiscs—uses, potential
comp.lang.apl	Discussion about APL
comp.lang.lisp	Discussion about LISP
comp.lang.lisp.mcl	Discussing Apple's Macintosh Common Lisp
comp.lang.logo	The LOGO teaching and learning language
comp.mail.multi-media	Multimedia Mail (MIME)
comp.multimedia	Interactive multimedia technologies of all kinds
comp.org.eff.news	Electronic Frontier Foundation (EFF) News
comp.org.eff.talk	Discussion of EFF goals, strategies
comp.org.fidonet	FidoNews digest, official news of FidoNet
comp.periphs.scsi	Discussion of SCSI-based peripheral devices
comp.speech	Computer generated speech—hardware and software
comp.text.desktop	Technology and techniques of desktop publishing
rec.arts.books	Books of all genres and the publishing industry
rec.video.production	Professional video production
sci.cognitive	Perception, memory, judgment and reasoning
sci.edu	The science of education

Education—International

alt.culture.kerala	The culture of the Keralite people worldwide
alt.culture.tuva	Topics related to the Republic of Tuva
bit.listserv.euearn-l	Computers in Eastern Europe
bit.listserv.mideur-l	Middle Europe Discussion
bit.listserv.seasia-l	Southeast Asia Discussion
bit.listserv.slovak-l	Slovak Discussion
comp.society.development	Computers in developing countries (Moderated)
misc.news.southasia	News from Bangladesh, India, Nepal
soc.culture.afghanistan	Discussion of the Afghan society
soc.culture.african	Discussions about Africa
soc.culture.arabic	Technological and cultural issues
soc.culture.asean	Association of Southeast Asian Nations
soc.culture.australian	Australian culture and society
soc.culture.bangladesh	Issues and discussion about Bangladesh
soc.culture.bosna-herzgvna	Bosnia-Herzegovina culture and society
soc.culture.brazil	People and country of Brazil
soc.culture.british	Britain and people of British descent
soc.culture.bulgaria	Discussing Bulgarian society
soc.culture.canada	Discussions of Canada and its people
soc.culture.caribbean	Life in the Caribbean
soc.culture.celtic	Irish, Scottish, Breton, Cornish, and Welsh

soc.culture.china	About China and Chinese culture
soc.culture.croatia	Croatian peoples and culture
soc.culture.czecho-slovak	Bohemian, Slovak, and Moravian life
soc.culture.europe	All aspects of all-European society
soc.culture.filipino	Group about the Filipino culture
soc.culture.french	French culture, history, related discussions
soc.culture.german	Discussions about German culture and history
soc.culture.greek	Group about Greeks
soc.culture.hongkong	Discussions pertaining to Hong Kong
soc.culture.indian	India and things Indian
soc.culture.iranian	Iran and things Iranian/Persian
soc.culture.italian	The Italian people and their culture
soc.culture.japan	Everything Japanese, except Japanese language
soc.culture.korean	Discussions about Korea and things Korean
soc.culture.latin-america	Topics about Latin-America
soc.culture.lebanon	Discussion about things Lebanese
soc.culture.magyar	The Hungarian people and their culture
soc.culture.mexican	Discussion of Mexico's society
soc.culture.misc	Group for discussion about other cultures
soc.culture.nepal	People and things in and from Nepal
soc.culture.netherlands	People from the Netherlands and Belgium
soc.culture.new-zealand	Discussion of topics related to New Zealand
soc.culture.nordic	Discussion about culture up north
soc.culture.pakistan	Topics of discussion about Pakistan
soc.culture.polish	Polish culture, past, and politics
soc.culture.portuguese	Discussion of the people of Portugal
soc.culture.romanian	Discussion of Romanian and Moldavian people
soc.culture.soviet	Topics relating to Russian or Soviet culture
soc.culture.spain	Culture on the Iberian peninsula
soc.culture.sri-lanka	Things and people from Sri Lanka
soc.culture.taiwan	Discussion about things Taiwanese
soc.culture.tamil	Tamil language, history, and culture
soc.culture.thai	Thai people and their culture
soc.culture.turkish	Discussion about things Turkish
soc.culture.vietnamese	Issues and discussions of Vietnamese culture
soc.culture.yugoslavia	Discussions of Yugoslavia and its people
talk.politics.china	Political issues related to China
talk.politics.mideast	Debate over Middle Eastern events
talk.politics.soviet	Soviet politics, domestic and foreign

Education—K12

alt.child-support	Raising children in a split family
alt.kids-talk	A place for the pre-college set on the Net
alt.parents-teens	Discussions about raising teenagers
alt.sexual.abuse.recovery	Helping others deal with trauma

k12.chat.elementary	Informal discussion for grades K-5
k12.chat.junior	Informal discussion for grades 6-8
k12.chat.senior	Informal discussion for high school students
k12.chat.teacher	Informal discussion for K–12 teachers
k12.ed.art	Art curriculum
k12.ed.business	Business education curriculum
k12.ed.comp.literacy	Teaching computer literacy
k12.ed.health-pe	Health and Physical Education curriculum
k12.ed.life-skills	Home Economics and Career education
k12.ed.math	Mathematics curriculum
k12.ed.music	Music and Performing Arts curriculum
k12.ed.science	Science curriculum
k12.ed.soc-studies	Social Studies and History curriculum
k12.ed.special	Students with disabilities, special needs
k12.ed.tag	Talented and gifted students
k12.ed.tech	Industrial Arts and vocational education
k12.lang.art	Language Arts curriculum
k12.lang.deutsch-eng	Bilingual German practice with native speakers
k12.lang.esp-eng	Bilingual Spanish practice with native speakers
k12.lang.francais	Bilingual French practice with native speakers
k12.lang.russian	Bilingual Russian practice with native speakers
misc.education	Discussion of the educational system
misc.kids	Children, their behavior and activities
sci.edu	The science of education

Education—Multicultural

alt.culture.us.asian-indian	Asian Indians in the U.S. and Canada
alt.discrimination	Quotas, affirmative action, bigotry, persecution
alt.native	Issues for and about Native Americans
soc.culture.african.american	Discussions about Afro-American issues
soc.culture.asian.american	Discussion about Asian-Americans
soc.culture.intercultural	A discussion on the pros and cons of multiculturalism
soc.culture.jewish	Jewish culture and religion
soc.culture.misc	Discussion about other cultures
soc.culture.usa	Culture of the United States of America

Education—Special

alt.education.disabled	Learning experiences for the disabled
bit.listserv.autism	Autism and Developmental Disabilities
bit.listserv.deaf-l	Deaf List
bit.listserv.l-hcap	Handicap List (Moderated)
k12.ed.special	Students with disabilities, special needs
misc.handicap	Items about the handicapped and Education

Arts

alt.artcom	Artistic Community, arts and communication
alt.binaries.pictures.fine-art.d	Fine-art binaries
alt.binaries.pictures.fine-art.digitized	Art from conventional media
alt.binaries.pictures.fine-art.graphics	Art created on computers
alt.binaries.pictures.fractals	Postings of fractal-pictures
alt.emusic	Ethnic, exotic, electronic, elaborate, etc., music
alt.exotic-music	Exotic music discussions
alt.fractals	Fractals in math, graphics, and art
alt.movies.visual-effects	Learn about the ins and outs of special effects
bit.listserv.allmusic	Discussions on all forms of Music
bit.listserv.cinema-l	Discussions on all forms of Cinema
bit.listserv.emusic-l	Electronic Music Discussion List
bit.listserv.film-l	Filmmaking and reviews List
comp.music	Applications of computers in music research
rec.arts.comics	Comic books, graphic novels, sequential art
rec.arts.dance	All aspects of dance discussed
rec.arts.fine	Fine arts and artists
rec.arts.misc	Discussions about the arts not in other groups
rec.arts.movies	Discussions of movies and movie making
rec.arts.movies.reviews	Reviews of movies (Moderated)
rec.arts.theatre.misc	All aspects of stage work and theatre
rec.arts.tv	TV—its history, past and current shows
rec.audio.high-end	High-end audio systems (Moderated)
rec.music.classical	Discussion about classical music

Computer

alt.3d	Three-dimensional imaging
alt.comp.acad-freedom.news	Academic freedom—computers (Moderated)
alt.comp.acad-freedom.talk	Academic freedom issues—computers
alt.folklore.computers	Stories and anecdotes about computers
alt.gopher	Discussion of the gopher information service
alt.religion.computers	People who believe computing is "real life"
alt.sources.wanted	Requests for source code
alt.uu.virtual-worlds.misc	Virtual worlds, virtual reality
alt.wais	The Wide Area Information Service (WAIS)
bionet.software	Information about software for biology
bionet.software.sources	Software Source relating to biology
bit.listserv.apple2-I	Problems and concerns regarding Apple II computers
bit.listserv.big-lan	Campus-Size LAN Discussion Group (Moderated)
bit.listserv.dasig	Database Administration
bit.listserv.bitnews	BITNET News
bit.listserv.c+health	Computers and health
bit.listserv.cdromlan	CD-ROM on Local Area Networks

bit.listserv.decnews	Digital Equipment Corporation News List
bit.listserv.edi-l	Electronic Data Interchange Issues
bit.listserv.ethics-l	Discussion of Ethics in Computing
bit.listserv.euearn-l	Computers in Eastern Europe
bit.listserv.pacs-l	Public-Access Computer System Forum
bit.listserv.valert-l	Virus Alert List (Moderated)
biz.comp.services	Using your computers to improve your business
biz.comp.software	The latest software news can usually be found here
comp.admin.policy	Discussions of site administration policies
comp.ai	Artificial intelligence discussions
comp.ai.neural-nets	All aspects of neural networks
comp.ai.vision	Artificial Intelligence Vision Research
comp.archives	Descriptions of public access archives
comp.databases	Database and data management
comp.dcom.telecom	Telecommunications digest (Moderated)
comp.doc	Archived public-domain documentation
comp.edu	Discussion of computers and education
comp.human-factors	Issues related to human-computer interaction
comp.lang.perl.misc	Discussion of Larry Wall's Perl system
comp.lang.postscript	The PostScript Page Description Language
comp.mail.misc	General discussions about computer email
comp.protocols.misc	Various forms and types of FTP protocol
comp.risks	Risks to public from computers and users (Moderated)
comp.simulation	Simulation methods, problems, uses
comp.society.futures	Events in technology affecting computing
comp.sys.transputer	Machine translation research
comp.text.sgml	SGML, structured documents, markup languages
comp.virus	Virus discussion list
info.ietf.isoc	Internet Society discussion
info.labmgr	Computer lab managers list
misc.books.technical	Discussion of books about technical topics
misc.legal.computing	Legal climate of the computing world
sci.comp-aided	Use of computers as tools in scientific research
sci.crypt	Different methods of data en/decryption
sci.image.processing	Scientific image processing and analysis
sci.virtual-worlds	Modeling the universe (Moderated)

Future Studies

alt.cyberspace	Cyberspace and how it should work
alt.sci.physics.new-theories	Scientific theories not found in journals
alt.society.futures	Events in technology affecting computing
alt.uu.virtual-worlds.misc	Virtual worlds, virtual reality
bit.listserv.fnord-l	New Ways of Thinking List
bit.listserv.xtropy-l	Extopian List

comp.society   Impact of technology on society (Moderated)
comp.society.privacy   Effects of technology on privacy (Moderated)
rec.arts.sf.science   Aspects of Science Fiction (SF) science

Help

alt.algebra.help   Aid for those algebra-plagued students
alt.child-support   Raising children in a split family
alt.school.homework.help   An online homework helper
alt.sexual.abuse.recovery   Helping others deal with trauma
alt.parents-teens   Discussions about raising teenagers
comp.answers   Answers to basic computer, Internet questions
misc.answers   More answers to basic computer, Net questions
misc.misc   Discussions not fitting in any other group
news.announce.conferences   Calls for papers and conference announcements
news.announce.important   General announcements of interest to all
news.announce.newgroups   Calls for newgroups and announcements of same
news.announce.newusers   Explanatory postings for new users (Moderated)
news.groups   Discussions and lists of newsgroups
news.lists   News-related statistics and lists (Moderated)
news.lists.ps-maps   Maps relating to USENET traffic flows (Moderated)
news.misc   Discussions of USENET itself
news.newusers.questions   Q & A for users new to the Usenet
news.software.nn   Discussion about the "nn" news reader package
news.software.nntp   The Network News Transfer Protocol
news.software.readers   Discussion of software used to read network news

History and Humanities

bit.listserv.c18-l   18th Century Interdisciplinary Discussion
bit.listserv.hellas   The Hellenic Discussion List (Moderated)
bit.listserv.history   History List
k12.Ed.soc-studies   Social Studies and History curriculum in K–12
sci.classics   Studying classical history, languages, art and more
soc.history   Discussions of things historical

Language—Communication Studies

alt.news-media   News media discussion and debate

Language—International

alt.chinese.text	General postings of Chinese in standard form
alt.uu.lang.esperanto.misc	Learning Esperanto
k12.lang.deutsch-eng	Bilingual German with native speakers
k12.lang.esp-eng	Bilingual Spanish with native speakers
k12.lang.francais	Bilingual French with native speakers
k12.lang.russian	Bilingual Russian with native speakers
sci.lang	Natural languages, communication, etc
sci.lang.japan	Japanese language, spoken and written
soc.culture.esperanto	The neutral international language Esperanto

Language—Linguistics

comp.ai.nlang-know-rep	Natural Language, Knowledge Representation (Moderated)
comp.editors	Topics related to computerized text editing
comp.text	Text processing issues and methods
sci.lang	Natural languages, communication

Language—Literature

alt.mythology	Understanding human nature through mythology
alt.postmodern	Postmodernism, semiotics, deconstruction, etc.
bit.listserv.gutnberg	GUTENBERG Project Discussion List
bit.listserv.literary	Discussions about literature
rec.arts.sf.misc	Science fiction lovers' newsgroup

Language—Writing

alt.hypertext	Discussion of hypertext (World Wide Web) uses, transport
alt.prose	Original writings, fictional and otherwise
alt.prose.d	Discussions about postings in alt.prose
alt.pulp	Paperback fiction, newsprint production discussion
alt.usage.english	English grammar, word usages, related topics
bit.listserv.mbu-l	Megabyte University—Computers and Writing
bit.listserv.words-l	English Language Discussion Group
comp.edu.composition	Writing instruction in computer-based classrooms
misc.writing	Discussion of writing in all of its forms
rec.arts.int-fiction	Discussions about interactive fiction
rec.arts.poems	For the posting of poems

Library and Information Retrieval

alt.wais	The Wide Area Information Service (WAIS)
alt.gopher	Discussion of the gopher information service

bit.listserv.advanc-l	Geac Advanced Integrated Library System Users
bit.listserv.buslib-l	Business Library List
bit.listserv.cdromlan	CD-ROM on Local Area Networks
bit.listserv.circplus	Circulation Reserve and Related Library Issues
bit.listserv.cwis-l	Campus-Wide Information Systems
bit.listserv.govdoc-l	Discussion of Government Document Issues
bit.listserv.libref-l	Library Reference Issues
bit.listserv.libres	Library and Information Research List (Moderated)
bit.listserv.medlib-l	Medical Libraries Discussion List
bit.listserv.notabene	Nota Bene List
bit.listserv.notis-l	NOTIS/DOBIS Discussion group List
bit.listserv.pacs-l	Public-Access Computer System Forum (Moderated)
bit.listserv.slart-l	SLA Research and Teaching
bit.listserv.spires-l	SPIRES Conference List
comp.archives	Descriptions of public access archives (Moderated)
comp.archives.admin	Issues in computer archive administration
comp.doc	Archived public-domain documentation (Moderated)
comp.doc.techreports	Lists of technical reports (Moderated)
comp.infosystems	Any discussion about information systems
comp.internet.library	Discussing electronic libraries (Moderated)
soc.libraries.talk	Discussing all aspects of libraries

Philosophy

alt.sci.physics.new-theories	Scientific theories not found in journals
bit.listserv.ethics-l	Discussion of Ethics in Computing
bit.listserv.fnord-l	New Ways of Thinking List
comp.ai.philosophy	Philosophical aspects of Artificial Intelligence
sci.philosophy.meta	Discussions within the scope of "MetaPhilosophy"
sci.philosophy.tech	Technical philosophy: math, science, logic, etc.
sci.logic	Logic—math, philosophy, and computational aspects
sci.skeptic	Skeptics discussing pseudo-science
talk.origins	Evolution versus creationism
talk.philosophy.misc	Philosophical musings on all topics
talk.religion.misc	Religious, ethical, and moral implications
talk.religion.newage	Esoteric and minority religions and philosophies

Science

alt.fractals	Fractals in math, graphics, and art
alt.sci.astro.aips	National Radio Astronomy Observatories' AIPS
alt.sci.astro.fits	Technical—Flexible Image Transport Systems
bionet.agroforestry	Discussion of Agroforestry
bionet.announce	Announcements of interest to biologists (Moderated)
bionet.biology.computational	Computer and math applications (Moderated)

bionet.biology.tropical	Discussions about tropical biology
bionet.genome.chromosomes	Discussion of Chromosome 22
bionet.immunology	Discussions about research in immunology
bionet.info-theory	Discussions about biological information
bionet.jobs.offered	Scientific Job opportunities
bionet.journals.contents	Contents of biology journal publications
bionet.molbio.ageing	Discussions of cellular and organismal aging
bionet.molbio.bio-matrix	Computer applications to biological databases
bionet.molbio.embldatabank	Information about the EMBL Nucleic acid database
bionet.molbio.evolution	How genes and proteins have evolved
bionet.molbio.genbank	Information about the GenBank Nucleic acid database
bionet.molbio.genbank.updates	Hot off the presses (Moderated)
bionet.molbio.gene-linkage	Discussions about genetic linkage analysis
bionet.molbio.genome-program	Discussion of Human Genome Project issues
bionet.molbio.hiv	The molecular biology of HIV
bionet.molbio.methds-reagnts	Requests for information and lab reagents
bionet.molbio.proteins	Research on proteins and protein databases
bionet.neuroscience	Research issues in the neurosciences
bionet.plants	Discussion about all aspects of plant biology
bionet.population-bio	Discussions about population biology
bionet.sci-resources	Information about funding agencies
bionet.users.addresses	Who's who in Biology
bionet.women-in-bio	Women in Biology
bionet.xtallography	Discussions about protein crystallography
bit.listserv.frac-l	FRACTAL Discussion List
bit.listserv.medforum	MEDNEWS—Health Info-Com Network Newsletter
comp.theory	Theoretical Computer Science
comp.theory.cell-automata	Discussion all aspects of cellular automata
comp.theory.dynamic-sys	Ergodic Theory and Dynamical Systems
comp.theory.info-retrieval	Information Retrieval topics (Moderated)
comp.theory.self-org-sys	Topics related to self-organization
info.nsf.grants	NSF grant notes (Moderated)
info.theorynt	Theory list (Moderated)
k12.ed.math	Mathematics curriculum in K–12
k12.ed.science	Science curriculum in K–12
rec.arts.sf.science	Real and speculative aspects of SF science
sci.aeronautics	Science of aeronautics and related technology
sci.aquaria	Only scientifically oriented postings re: aquaria
sci.astro	Astronomy discussions and information
sci.astro.hubble	Processing Hubble Space Telescope data (Moderated)
sci.bio.misc	Biology and related sciences
sci.bio.technology	Any topic relating to biotechnology
sci.chem	Chemistry and related sciences
sci.comp-aided	Use of computers as tools in scientific research
sci.cryonics	Theory/practice of biostasis, suspended animation
sci.electronics.misc	Circuits, theory, electrons and discussions

sci.energy	Discussions about energy, science, and technology
sci.engr	Technical discussions about engineering tasks
sci.engr.biomed	Discussing the field of biomedical engineering
sci.engr.chem	All aspects of chemical engineering
sci.engr.civil	Topics related to civil engineering
sci.engr.mech	The field of mechanical engineering
sci.geo.fluids	Discussion of geophysical fluid dynamics
sci.geo.geology	Discussion of solid earth sciences
sci.geo.meteorology	Discussion of meteorology and related topics
sci.logic	Logic—math, philosophy and computational aspects
sci.materials	All aspects of materials engineering
sci.math	Mathematical discussions and pursuits
sci.math.num-analysis	Numerical Analysis
sci.math.research	Discussion of current mathematical research (Moderated)
sci.math.stat	Statistics discussion
sci.math.symbolic	Symbolic algebra discussion
sci.med	Medicine and its related products and regulations
sci.med.aids	AIDS treatment, HIV pathology/biology, prevention
sci.med.physics	Issues of physics in medical testing/care
sci.misc	Short-lived discussion on subjects in the sciences
sci.nanotech	Self-reproducing molecular-scale machines (Moderated)
sci.optics	Discussion relating to the science of optics
sci.physics	Physical laws, properties
sci.physics.fusion	Information on fusion, especially "cold" fusion
sci.research	Research methods, funding, ethics, and whatever
sci.research.careers	Issues relevant to careers in scientific research
sci.space.policy	Space, space programs, space research
sci.space.news	Announcements of space-related news items (Moderated)
sci.space.shuttle	The space shuttle and the STS program

Science—Social

alt.folklore.science	Folklore of science, not science of folklore
alt.folklore.urban	Urban legends
alt.society.civil-disob	Discussions on civil disobedience
alt.society.civil-liberty	Civil Liberties Discussion
bit.listserv.biosph-l	Biosphere, ecology, Discussion List
bit.listserv.envbeh-l	Forum on Environment and Human Behavior
bit.listserv.qualrs-l	Qualitative Research of the Human Sciences
bit.listserv.sos-data	Social Science Data List
comp.text	Text processing issues and methods
sci.anthropology	All aspects of studying humankind
sci.archaeology	Studying antiquities of the world
sci.cognitive	Perception, memory, judgment and reasoning
sci.econ	The science of economics

sci.edu	The science of education
sci.environment	Discussions about the environment and ecology
sci.psychology.misc	Topics related to psychology
sci.psychology.digest	PSYCOLOQUY: Refereed Psychology Journal
sci.systems	The theory and application of systems science
soc.misc	Socially oriented topics not in other groups
soc.politics	Political problems, systems, solutions. (Moderated)
talk.environment	State of the environment and what to do
talk.politics.misc	Political discussions and ravings of all kinds
talk.politics.theory	Theory of politics and political systems

Statistics

bit.listserv.sos-data	Social Science Data List

Women's Studies

bionet.women-in-bio	Women in biology
soc.feminism	Discussion of feminism and feminist issues (Moderated)
soc.women	Women's issues, their problems and relationships
talk.rape	Discussions on stopping rape

"The universe is full of magical things patiently waiting for our wits to grow sharper."

Eden Phillpots

WORLD WIDE WEB TOUR

Snapshots of the top 50 educational sites on the Web

The most exciting and easy-to-use Internet navigational tool is the World Wide Web, also called the Web or WWW. With the click of a button, students and educators can visit colorful Web pages packed with educational information of all kinds on computers all over the world.

As of March 1996 8,000 K–12 schools in the United States were estimated to be using the Internet, and more than 300,000 of their students were surfing the Web.

The appeal of the Web over other Internet tools, besides its ease of use, is its multimedia capability. Besides accessing text and graphics, Web users can watch videos and listen to music or speeches. The Web's simple "point, click, and you're there" approach means users don't have to struggle with as many technical aspects of the Internet when they search for and retrieve information.

Classroom Connect's writers/Net surfers have scoured the Web, looking for sites teachers can use for and with students. What follows is a tour of more than 50 of the best educational WWW sites on the Internet. Each snapshot includes a computer screen capture of the site, its URL address, and a brief description of its value to educators and students. They're in alphabetical order by name of site or by subject. (For details on how you can get the Web browser software you need to use the WWW, see the World Wide Web section of Appendix B, Internet Tutorials.)

The Web is growing so rapidly that hundreds of new educational sites—some of them schools!—will be on the Internet by the time this book is printed. Software for making a "Web page" or "home page" is easily accessible on the Internet, and teachers and students are already designing their own home pages and putting them online. Anyone in the world with access to the Web can visit public school students in Boulder, Colorado, or read school newspapers and meet teachers and students at the Ralph Bunche School in New York City. Dozens of other K–12 schools are available for virtual visits. (See Appendix B for information on how to make a Web page.)

If your school has made a Web page but can't post it on the Internet, we'll mount it on *Classroom Connect's* Web site. A portion of the site, called ClassroomWeb, is devoted solely to Web pages from K–12 schools. For details, send email to **classweb@wentworth.com** and type **School Web Page** in the subject line. To visit ClassroomWeb, go to **URL: http://classroom.net/classweb/**

To keep up with the latest in Web pages and how to use them in the classroom, check the *Classroom Connect* newsletter.

Academy One

URL:
http://nptn.org/cyber.serv/AOneP/
academy_one/menu.html

An international, online resource for students, educators, parents and administrators of grades K–12. Academy One sponsors dozens of Internet projects throughout the school year, including space shuttle simulations, virtual track meets, stock market simulations, Student Research Center, Bridge Building Contest, Bird Migration Watch, foreign language exchanges, Iditarod Dogsled Race project, the Student News Network, and a sonnet-writing contest. It also includes a Curriculum Database & Index to Online Projects, the Academy One Teacher's Manual, and more. For more information, call (714) 527-5651 or send email to **info@nptn.org.182**

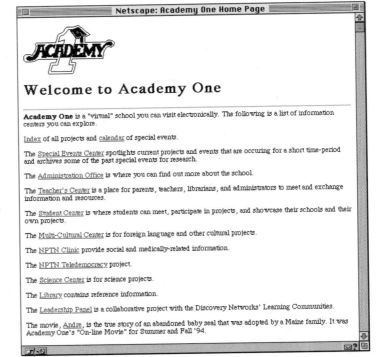

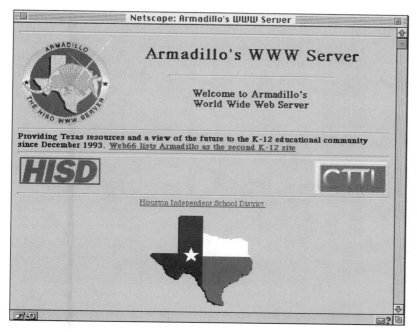

Armadillo

URL:
http://chico.rice.edu/armadillo/
Full of resources and instructional materials related to Texas, the Lone Star State. The content supports an interdisciplinary course of study with a Texas theme and includes hyperlinks to dozens of other Web and gopher servers related to education.

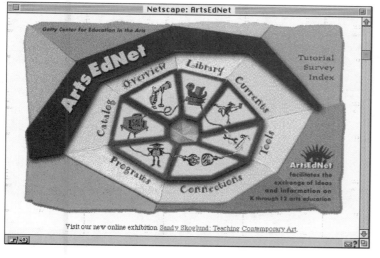

ArtsEdNet

URL: http://www.artsednet.getty.edu
ArtsEdNet, developed by the Getty Center for Education, is a new electronic resource designed to support the needs of the K–12 arts education community. This expertly designed site includes departments such as Currents, where you'll find articles, news releases, and teaching trends and advocacy issues; Tools, which feature lesson plans and other curriculum materials; and the Library, which houses resources such as an image bank, and excerpts of various art education books.

Bartlett's Familiar Passages, Phrases, and Proverbs

URL: http://www.cc.columbia.edu/ acis/bartleby/bartlett/

You'll find a complete, unabridged, and searchable database of the ninth edition of Bartlett's Familiar Quotations. In the real world, this book weighs in at more than 1,100 pages. The online version is easy to access and is very easily searched by keyword so you can find famous quotes and sayings of hundreds of famous authors, politicians, poets, and other notables.

Busy Teacher's K-12 WebSite

URL: http://www.gatech.edu/lcc/idt/ Students/Cole/Proj/K–12/TOC.html

This Web site is designed to provide K–12 educators with a direct source of online teaching materials, lesson plans, and classroom activities. It's also in existence to provide an enjoyable and rewarding experience for the teacher who is just learning to use the Internet.

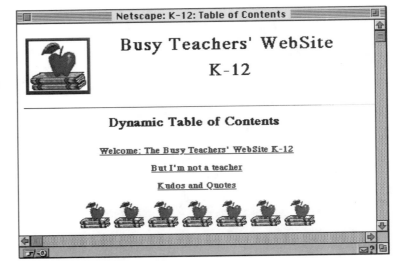

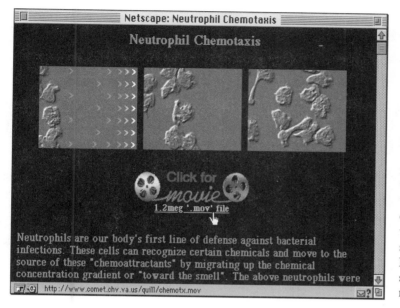

Cells Alive

URL:

http://www.comet.chv.va.us/quill/

This "microscopy of living cells and organisms" site is packed with information and images of viruses, parasites, bacteria, and even "foodborne pathogenic microorganisms." Yuk! Uncover the truth about cryptosporidium parvum, which lurks in our water supplies, and discover how streptococci threaten white blood cells. After exploring the site, click on the link to Tom Terry's Microbiology Course which contains short quizzes and tests related to the material.

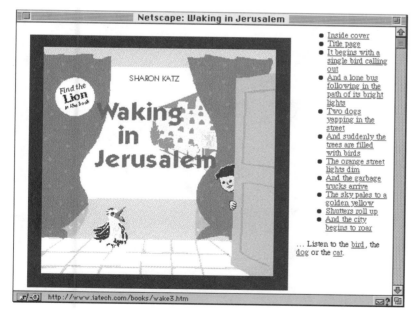

Children's Books

URL: http://www.digimark.net/ iatech/books/

Concertina Publishing offers electronic versions of its popular children's books via this site. Young students will love flipping through these colorful online books, and so will you!

Child Safety on the Information Highway

URL: http://www.omix.com/magid/child.safety.online.html

Internet-savvy educators have been aware for some time of the necessity of controlling student access to inappropriate material on the Internet. This important document outlines how to control student access to inappropriate Internet content, both from home and school.

EDITOR'S CHOICE

Classroom Connect

URL: http://www.classroom.net

This is your one-stop source of information about using the Internet in the K–12 classroom. Includes sample articles from the premier newsletter for online educators of the same name, tap more than a thousand links to educational material online, and bookmark the searching page for the best Net search tools. You'll also find information about national educational conferences and Classroom Connect products.

ClassroomWeb

URL: http://www.classroom.net/classweb/

Send your school's Web pages to Classroom Connect, and we'll mount them online for free for the whole world to see! Thousands of K–12 schools worldwide already have homes on ClassroomWeb. Visit the ClassroomWeb site to see how they're making use of this global publishing opportunity.

Developing Educational Standards

URL: http://putwest.boces.org/ Standards.html

All educators have certain standards in mind when they create new lesson plans. While these standards are conceptually nothing new, lately they have received a new emphasis through dozens of state initiatives and through the passage of the Goals 2000 Educate America Act. This site has been created to help educators keep up to date with the latest educational standards information, and contains more than 850 links to related information nationwide.

Dinosaur Exhibit

URL:
**http://www.hcc.hawaii.edu/
dinos/dinos.1.html**

For the first time, Hawaiians (and anyone else) can visit a free, permanent exhibit of dinosaur fossils for public viewing — on the Web. Honolulu Community College give K–12 students a look at the fossils of some of the largest creatures that ever lived, and even includes an audio tour. The fossils are replicas of the originals at the American Museum of Natural History in New York City, with one of the largest and finest collections of dinosaur fossils in the world.

Discovery Channel Online

URL: http://www.discovery.com

The Discovery Channel, known for its award-winning educational programming, now offers a Web site boasting original interactive content with film, music, photography, and illustration. Recent offerings include news bites with photographs of new species discovered in the Galapagos, information on Haiti's continuing political upheavals, and a guide to the cable channel's daily programming.

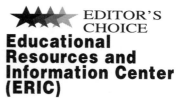
Educational Resources and Information Center (ERIC)

URL: http://ericir.syr.edu

Sponsored by the U.S. Office of Educational Research and Improvement, ERIC is a one-stop source of the latest education information—from thousands of free lesson plans to full-text articles about K–12 education in the United States and abroad. The site is searchable by keyword. Email the staff for information on how to submit education-related Internet questions. **Email to: askeric@ericir.syr.edu**

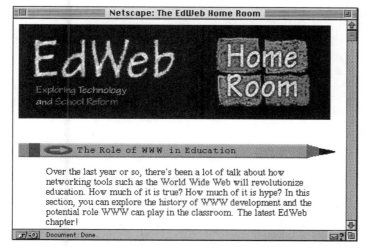

EdWeb

URL: http://edweb.cnidr.org:90

The purpose of this online "hyperbook" is to explore the worlds of educational reform and information technology. With EdWeb, you can hunt down online educational resources around the world, learn about trends in education policy and information infrastructure development, and examine success stories of computers in the classroom. EdWeb is a dynamic work-in-progress, and numerous changes and additions occur on a weekly basis.

Encyclopedia Britannica Online

URL: http://www.eb.com

At 44 million words, the Encyclopedia Britannica is recognized as the world's most comprehensive reference. Now, advanced search and retrieval capabilities and hypertext linking via the WWW make this reference tool even more powerful. Britannica Online is a fully searchable and browsable collection of authoritative references, including Britannica's full encyclopedic database, Merriam-Webster's Collegiate Dictionary, the Britannica Book of the Year, and more. Visitors may try the site, but users who wish to make regular searches must pay a fee to subscribe.

Exploratorium

URL: http://www.exploratorium.edu

Housed within the Palace of Fine Arts in San Francisco, California, the Exploratorium is a collage of 650 interactive exhibits in science, art, and human perception. Students can explore many of them via this site. The exhibits fall into 13 broad subject areas, including light color, sound, music, motion, animal behavior, electricity, heat and temperature, language, patterns, hearing, touch, vision, waves and resonance, and weather.

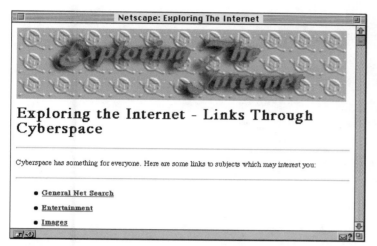

Exploring the Internet Basic Training

URL:
http://www.hcc.hawaii.edu/hccinfo/ tutorials/tutorials.html

Need a refresher course on the basics of navigating the Internet?

Dr. Kenneth Hensarling (ken@pulua.hcc.hawaii.edu) at Honolulu Community College placed his Internet college course online for all to use. A great resource for trainers bringing educators onto the World Wide Web for the first time. Covers everything from email to the Web.

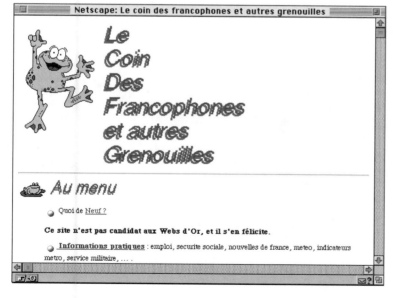

French Language Web

URL: http://web.cnam.fr/fr/

This link to all things French is maintained by a major French university. Includes pointers to practical information about getting around in France, hyperlinks to popular French tourist attractions, language tips, and much more.

EDITOR'S CHOICE

Frog Dissection Kit

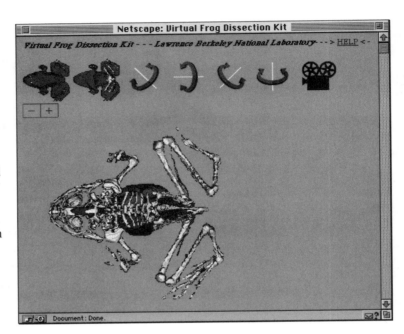

URL: http://george.lbl.gov/ ITG.hm.pg.docs/dissect/dissect.html

Designed for high school biology classes, this site allows students to explore the anatomy of a frog without dissecting a real animal. They can turn the frog over, remove skin, and highlight various organs and systems. Researchers used data from high-resolution imaging to create this one-of-a-kind site.

Global Community of Educators (Iris)

URL: http://www.tmn.com/Organizations/ Iris/home.html

Iris promotes excellence in education by providing a rich source of student-centered telecommunication projects, professional information, an inviting place to meet colleagues with similar educational interests, and a forum for developing new and innovative curriculum resources.

Global SchoolNet Foundation

URL: http://gsn.org

Global SchoolNet hosts nearly 100 innovative K–12 Internet projects each year, and continues to find innovative classroom applications for the Internet. You and your class can join in right away via this site. Their latest project involves connecting schools worldwide via inexpensive videoconferencing tools such as CU-SeeMe.

Grand Canyon National Park

URL: http://kbt.com/gc/

Take your class on a virtual tour of one of the most incredible places on earth. The Grand Canyon of the Colorado River is one of the seven natural wonders of the world and one our planet's most astounding accomplishments. Hundreds of pictures of wildlife and areas of the canyon await you.

Grassroots Project

**URL:
http://www.hiwaay.net/sunrise/
grassrts/home.htm**

Using this site, students and educators participate in a virtual, Internet-based "neighborhood" where they can explore, interact, and learn. The site's creators encourage participants to contact them regarding constructing "rooms" of their own, thereby gaining hands-on experience in building their own online community.

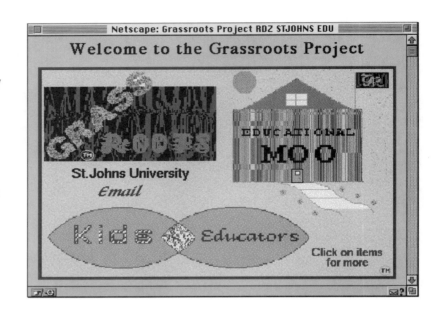

Health Information

**URL:
http://www.tcom.ohiou.edu/
family-health.html**

Students can use this site to listen to health information. It's an ideal opportunity for students with impaired vision to access the World Wide Web. Family Health is a daily, online series of 2.5 minute audio programs featuring practical, easy-to-understand answers to some of the most frequently asked questions about health and health care.

Hurricane Storm Science

URL: http://www.miamisci.org/hurricane/

Developed with the elementary student and teacher in mind, youngsters can use this site to discover how hurricanes form and learn about weather instruments. Lots of fun and educational activities are provided, including "Andrew in 3D," a project in which students make their own 3D glasses to view a Web image of Hurricane Andrew's inner workings.

Intercultural E-Mail Classroom Connections (IECC)

**URL:
http://www.stolaf.edu/network/iecc/**

The IECC site is provided by St. Olaf College as a free service to help teachers and classes link with partners in other countries and cultures for keypal (online penpals) and project exchanges. A must visit for all online educators.

Internet in Education Statistics via Janice's K–12 Outpost

URL: http://k12.cnidr.org/ janice_k12/

Includes the latest statistics on K–12 Internet use, which schools are connected to the Internet and how, and in-depth profiles of more than 12 U.S. schools leading the charge to bring the latest telecommunications tools into the classroom. The site is full of ammunition to bring to the school board or principal to show them that the Internet is needed at all schools.

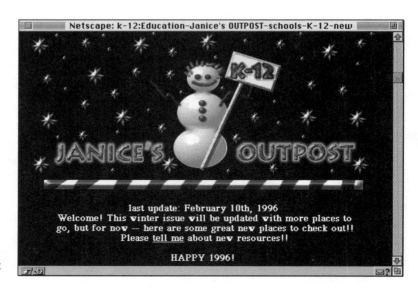

Kids' Crambo

URL: http://www.primenet.com/ ~hodges/kids_crambo.html

Kids' Crambo is a children's word game your young students will adore. Check out the "rules" for the games, see how other people have played the game, and then jump in and play the game yourself. You will have fun playing crambo, ziggy piggy, and doggerel.

Latitude 28 Schoolhouse

URL: http://www2.opennet.com/ schoolhouse/

The award-winning Latitude 28 Schoolhouse is designed to make educational materials accessible to students of all ages. It's creators encourage you to let them know about your favorite educational resource on the Internet.

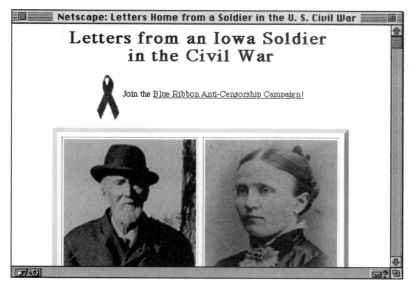

Letters from an Iowa Soldier in the Civil War

URL: http://www.ucsc.edu/ civil-war-letters/home.html

A valuable site for all students studying America's Civil War, the Letters from an Iowa Soldier in the Civil War site contains hundreds of letters and photographs. The site also includes portraits of Confederate and Union officers and enlisted men.

National Aeronautics and Space Administration

URL:
http://www.nasa.gov

NASA operates dozens of Web sites of interest to educators. This new NASA home page is a one-stop link to all of them—from the Johnson Space Center to images from the Hubble Space Telescope.

Online Internet Institute (OII)

URL: http://prism.prs.k12.nj.us/ WWW/OII/OIIhome.html

Two leading online educators created the OII, which contains an impressive collection of professional development information for schools integrating the Internet and other computer technology into their curriculum.

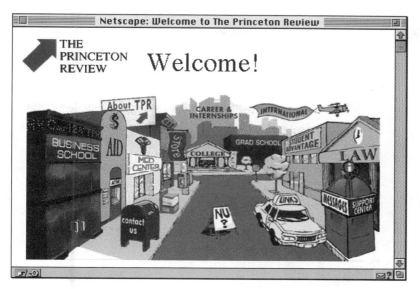

Princeton Review

URL: http://www.review.com

High school students can use this site to prepare for the SAT, GRE, and more! Each year, the Princeton Review helps more than 60,000 students get ready for college. The site includes rankings of the best colleges, and graduate, business, law, and medical schools, along with financial aid information.

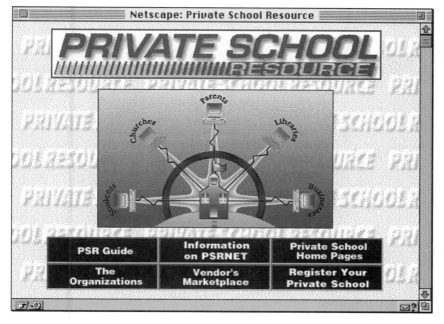

Private School Resource (PSR)

URL: http://www.psrnet.com/psrnet/

What Internet resource is free and also earns money for private schools? It's the Private School Resource. PSR provides private schools with free access to the Internet, while at the same time offering these schools new fund raising opportunities to pay for their computer and technology needs.

EDITOR'S CHOICE

Shakespeare Online

URL: http://the-tech.mit.edu/ Shakespeare.html

An interactive link to the life and complete works of William Shakespeare.

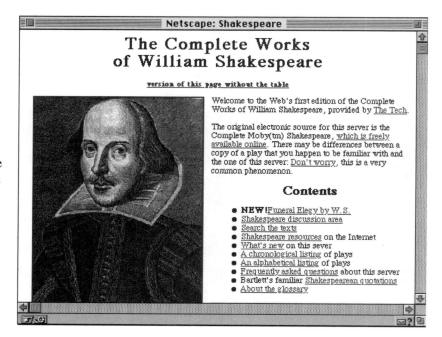

South Africa Tour

URL: http://osprey.unisa.ac.za/ south-africa/home.html

Take a colorful tour of South Africa via this well-designed site. Appropriate for all K–12 students.

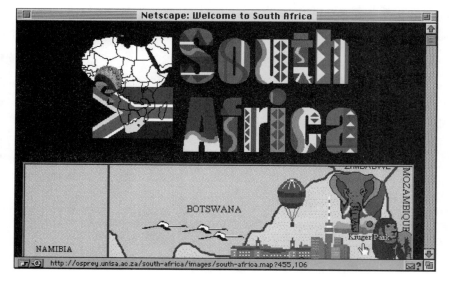

Soviet Archives at the Library of Congress

URL: http://sunsite.unc.edu/expo/ soviet.exhibit/entrance.html

This exhibit is the first public display of the highly secret internal record of Soviet Communist rule. The legendary secretiveness and inaccessibility of the Soviet archival system was maintained through the Gorbachev era. The willingness of the new Russian Archival Committee to cooperate with the Library of Congress dramatizes the break that a newly democratic Russia is attempting to make with its Soviet past. Material long used for one-sided political combat has become fodder for shared historical investigation into the post–Cold War era.

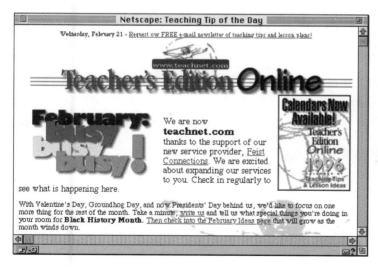

Teacher's Edition Online

**URL:
http://www.southwind.net/~lshiney/**

This site provides a forum for educators to network and share teaching strategies, knowledge, and wisdom. New, hands-on information about classroom management, room ideas, organization, and public school relations is added daily. Includes one new lesson plan and teaching tip every day of the school year!

Teachers Helping Teachers

URL:

http://pacificnet.net/~mandel/

The goal of this innovative online service is to provide basic teaching tips to inexperienced teachers (ideas that can be immediately implemented into the classroom), new ideas in teaching methodologies for all teachers, and to provide a forum for experienced teachers to share their expertise and tips with colleagues around the world.

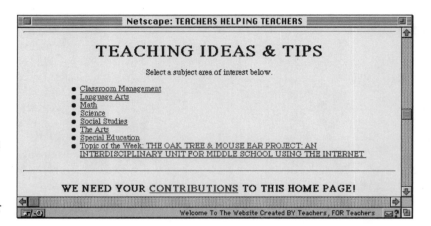

Theodore Tugboat Home Page

URL:

http://www.cochran.com

The online activity center for Theodore Tugboat, a Canadian TV show about a cheerful tugboat who likes to make friends and have adventures, will appeal to young students. They can access an interactive story, retrieve a page from an online coloring book, and send themselves or a friend an electronic postcard with Theodore's picture.

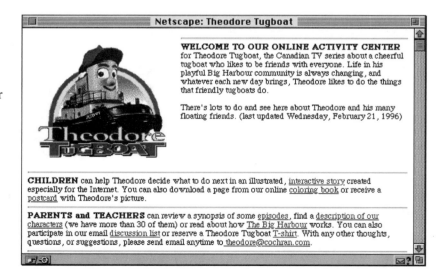

Thomas Congressional Database

URL: http://thomas.loc.gov

Through this site, named for Thomas Jefferson, the U.S. Congress offers access to the full text of all 1993–94 and recent 1995 House and Senate bills, including summaries and chronologies of pending legislation; the *Congressional Record,* updated daily; email directories for House of Representatives and Senate members and committees; and C-SPAN transcripts and broadcast schedules. A valuable stop for educators and students studying the U.S. government and the legislative process.

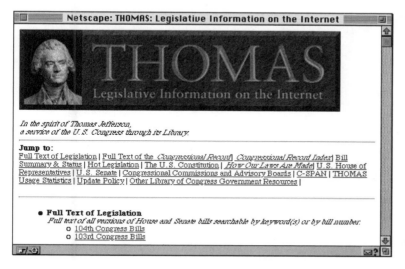

EDITOR'S CHOICE

Virtual TeleGarden Project

URL: http://cwis.usc.edu/dept/garden/

This telerobotic site allows students to view and interact with a California garden filled with living plants. Internet users can plant, water, and monitor the progress of the seedlings via the tender movements of an industrial robot arm. Your class can plant a seed in September and watch it grow over the course of a school year via the Net!

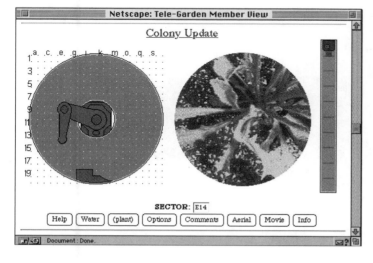

Virtual Tourist

URL:
http://www.vtourist.com:80/vt/
Click anywhere on this interactive world map and you'll be instantly transported to a large collection of online sites located in that continent, country, city, or town.

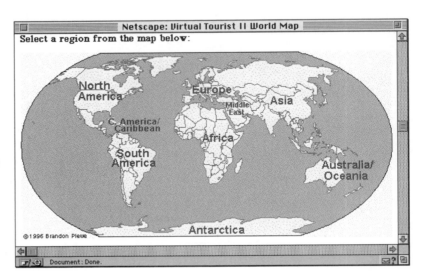

Visible Human Project

URL: http://www.nlm.nih.gov/ extramural_research.dir/ visible_human.html
The Visible Human Project has created a complete, anatomically detailed, three-dimensional representation of the male and female human body. The current phase of the project involves collecting CAT, MRI, and "cryosection" images of a male and female cadaver at one millimeter intervals. An interesting site for all students and teachers of anatomy.

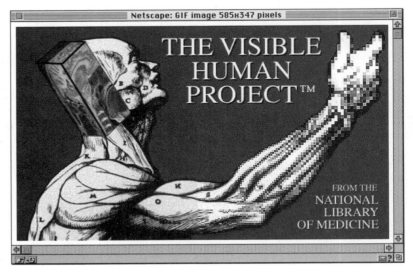

Volcano World

URL: http://volcano.und.nodak.edu

Perfect for students studying volcanos, NASA's Volcano World contains timely updates about volcanic activity worldwide, historical eruption reports, information on how volcanos work, and guidance on becoming a volcanologist.

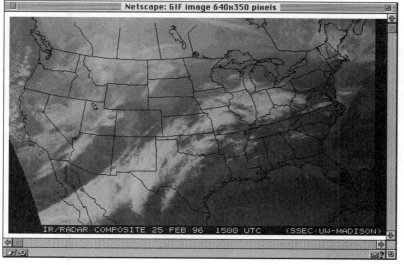

Weather Maps & Movies

URL: http://rs560.cl.msu.edu/weather/

View the latest weather satellite images from more than a dozen satellites circling the globe.

Web66

URL:
http://web66.coled.umn.edu

Web66 is a one-stop source for all the software and information needed to set up a World Wide Web server at a school. Includes the official Classroom Internet Server Cookbook, with recipes for setting up a WWW site on a Mac. It also includes Web66 SharePages, which are sample HTML pages you can download and use on your site, and several pages of pointers to Web-based resources appropriate for the K–12 classroom. These HTML pages can be used with any PC or Mac Web browser.

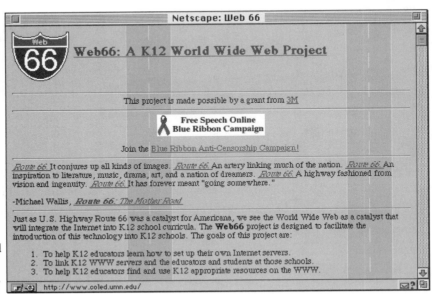

WebLouvre

EDITOR'S CHOICE

URL:
http://sunsite.unc.edu/wm/

This version of the Musee du Louvre, probably the most famous museum in the world, is free and open to the public 24 hours a day—no matter where you live! Visit the famous painting exhibition, the Louvre's Auditorium, and a medieval art exhibition. Students can also take a short tour of Paris.

White House Web

URL: http://www.whitehouse.gov

An interactive citizens' handbook to the White House. Students can take an interactive, graphical tour, listen to recorded messages from the president and vice president (and Sox the cat!), and read a detailed account of family life at the White House. Internauts can even leave a message for the president in the virtual guest book.

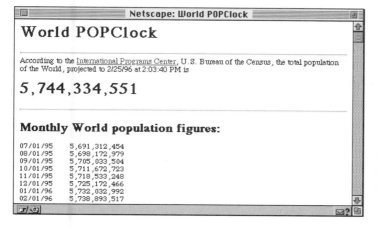

World Population Clock

URL: http://www.census.gov/ipc-bin/popclockw

Students studying the continuing worldwide population explosion will find this site interesting. Updated once every ten minutes, the site provides an estimated count of the world population, along with facts and figures on how the numbers are calculated and an archive of past figures.

"Never doubt that a small group of thoughtful, committed citizens can change the world. Indeed, it's the only thing that ever does."

Margaret Mead

FUNDING SOURCES

Finding the money for school telecommunications programs

It's a fact of life—school budgets are being squeezed to their breaking points. More than ever, school boards are pressured to keep spending to a minimum. At the same time, they are expected to maintain or raise the level of educational excellence while keeping their curricula up to date and relevant in an increasingly technical, computer-oriented society.

The educational reform movement, because it advocates change, offers many schools an opportunity to bring new instructional materials such as the Internet into the curriculum. Funding for an Internet connection *can* be extracted from the tightest of budgets, but only after its value becomes apparent to those who control the funds.

The best way to demonstrate the Internet's power is to take decision makers—school board members, administrators, and principals, for example—on a tour of the online world. Other "convincers" are resources such as this book, the *Classroom Connect* newsletter, the *Classroom Connect* Video Series, and the Global

Quest video from NASA, which is available through *Classroom Connect*. All of these materials feature many real-life examples of how schools all around the world are creating captivating learning experiences using the Internet.

Seeing is believing, and a tour of the Internet is very convincing. To set up a tour, ask a local Internet service provider or a local college with Internet access to allow you to use an account for a demonstration. Most are willing to cooperate for free. A graphical tour will be the most impressive, and that requires a direct or SLIP/PPP account. Ask for that kind of account and access to graphical software.

Another good strategy is to stockpile information as ammunition in the campaign to win support for an Internet connection. Begin a clipping file of articles about K–12 use of the Internet. Scour educational magazines, major newspapers, and national magazines and route copies of especially powerful articles to the major decision makers.

School-business partnerships

Don't overlook one of the easiest sources of money for technology—area businesses. Almost any local business can afford to pay to connect one classroom to the Internet for a year.

Create an ad-hoc committee of parents to explore ways of approaching businesses for funds. Ask them to inquire about the availability of educational funds where they work. As they canvass the business community, make sure they're prepared to show how each firm's generosity will be publicized. The promise of news coverage goes a long way to winning funds. Here are some successful techniques schools use when approaching local businesses.

• **Create and maintain a wish list of required equipment and funds.** Make this document a prominent part of any information given to businesses. That way, they know what other businesses have pledged or given, and what is still needed. Many newspapers will publish this list to raise community awareness of the school's needs and to help drive donations of money and equipment.

• **Initiate an adopt-a-classroom program with three levels of giving.** The first level ($200 or $300) would purchase one year of Net access for a classroom with all the necessary equipment already in place. The second level ($600) would pay for a phone line and Net access for a year for a classroom with a computer and modem. The third level ($1,800) would pay to install a computer, modem, telephone line, and Internet access via a local phone call into an adopted classroom for one year. These costs will vary depending upon geographic area, so adjust your levels accordingly.

• **Seek matching grants.** Many businesses are more likely to provide funding when they see an effort on a school's part to raise one-third to two-thirds of the money.

• **Set up a corporate participation plan.** Ask businesses to donate set amounts by category, such as bronze ($100), silver ($500), gold ($1,000) and platinum ($5,000). Offer certificates of participation, and publish a list of the participating businesses in the school newspaper and monthly newsletter to parents.

• **Canvass larger businesses who have Internet access.** Ask if they would provide access to schools through their system. Always ask if they have any old equipment or software they would be willing to donate.

• **Contact local phone companies.** Ask if they will donate phone lines and subsidize long distance charges that may be incurred when accessing the Internet.

• **Call local computer retailers, service companies, or consultants.** They are potential resources from which you can obtain funding, equipment, software, and in-kind computer counsel and services such as installation, maintenance, and repairs.

Grassroots fund raising

Many schools have paid for new computers and online connections using old-fashioned, low-tech fund raisers. Schools have raised thousands of dollars quickly through bake, candy, or sandwich sales, school "garage" sales, craft shows, and similar efforts. Many schools have used math-a-thons, jog-a-thons, walk-a-thons, and similar "-thons" to raise money. A school in San Francisco raised nearly $100,000 in a year by selling hot lunches prepared and served by students and teachers once a week.

Consider soliciting alumni contributions. Colleges and universities have used this technique successfully for decades. Alumni know the school and want to help make it better. Send a letter explaining your plans and how they will benefit students. Don't assume people know much about the online world, so keep the letter simple. Organize a phone-a-thon and call alumni to solicit pledges for the project.

These kinds of grassroots efforts spread the word about the technology project and generate the critical mass of community support necessary to have plans approved by the school board.

Grants and awards

In 1994, more than $600 million in grants and awards were given to educational projects of all kinds in the United States. More than $300 million of those funds came from government Chapter 1 and Chapter 2 funds— the most widely known sources of technology funding. Fortunately, many government agencies have expanded their efforts to accelerate the use of technology in all schools, from preschool through high school.

Hundreds of sources of private and public funds exist for bringing new computer technology into the classroom. Many are open for new applications year round and offer awards ranging from several thousand to several million dollars. The tough part is finding contact information for the government agencies and private companies providing the funds. The following extensive list of funding sources for K–12 schools is a good start. For more funding information, see the back of this book to find out about *Classroom Connect's* desktop reference guide, *Educator's Internet Funding Guide.*

Before making phone calls, check this list of tips and pointers. Keep them in mind when going through the information-gathering process.

For government funding
   • Call the agency involved to be sure the program still exists. Verify all application dates and eligibility.
   • Federal agencies prefer to fund projects that serve as models for other schools.
   • Local agencies require strong evidence of community support for projects, so be prepared to back up the application request with this kind of proof.
   • Government funds seem to go to those with a high tolerance for red tape and bureaucracy. Persistence is often rewarded.
   • To find information on a particular grant program offered by the government, contact the Federal Information Center at (301) 722-9098.

For corporate giving
   • Many firms prefer to give funds to schools in their local area where they have a presence or which is home to a large number of their employees.
   • Businesses may be more willing to contribute products or services instead of cash. Brainstorm what a company could donate before contacting them. Consulting, equipment, and telephone lines are non-cash contributions that could help.

- Request a copy of the company's giving guidelines. Smaller firms may not have a formal policy, so ask what type of projects they would consider funding. Tailor the request to closely match their objectives.

In general
- When calling a potential funding source for the first time, ask them to mail the application procedures, funding guidelines, and an annual report. These three key pieces of information help a school determine whether the funding organization is a close match for the project. They'll also learn the type of projects the source has funded in the past (perhaps telecommunications?), the average grant amount, and the names of past recipients.
- Many organizations may not be up to speed on the Internet and the online world. If so, backtrack and emphasize that what the school is really asking for is money to buy computers, software, modems, and networking hardware to bring the Net into the classroom.

Corporate sources of funding

Apple Partners in Education

Apple Computer has launched its 1996 Apple Partners in Education project. Last year, 11 K–12 schools and teacher training institutions received more than $1 million worth of Apple technology and free 11-day professional development retreats.
Apple Community Affairs
(408) 974-2974

Educational Assistance, Ltd.

EAL is a clearinghouse of computer and scientific equipment and software. After it inventories equipment donated by corporations, lists are faxed to educational institutions. Schools may then receive any item for just a ten percent handling fee. The equipment isn't brand new or the latest model, but it's still in working, usable condition. EAL's priority is higher education institutions, but K–12 schools may be eligible on a case-by-case basis.
EAL
c/o Michael Evans
P.O. Box 3021
Glen Ellyn, IL 60138
(708) 690-0010
Fax: (708) 690-0565

Gifts in Kind

A program very similar to Education Assistance, Ltd., but more supportive of K–12 schools. A great source of inexpensive equipment and computer supplies.
Gifts in Kind
700 North Fairfax St.
Alexandria, VA 22314
(703) 836-2121

Educational Partnerships

Funding for computer networking projects in the $100,000 to $250,000 range.
Educational Networks Division
555 New Jersey Ave., NW, Room 500
Washington, DC 20208-5644

Great Asante Grant Program

This new program awards five free computer networks to schools each year. The Asante grant package includes all the hardware and software necessary to interconnect 50 computers at a school. Retail value: $14,000. The network can be easily hooked to the Internet. Grant applicants must become familiar with the applications of a computer network. Essays and other eligibility criteria are judged by a panel of technology experts and educators.
JDL Technologies
(800) 535-3969
Email to: jdltech@mr.net

Johnson's Wax Fund

Administered by S.C. Johnson & Son Wax Co., this fund provides more than $1 million to schools in the Racine, Wisconsin, area. The money can be used in a variety of ways, including buying equipment to link schools to the Net.
Reva Holmes
S.C. Johnson & Son
1525 Howe St.
Racine, WI 53403
(414) 631-2267

Southern New England Telecommunications (SNET)

This firm offers about $500,000 every year to schools in the New Haven, Connecticut, area for technology projects.
SNET
(203) 771-2546

Toshiba America Foundation

This organization supports precollegiate science education and offers a number of grants to junior high and high schools for development of science, math, and technology projects. Projects could include hands-on laboratory experiments, interactive computer work on and off the Internet, and curriculum-development programs. Schools must provide a detailed description of their projects, including management and budget information. Grant requests of $5,000 or less may be submitted at any time. Requests for larger grants must be submitted for approval to the foundation's board of directors by a specific date.
Toshiba America Foundation
(212) 596-0600

Corporate Foundations

Many national corporations finance their own foundations. Contact each for a complete listing of funding opportunities and proposal deadlines.

AT&T Foundation
1301 Avenue of the Americas
New York, NY 10019
(212) 841-4747

Computer Learning Foundation
P.O. Box 60400
Palo Alto, CA 94306
(415) 327-3347

Ford Foundation
320 E. 43rd St.
New York, NY 10017
(212) 573-5000

GTE Foundation
One Stamford Forum
Stamford, CT 06904
(203) 965-3620

ITT Hartford Insurance Group Foundation
690 Asylum Ave.
Hartford, CT 06115
(203) 547-4972

Times Mirror Foundation
Times Mirror Square
Los Angeles, CA 90053
(213) 237-3936

U.S. West Foundation
7800 East Orchard Road
Englewood, CO 80111

Vulcan Materials Foundation
P.O. Box 530187
Birmingham, AL 35253
(205) 877-3229

Xerox Foundation
Attn: Evelyn Shockley
800 Long Ridge Road
P.O. Box 1600
Stamford, CT 06904
(203) 968-3000

Government sources of funding

Federal Activities Program
Funding for teacher training in all subject areas, including integration of computer technology.
Office of Educational Research and Improvement (OERI)
U.S. Department of Education
400 Maryland Avenue, SW
Washington DC 20202-7242
(202) 219-2087

Networking Infrastructure for Education
This program will award more than $8 million in grants in 1996 to alliances of K–12 school districts, professional organizations, state agencies, and others concerned with bringing computer networking technology into the classroom.
National Science Foundation
(703) 306-1651, ext. 5888

Rural Electrification Administration (REA)
The REA awards $10 million in grants each year for projects that use computer networks and telecommunications in the classroom. Each grant ranges from $10,000 to $500,000 and can be used to buy equipment or software. School districts and nonprofit organizations that operate libraries or schools can apply.
Joseph Binder
(202) 720-1400

Teacher Enhancement Program
Seeks to improve the knowledge of teachers concerning use of computer technology in the K–12 classroom. Schools can register to participate in a regional Teacher Enhancement Program.
Dr. Michael Haney
National Science Foundation
(703) 306-1625, ext. 6833

Technology for Individuals with Disabilities
Focuses on giving monetary aid to schools to purchase technology for disabled students.
Technology for Individuals with Disabilities
Division of Innovation and Development
400 Maryland Avenue, SW
Washington DC 20202-7242
(202) 205-8123

Technology in Education
Awards grants for use of technology in secondary schools. Past awards ranged from $36,000 to more than $400,000 per request.
U.S. Department of Education
(202) 205-9071 (recording)
Ask for Technology Education program 84.230

Other sources of funding

International Technology Education Association

The ITEA offers grants which apply directly to research projects to technology teachers across the United States.

Dr. W. Tad Foster

(203) 832-1851

Email to: foster@ccsua.ctstateu.edu

Pioneering Partners for Education Technology

Educators from eight Great Lakes region states can apply for $400,000 in grants and scholarships through this program. Grants are awarded to educators creatively using technology in the classroom. Winners receive a $3,000 grant and $2,000 in supplemental matching grants. Participating states include Pennsylvania, New York, Ohio, Minnesota, Illinois, Indiana, Michigan, and Wisconsin. The program has awarded more than $1.2 million in grants since its inception in 1991.

Mary Kinney

(317) 896-6494

Email to: **mkinney@greatlinks.cic.net**

Resources and reference materials

Corporate Giving Watch

Monthly magazine with news and information on corporate giving programs.

The Taft Group

(301) 816-0210

Directory of Computer and High Tech Grants

Lists more than 600 foundations that provide hardware, software, and high-technology grants to schools. The directory costs $60.

Research Grant Guides

P.O. Box 1214

Loxahatchee, FL 33470

(407) 795-6129

Education Funding News

This newsletter is a key source of current federal funding legislation benefiting K–12 public schools. Yearly subscriptions are $300.

Education Funding Research Council

4301 North Fairfax Drive, Suite 875

Arlington, VA 22203

(703) 528-1000

The Foundation Directory

This book is the standard reference work for information about private and community grantmaking foundations in the United States. Entries for more than 6,000 private and community foundations appear in this volume, representing more than one-fourth of all active grantmaking foundations in the United States. Between editions of *The Foundation Directory,* the publisher produces *The Foundation Directory Supplement,* which updates the Directory by providing the reader with significant changes, i.e., new addresses, contacts, and application guidelines. *The Foundation Directory* costs $195 (hardbound), $170 (soft) plus $4.50 for shipping and handling. *The Foundation Directory Supplement* costs $90 plus $4.50 for shipping and handling. For more information, call (800) 424-9836.

Grantwriter's Newsletter of Funding Resources

This newsletter is an inexpensive way to find grant sources. Written and published by an educator, the monthly offers timely information on grants and contests. Cost: $36 for 12 issues.
Grantwriter's Newsletter of Funding Resources
617 Wright Ave.
Terrytown, LA 70056

Funding Update

Published 12 times a year, this newsletter gives information and deadlines for new educational funding sources for three-month periods. Cost: $60.
Education Funding Resources
Attn: Marcella Sherman
11265 Canyon Dr.
San Jose, CA 95127
Fax: (408) 258-8020

Government Assistance Almanac

Published periodically, this publication contains a wealth of information on all kinds of grants and funding. Cost: $135.
Omnigraphics Publishing
(313) 961-1340

Grants: Where to Look and How to Win!

This educational resource guide is available through the Eisenhower Mathematics and Science Technical Assistance and Leadership Development Project. It lists grant opportunities, other funding source publications, and tips and tricks for successful grant writing. Individual copies cost $1.50. Call (301) 220-0879 (voice mail).

Grassroots Funding Journal

Articles on alternative sources of funding, book reviews, and bibliographies.
GFJ
P.O. Box 11607
Berkeley, CA 94701

Funding resources online

All of the major commercial online services—America Online, CompuServe, Prodigy, Delphi, and AppleLink—have education departments or forums that list sources of funds for technology. Look for an icon or main department labeled "education" when you first login. Also, type the keyword "education" when using the service's keyword or department searching option.

Beyond the commercial services, the Internet also holds several large databases of information pertaining to educational grants.

Catalog of Federal Domestic Assistance

Access this online database of government assistance programs of all kinds.

Gopher to: marvel.loc.gov

Look in *Government Information, Federal Information Resources, Information by Branch of Federal Government, General Information Resources*

Grants Bulletin Board System

Information about grants from the U.S. Department of Education is now accessible via an electronic bulletin board. It is open to public access.

Modem: (202) 260-9950

OERI Gopher Information System

The Office of Educational Research and Improvement (OERI) operates a jam-packed Internet gopher site which provides public access to educational research, statistics, and the latest news on U.S. Department of Education funding opportunities. Available menus include: *Department of Education Programs—General Information, Goals 2000 Initiative, Educational Research, School-to-work, Vocational, and Adult Education,* and a large database of education-oriented software for all computer platforms.

OERI

(202) 219-1547

Gopher to: gopher.ed.gov

Plymouth State College Gopher System

The Grants Information Bulletin Board keeps abreast of the latest grant opportunities.

Gopher to: oz.plymouth.edu

Look in *Plymouth State College Gopher Service, PSC Grant Office*

Science & Technology Information System (STIS)

Available via the Internet, the STIS is an electronic distribution system that provides easy access to National Science Foundation publications, including information about available grants.

STIS

Modem: (202) 357-0359

Login: **public**

Email to: stis@nsf.gov

Gopher or telnet to: stis.nsf.gov

Login: **public**

Ftp to: stis.nsf.gov

Retrieve the *index* and *nsf9410* files.

THE INTERNET DEFINED

Origin and overview

It's hard to define the Internet in a few sentences. Technically, the Net is an interconnected, spiderweb-like system of millions of computer networks linked with telecommunications software and hardware.

To the people who use it, the Internet is the sum of all individuals and institutions that connect their computers to other computers anywhere in the world with devices called *modems*. A computer with a modem can plug into any phone line, and that simple connection is enough to bring together people and information around the world via the Internet.

Who built this Information Superhighway? The U.S. military laid the foundation in the late 1960s as a global, fail-safe communications network designed to operate if one or more links became inoperative. Universities and research laboratories were granted access to the Internet when they began to do more business with the government. Funded mostly by government money, the Internet was used exclusively by the government, research institutions, and colleges and universities for two decades.

But in early 1992, policies regulating commercial use of the Internet were relaxed, allowing unrestricted use for commercial purposes. Now, commercial and nonacademic traffic on the Internet is growing rapidly, partly because the government is backing away from subsidizing the network. The government still funds many parts of the Internet used by federal and educational institutions for research, government, and academic work.

The Internet community

Within a year of the policy change, dozens of entrepreneurs formed companies offering low-cost Internet access to individuals and businesses. Business people discovered that the Internet holds rich resources for research, public relations, marketing, customer service, and retail sales. But even as commercial use of the Net burgeons, a debate rages about whether this is an appropriate use of the network. The fact is that unless the government enacts legislation to the contrary, commercial traffic will continue to increase.

According to recent estimates, more than 40,000 new Internet services and information locations come online each month. Almost all of these resources—including documents, software, and databases—are *free,* due in large part to the Internet's culture of sharing information and helping people solve problems.

The operational philosophy of the Internet is that of a free sharing of information. Virtually all of the universities, libraries, schools, government agencies, and even most businesses online allow users to access their information at no cost. Likewise, individuals give advice and information expecting nothing but thanks in return. The battle cry of the Internet community is "Information wants to be free!" While this is changing as more "pay-per-use" commercial services spring up, many new users still experience an almost giddy feeling of camaraderie when they become part of this enormous yet personal global community.

Netiquette: rules of the road

With this frenzy of global activity, some kind of order is needed. No Internet police force patrols the Internet, though numerous organizations such as the Internet Society and InterNIC play key roles in its continuing development.

The lack of established rules has brought the evolution of an informal code of conduct called *netiquette* which users are expected to agree to abide by during their activities on the Net. Some of this code is written, though it's ironic that users often must *be* online to find guidelines for online behavior. You can find extensive netiquette information at two Web sites. Arlene Rinaldi, of Florida Atlantic University, sets down netiquette guidelines at **URL: http://rs6000.adm.fau.edu/faahr/netiquette.html**. Also visit the Raindrop Labs Web page at **URL: http://agora.rain.com/the-net/netiquette**.

For the most part, the atmosphere on the Net is congenial and open. But the very anonymity of electronic communication requires that each user have a heightened sense of personal responsibility regarding his or her behavior online. Users who violate netiquette with thoughtless or inappropriate behavior are often *flamed* by angry users. They quickly receive dozens or even hundreds or thousands of email reprimands clogging their mailboxes as punishment.

Realize that what users access or send over the Internet directly affects other computer networks and their system administrators. Many of the rules of the Net have to do with the amount and kind of data transferred across thousands of networks. Computers and networks can only handle so much traffic, which is one of the reasons users consider the sending of "junk" over the Internet a violation of netiquette.

To make sure every user is aware of such issues, each computer network on the Internet has its own set of rules visitors must follow while on the system. System operators can remove a user's "right" to access their resources if the user repeatedly violates their rules. Most policies forbid putting unlawful materials, such as pirated software, on the system. They also ban abusive language or behavior and *flame baiting,* such as the posting of racial comments. Transmitting messages or programs designed to slow down or incapacitate another's computer or network is also prohibited.

Beyond these basic tenets, a particular netiquette exists when using specific tools such as gopher, ftp, email, and so on. See the Internet Tutorials in Appendix B for netiquette as it applies to these tools.

The Ten Commandments of Computer Ethics

1. Thou shalt not use a computer to harm other people.
2. Thou shalt not interfere with other people's computer work.
3. Thou shalt not snoop around in other people's files.
4. Thou shalt not use a computer to steal.
5. Thou shalt not use a computer to bear false witness.
6. Thou shalt not use or copy copyrighted software for which you have not paid.
7. Thou shalt not use other people's computer resources without authorization.
8. Thou shalt not appropriate other people's intellectual output.
9. Thou shalt think about the social consequences of the program you write and the messages you post.
10. Thou shalt use a computer in ways that show consideration and respect.

(Source: The Computer Ethics Institute)

Understanding Internet addresses

Before setting out on the Information Superhighway, it's helpful to know how the Internet's founders organized the "addresses" of online computers. Understanding a street address in the "real world" is important. It's also crucial in the "virtual world" that users be able to identify Internet addresses and use them to access Net computers and reach other users.

Email addresses

Almost everyone on the Internet has an email address. Chances are that when you begin navigating the Net and making friends using email, your electronic mailbox will begin to fill up. Here's an example of a standard email address:

llane@smallville.highschool.edu

The first part of the email address—the information before the @ sign (which is called the "at" sign)—is a user's unique *user identity*, or "user ID" for short. In this case, Ms. Lane shortened her real name from Lucy Lane to just "llane" for her email address.

The part after the @ sign is the actual Internet *domain* where she receives her email. Domains are the names of Internet computers in the schools, businesses, and other organizations and institutions on the Net. Each computer has a unique domain name. The fictitious Smallville High School is **smallville.highschool.edu**; the real-world Cornell University is **cornell.edu**; the U.S. Navy is **navy.mil**; FidoNet is **fidonet.org**; and Apple Computer is **apple.com**.

Notice that the rightmost parts of the preceding domain names are different. In the United States, the three letters after the last period signify various types of entities—educational, commercial, military, nonprofit, or some other type of organization.

Common domains on the Internet

DOMAIN	TYPE
.com	Commercial
.edu	Educational
.gov	Governmental
.int	International
.mil	Military
.net	Internet resource
.org	Nonprofits

Domains outside the United States generally end in a two-letter country suffix. In an address such as **klinefelter@ting.umad.de** the "de" indicates that this person sent a message from a computer in Germany. If there is no country "extension" to an address, assume the user is in the United States.

Unlike the postal service, the Internet system won't deliver mail with an "almost perfect" address. So, when sending email, be sure to type the recipient's complete email address with no mistakes. Otherwise, the message will "bounce" and be returned with a message saying the user is unknown. Most email addresses are case insensitive, meaning that it doesn't matter whether you type in upper or lower case. Experts advise, however, that you type an address exactly as it appears.

International domains on the Internet

DOMAIN	COUNTRY
.au	Australia
.ca	Canada
.ch	Switzerland
.de	Germany
.dk	Denmark
.es	Spain
.fr	France
.il	Israel
.it	Italy
.jp	Japan
.mx	Mexico
.nz	New Zealand
.pl	Poland
.ru	Russia
.tr	Turkey
.uk	United Kingdom
.us	United States
.va	Vatican

Identifying other Internet addresses

After using email for a while, users begin to come across other types of Internet addresses. To explain what they mean, take a look at the several addresses for Wentworth Worldwide Media.

Email to: connect@classroom.net
Email to: info@classroom.net
Ftp to: ftp.classroom.net
  Go to the *wentworth* subdirectory
URL: http://www.classroom.net

Notice that there are two email addresses. The first, **connect@classroom.net**, is an email address anyone can write to that a human will read and answer. The second, **info@classroom.net**, is the address for an auto-reply *mailbot*, or *infobot*.

Mailbots and infobots are "smart" email addresses that allow users to retrieve information by email. Thousands of organizations and businesses have info@ addresses. If you send a message to any info@ address and leave the subject line and body blank, the infobot will automatically send a prepared message to your email address. That first reply may contain general information and an index of other available documents. Generally, you can retrieve additional documents by sending a subsequent email message to the info@ address. You usually reference a document name or number in the subject line or body of the message. The infobot reads the request and sends its reply via email.

After WWM's email addresses is an ftp address. You enter this address into your ftp software to access this site to transfer or download files. Once connected to the site, you would change directories to the *wentworth* subdirectory to reach the referenced information. Ftp software does this in a variety of ways, so consult your documentation.

After the ftp address is the URL, or Universal Resource Locator. URLs are addresses of sites users access with a World Wide Web (WWW) browser such as Mosaic, Netscape, MacWeb, WinWeb, or Lynx. Basically, you would enter **http://www.classroom.net/** into the Web browser software, which links you to the site's home page.

Sometimes a *modem* number will be listed. That means you dial the phone number with your computer's modem to access an online computer system or computer bulletin board system (BBS).

Other common addresses used to navigate the Net are for telnet and gopher sites. In most cases, the method of access will be typed in front of the address so you know how to get at it. For example:

Gopher to: copernicus.bbn.com
Telnet to: ericir.syr.edu

INTERNET
TUTORIALS

How to use Internet navigation tools

Internet users communicate with people in more than 160 countries, search through and retrieve information, and simply browse the global network of more than four million computers by using software commonly referred to as "navigation tools." These tools include email, gopher, telnet, ftp, and, increasingly, World Wide Web browsers. This Appendix will give you brief tutorials on how to use these Internet essentials and suggests ways to use them effectively, including pointers to related resources. If you need help understanding the terms we use, consult the glossary at the end of the appendices.

Software used by personal computers to access the Internet is developing rapidly. Thankfully, newly developed and inexpensive graphical software is available for Windows and Mac computers. This software provides an easy-to-use, graphical, point-and-click interface to all the resources on the Internet. But navigating the Net has not always been so easy—it has its roots in text-based Unix computing. Many users still don't have access to graphical versions of Internet tools, and must contend with using text-based commands.

It's important to realize that the appearance of each tool may differ from user to user, even though it performs the same function. That's because the Internet offers two basic interfaces, or "looks": text-only and graphical. Which interface you use depends on the provider of your Internet connection, the type of Internet account you have, and the software you use.

Text-only interfaces, used by Internauts with basic dial-up accounts, usually begin with a blank screen and a blinking prompt. Users must know and enter a series of commands to get around the Internet. Graphical interfaces, used by Internauts whose providers offer SLIP or PPP accounts, are an easy-to-use, point-and-click method of moving around the Internet. Users familiar with Windows or Macintosh computers will find learning to use graphical Internet tools a short lesson.

The Internet is becoming more graphical for more people as SLIP accounts become more affordable. Many commercial online services are beginning to offer graphical Internet navigation tools. In fact, the explosion in growth of the World Wide Web—a completely graphical, multimedia interface—means that soon a generation of users won't imagine navigating the Net any other way!

Email

Email is the most widely used online tool. Virtually every Internaut gets started by experimenting with electronic mail. Email is a valuable communication tool for numerous reasons:

- Unlike postal or "snail mail," messages can be delivered at any time, regardless of carrier services, holidays, or weekends.
- Incoming messages can be immediately saved to a disk, printed, forwarded, or deleted.
- Outgoing messages can be carefully composed offline, delivered instantly, and even sent at specific times via software timers.
- An email message—unlike a telephone call—can be delivered independent of time zones, without long distance charges.
- Messages can be sent out to dozens, even thousands of people at once.
- Many users soon discover that they can eliminate annoying and time-wasting problems such as "telephone tag" and bad faxes.
- Millions of people who aren't even "on the Internet" can send and receive email. Anybody with an account with a commercial online service such as America Online or Prodigy, or anyone with access to one of thousands of local bulletin boards or networks with email gateways is a potential recipient of an email message.

As an education tool, however, email is invaluable. With a little creativity, students and teachers can instantly visit people and places all over the globe. Classes can communicate and do projects with students and teachers in other nations, send questions to geologists in California, or ask the president about his foreign policy. Thousands of students already use email to share school information, practice foreign languages, exchange school newspapers, and learn about distant cities, cultures, and climates.

To send email, users access their email software and choose the option that allows them to "create" a message. In the "To" area, you simply type in the email address of the person you're writing to, i.e., **llane@school.edu**.

The majority of email messages transmitted around the globe consist of only text. But new software allows users to transmit graphics, sound, and even video over the Internet to other schools, teachers, and students. To do this, a user needs an encoding program that temporarily converts graphics, video, or sound to text, which is decoded on the receiving end. Similar software using MIME, or *Multipurpose Internet Mail Extension,* allows email users to send multimedia files such as graphics, non-English character sets, sound, or even video clips along with basic text messages. Most newer email software comes with these features built in.

Such technology makes the learning potential of email even more powerful. Students can exchange computer images of themselves with a class in Europe. Art students can send computerized works back and forth for critique. School newspaper or yearbook editors can exchange desktop files and evaluate each others' work. Teachers can share lesson plans and overhead slides. The possibilities are endless.

The Net via email

Schools that have only email access need not limit themselves to simple correspondence. They can use email to access and execute other Internet functions, such as newsgroup postings, file transfers, and even information searches. All they need is email software, a modem, and some type of an Internet or commercial online service account. Some Internet providers will set up email-only accounts for schools that want to take advantage of this technology. These books are great starting points for more information on email and Internet functions.

The Internet by Email
Clay Shirky
Ziff-Davis Press
$19.95

The Email Companion
John S. Quarterman
Smoot Carl-Mitchell
$19.95

Internet by Email
Email to: listserv@ubvm.cc.buffalo.edu
Type **GET INTERNET BY-EMAIL NETTRAIN F=MAIL**
in the body of the message.

Email netiquette

Certain rules of netiquette apply to email, and it's important to be familiar with them. Email is easily stored and forwarded, so be professional and careful about what you say about others. Never assume your email is private, and never send anything that you would not mind seeing on the evening news.

Use discretion when forwarding mail to group addresses or distribution lists. It is considered extremely rude to forward personal email to mailing lists or Usenet newsgroups without the original author's permission.

Cite all quotes, references, and sources. It's preferable to reference the source of a document and provide instructions on how to obtain a copy. Respect copyright and license agreements. Don't use academic networks for commercial work.

When writing messages, keep paragraphs and messages short and to the point. Focus on one subject per message. Follow chain of command procedures for corresponding with superiors. Don't send a complaint via email directly to the top just because you can. Check your email daily—Internauts appreciate a quick reply. Email can pile up quickly and take up huge amounts of disk space, so delete unwanted messages immediately.

When quoting another person, edit out whatever isn't directly applicable to your reply. Including irrelevant portions of the original article will annoy others, so simply copy the pertinent portions of the message and paste them into your reply. Most email software automatically sets off the excerpt with carets.

Always include your *signature* at the bottom of email messages. Your signature should include your name, position, affiliation, and Internet addresses. Signature files are like customized business cards. You can attach them to newsgroup or mailing list posts and to email messages. Signature files should be no more than four lines long. For professional purposes, a signature should have the same information as a business card: name, title, postal and/or email address, and a telephone or fax number. For personal or fun uses, a signature file could contain a favorite quote or musical lyric, a poem, or even a short piece of ASCII art created with keyboard characters. But keep it short.

Express yourself

A cardinal rule for communicating on the Internet is *keep it short.* Does that leave the Net without personality, emotion, or humor? Absolutely not. There are several ways to express your feelings. Two primary means are your signature file (mentioned above) and *smileys,* also called *emoticons.* Both can be used in any email communication.

Smileys are normal type characters that, when viewed sideways, resemble facial expressions. Here are some of the more common ones and their meanings. You can come up with dozens more.

:-)   A basic smile, used to express happiness or sarcasm.
;-)   A whimsical smile or "inside joke" expression.
:-(A frown.
B-)   Wearing glasses.

A warning: be careful using sarcasm and humor. Without face-to-face communications, an email joke may be viewed as criticism.

Another way to express emotion is to capitalize words, but do so only to highlight an important point or to distinguish a title or heading. Some users consider all caps to be SHOUTING. *Asterisks* surrounding a word also can be used to add emphasis and make a stronger point.

Mailing lists

A *mailing list* is an email-based public or private forum on a particular topic, and there are 6,000 different ones! Each one is like an electronic newspaper or newsletter consisting entirely of reader submissions. Educators can join any of the hundreds of mailing lists having to do with education. (See Chapter 3, Educational Resources, for an exhaustive list.)

Mailing lists are interactive because a subscriber anywhere in the world can read messages posted to it and can send messages to the list. Anyone with an email account can join a mailing list, though some are only open to members of certain organizations. Users of commercial online services such as America Online, Prodigy, Delphi, and CompuServe can subscribe to lists as can users of bulletin board services (BBSs) with Internet email access.

How to join a list

To join a mailing list, you must email a message to a mailing list's "subscription" email address and request to be added to the subscriber list. After the message is received you are automatically added to the list.

The first message you'll receive will be a confirmation message from the list's owner. Hang onto this message. It contains important information, including instructions on how to send messages to the list and guidelines or rules for subscribers. It also tells you how to temporarily suspend mailings (something you might do if you go away on an trip for a while) and permanently unsubscribe, or delete your name, from the list.

Subscribers participate in discussions by reading messages and posting their response to the list itself rather than by replying individually to the other subscribers. The list automatically rebroadcasts a copy of any posted message to all subscribers.

Two types of lists

Mailing lists can be moderated or unmoderated. On unmoderated lists, messages (also called "posts") are automatically broadcast to every subscriber. On moderated lists, posts are monitored by the list owner, who serves as a gatekeeper. Only messages the moderator believes are appropriate are broadcast to all subscribers on the list. A rejected message is returned with a message explaining why it was refused. This gives the subscriber a chance to change it and resend it.

Educators will find mailing lists to be a great resource for professional development and networking. You can ask questions, discuss teaching methods and curriculum development, and launch online classroom projects with others around the world.

Students studying other languages can interact with native-speaking students from other lands. There are dozens of age-appropriate and topic-specific mailing lists offering information on many topics. Schools can even start their own mailing lists.

Subscribing to a mailing list is simple. For instance, if you wanted to subscribe to the AAAE (American Association for Agricultural Education) list, you would send an email message to this address.

Email to: listserv@listserv.net

Next, you would type **subscribe AAAE John Smith** on the first line of the body of the message. (Where you see John Smith you would type your name.)

To sign up for any other list, simply replace **AAAE** with any other mailing list name and replace **<John Smith>** with your first and last name. You will be added to the subscriber list immediately and receive your first messages within hours.

Spend several days reading posts to the list until you get a feel for the "personality" of the list. Your first post should be a short introduction of yourself so other subscribers can get to know you. After that, feel free to post regularly, but be sure to stay within the context of the list topic.

Mailing list netiquette

Some mailing lists have low rates of traffic, while others can flood an email box with several hundred messages per day. The barrage of messages for multiple subscribers of mailing lists at the same school requires extensive system processing and disk space, which can tie up valuable resources.

Allowing all interested teachers to individually subscribe to a list can overwhelm the school's system. It may be better for one teacher or librarian to subscribe and then allow everyone to access the list's posts. When you subscribe, use your personal email account. Don't subscribe using a shared school account unless you know everyone wants to read the list. When signing up for a group, save your subscription confirmation letter for reference. The message cites the rules of the list as well as instructions on how to suspend mail and unsubscribe from the list.

When going away for more than a week, unsubscribe or suspend mail from any mailing lists or listserv services. Occasionally, subscribers who are unfamiliar with netiquette will submit requests to SUBSCRIBE or UNSUBSCRIBE directly to the list itself. Such requests should be made to the appropriate address, not the list posting address itself.

Keep your questions and comments sent to the list relevant to the focus of the discussion group. Resist the temptation to "flame" others on the list. These discussions are public and meant for constructive exchanges. Treat others as you would want them to treat you. When requesting a list of information from subscribers, ask that responses be directed to you personally, offering to post a summary or answer to your question to the group later.

When replying to a message posted to a discussion group, check the address to be certain your reply will go only to the intended location, person, or group. Simply selecting "Reply" will usually send your message to the entire subscriber list. Many times it is more appropriate to answer another subscriber's question or to communicate with that subscriber by sending email to him or her directly. This will reduce the extraneous traffic on the list. Twenty people answering the same question on a large list can quickly fill your mailbox, and those of everyone else on the list.

Net talk

Brevity is prized on the Internet, so Internauts have come up with numerous abbreviations or acronyms for commonly used phrases.

CUL	See you later
BTW	By the way
FAQ	Frequently Asked Question
FYI	For your information
FYA	For your amusement
IMHO	In my humble opinion
IOW	In other words
OTOH	On the other hand
TIA	Thanks in advance

Newsgroups

Newsgroups, or Usenet newsgroups, follow the same principle as email or mailing lists, except that users don't receive individual messages in their email boxes. Newsgroups are like a giant, worldwide bulletin board that anyone on the Internet, on a commercial online service, or on a computer bulletin board can read or post to.

A newsgroup exists for just about anything imaginable—there are almost 10,000 distinct newsgroups. Due to the subject matter of some groups, many are *not* appropriate for K–12 users, so supervision is critical. A user must have software called a "newsreader" to access the groups. Which newsgroups are available to you depends on your Internet service provider. Certain groups are carried by almost every Internet service provider, while other groups are distributed only to regional areas.

Users can choose to read any article from any newsgroup and post a reply. Articles can be printed, saved, replied to, or deleted. Like email, users can post graphics, video, or sound files in addition to plain text.

There are two basic ways to access Usenet newsgroups. You can logon to a computer that allows you to use its newsreader, or you can use your own newsreader software to select a newsgroup and view its contents. Educators can use software that filters out unwanted groups by allowing them to preselect groups appropriate for the classroom.

As with mailing lists, most newsgroups post a general information document highlighting what's acceptable and what's not. In some groups anything is acceptable, including advertisements, while others attempt to enforce stringent requirements. The rules are usually outlined in the group's Frequently Asked Questions (FAQ) document. Users that blatantly violate the rules will most likely be *flamed*—others will respond to them with nasty, hateful messages. Monitor a newsgroup to get a feel for its atmosphere and the sort of conduct that is acceptable before becoming active. (See Chapter 3, Educational Resources, for a comprehensive list of newsgroups for education.)

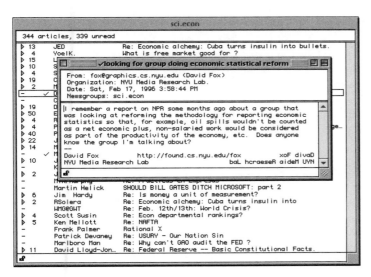

This posting is from the **sci.econ** newsgroup, a forum devoted to discussing the science of economics.

Newsgroup classifications

alt.	Alternatives to the mainstream groups. They're easier to create, so the door is open to all sorts of off-the-wall, strange, or downright chaotic discussions.
comp.	About computers and frequented by computer professionals and hobbyists.
misc.	Groups that don't fit into any other category.
news.	Concerning the Usenet news network itself.
rec.	Recreational, such as rec.hobby.sewing.
sci.	Discussions on the sciences, ranging from biology to nuclear physics.
soc.	Social science issues.
talk.	Continuing debates or flame wars on a variety of topics.

Telnet

Telnet allows Internet users to connect with and use a computer anywhere—in the next room or halfway around the world—as if they were sitting at its keyboard.

With telnet, you can conduct real-time searches on full-text databases, use software installed on a remote computer, and accomplish much more. If you access the Net using a graphical interface (SLIP or PPP), telnetting is easy. Just follow the telnet software's instructions—there's usually a menu choice to click on. However, if you're using a text-based online account, you need to know two primary commands: **telnet** and **open**.

> **telnet** Opens a telnet session.
> **open ds.internic.net** Opens a telnet session with the computer at the location **ds.internic.net**

Once you've accessed a site, the software will display a menu. Use the menu to find the information you want. Telnet sites vary widely, with different menus, content, instructions, and navigating capabilities, so consult **help** files on the menu whenever you find them.

After you login to the remote computer via telnet, you can access the programs, databases, and resources stored on that host computer. For example, you could telnet to the U.S. Geographic Names Database computer. (**Telnet to: martini.eecs.umich.edu 3000**) By following the simple, on-screen instructions, you can select menus that will lead you to information about geographic coordinates, state populations, elevation, and even zip codes. Telnet is often used to launch other Internet applications, such as email, gopher searches, and IRC or Internet Relay Chat sessions. Some telnet sites are restricted, but thousands allow the public to login and scan their databases. (See Chapter 3, Educational Resources, for a long list of worthwhile telnet sites.)

Gopher

Gopher is an Internet tool that does what the name implies: it *goes for* information. Gopher software allows Internet users to move through an easy-to-navigate collection of menus to search and retrieve data.

Gopher sites are those collections, some 5,000 databases of diverse types of information organized into menus and directories mounted on as many computers around the world. Many sites allow users to carry out real-time searches of their information, as well as to connect to other gopher sites around the world. (See Chapter 3, Educational Resources, for a list of gopher sites of value to educators.)

If you're accessing the Net using a graphical interface (SLIP or PPP), using gopher should be a simple matter of point-and-click menu choices. If you're using a text-based, online account that offers gopher access, you will use two key gopher command: **gopher** and **open**.

> **gopher** Opens a gopher session and returns a new prompt
> **open infopath.ucsd.edu** Opens a gopher session with the computer at **infopath.ucsd.edu**

Once you've logged in, you'll see the gopher site's main menu. Move through the menu items to get to the information you want. If your online account doesn't offer gopher access, you can telnet to a site that features public gopher access and log in as **gopher**. From there, you can access gopher sites using that computer's gopher software. Here are two sites that offer public gopher access.

Telnet to: is.internic.net
Telnet to: boombox.micro.umn.edu

File Transfer Protocol

File Transfer Protocol or *ftp* is a navigational tool that allows an Internet user to connect to a remote computer to transfer programs (upload or download). A computer that allows others to access files via ftp is referred to as an *ftp site*. Ftp sites that allow public access are known as *anonymous ftp sites*. When logging into such a site, type **anonymous** as your login name and enter your email address as your password.

If you access the Net via a graphical interface, using ftp is a snap. There's usually a menu item called *ftp*, which opens up a window where you simply type in the ftp site address. However, if you're using a text-based online account, you need to type in commands to use ftp. DOS users may find some of them familiar. (See box on next page.)

Ftp sites are rich resources for educators. Clip art, software programs, the full text of the CIA World Factbook—all are available for downloading at your command. But remember: many organizations with ftp sites are generously making their computer networks accessible to the public, so be considerate. Try not to download huge files during peak working hours, and limit your visit at the site so other users can access it. (See Chapter 3, Educational Resources, for a list of ftp sites with material helpful to educators.)

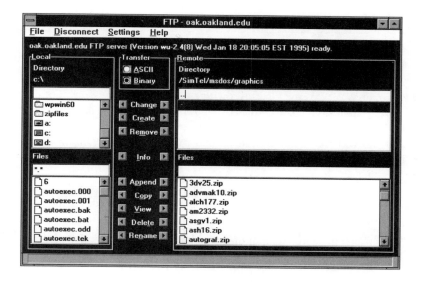

The University of Oakland's ftp server (a sample screen is shown above) is one of the busiest because it houses thousands of freeware, shareware, and public domain programs. The right column is a directory of educational programs you could download; the left column shows directories and files on your machine. Always retrieve the indexes first to save time. In this case, you would retrieve *00_index.txt*.

Common ftp commands

ftp Begins the ftp session.

help Gives you a list of ftp commands.

open oak.oakland.edu Opens an ftp session with the site at this address, **oak.oakland.edu**

cd pub/msdos/finance The change directory command. Changes to the finance subdirectory under the *pub* and *msdos* subdirectories.

dir The directory command. Lists the contents of the current subdirectory.

cd up Moves up one subdirectory.

cd down Moves down one subdirectory.

binary Changes the retrieval (download) setting to binary. Type this command and hit enter before issuing a **get** command for a nontext file such as a software program or graphics file.

get math.zip Retrieves (downloads) the *math.zip* file

ascii Changes the retrieval (download) settings to ASCII (a text-only computer language). Type this command and hit enter before issuing a **get** command for a text file.

exit Ends an ftp session.

World Wide Web

The *World Wide Web*, or WWW, is the fastest growing, most exciting component of the Internet. Fully graphical, including text, graphics, video, and sound, the Web gives users the ability to simply click on a word or graphic to travel to another computer anywhere on the Internet.

Each page, or site on the Web, has a unique address, referred to as a *Universal Resource Locator* or *URL*. The URL for the White House in Washington, D.C. is: **http://www.whitehouse.gov**

To illustrate how Web pages are *hyperlinked*, let's say that you type in the World Wide Web address for the White House. At that site, you might find information about the building's history, photos of rooms or decorations, a list of dignitaries expected to visit the president that week, whatever the people running the White House's Web server decide to include. That "home" page would also contain *hyperlinks*, highlighted words or pictures that you can click on to instantly travel to another Web document, say the Library of Congress to view the original plans for the building's construction.

Educational resources abound on the Web. Complete, hyperlinked texts of classic novels; short video clips of physics projects; dozens of museums, including the Louvre; sound clips of works by Mozart; detailed graphics of insects; even other K–12 schools. These are only a few of the sites educators and students can visit. (See Chapter 4, World Wide Web Tour, for some great places you can take your students.)

Students in hundreds of schools are learning to create and mount their own Web pages—an easier task than you would imagine—which gives them a global audience for their projects, school newspapers, and other work. Creating Web pages requires using *HTML, Hypertext Markup Language*. Learning HTML isn't difficult. Programs for creating Web pages, called *html authoring software,* are available via ftp.

Ftp to: **ftp.classroom.net**

Look in the *wentworth/Internet-Software* subdirectory

Software for the Web

To traverse the Web, Internet users need software called a *Web browser*. Browsers are available in text-only or fully graphical versions. Popular graphical browsers include Netscape, Microsoft Internet Explorer, Mosaic, and Netshark. They can be used by Internauts with a direct connection to the Internet via a SLIP or PPP account. Users who access the Net through what is called a "dial-up shell account" will most likely use Lynx, a text-only browser. A special piece of Windows-compatible software called SlipKnot allows text-only users to cruise the Web as if they had a graphic browser.

The Web is entirely searchable, and several online Web "search engines" allow keyword searches for Web documents around the world. Web browser software provides access to other Internet programs such as gopher, telnet, and ftp without launching separate programs. New Web software incorporates all of the best tools for using the Internet into one friendly, graphical application.

Much of this software is available at the *Classroom Connect* ftp site.

Ftp to: ftp.classroom.net

Go to the *wentworth/Internet-Software* subdirectory. Choose the *Mac* or *IBM* directory to find the software you need. MacWeb and WinWeb are also available.

Netscape has advanced features and can be retrieved via ftp from following ftp site.

Ftp to: ftp8.netscape.com

You can also download the latest version from the developer's home page.

URL: http://home.netscape.com

Mosaic, the original Web browser, can be downloaded from the National Center for Supercomputing Applications, where it was developed. Versions for Mac, Windows, and Unix are available.

Ftp to: ftp.ncsa.uiuc.edu

Go to the *Web/Mosaic* subdirectory.

Lastly, educators who want to learn to make their own World Wide Web pages can do so through tutorials at several sites.

URL: http://www.infomedia.com/BUILDWEB/tutorial/tutorial.html

URL: http://web66.coled.umn.edu/

Related tutorials can be found on *Classroom Connect's* Web site.

URL: http://www.classroom.net

Only a few years ago, navigating the Web meant retrieving line after line of plain text. Today, Web browsers such as Mosaic, Netscape, and WinWeb or MacWeb, combined with computer networking advances, let users flip through Web pages in their full multimedia glory. This screen shows the White House home page.

Internet Relay Chat

Internet Relay Chat, or *IRC* is real-time Internet "talk." Internauts from around the world can join live, online discussion channels and converse with hundreds or thousands of people, all from their keyboards. As quickly as a person types out a thought, everyone else on the "channel" can read and respond to it, sort of like a global conference call.

What can you do with IRC? You can:

• Communicate in real-time with other students, keypals, or partner classes anywhere in the world.
• Conduct online conferences or seminars with other teachers and schools.
• Locate and query experts in a particular field.
• Develop interpersonal skills while learning about the Internet.

A variety of projects are possible. Students can chat in German with a class in Germany and get immediate feedback on their language skills and cultural insight. Or you could arrange a virtual visit with a guest scientist in the Antarctic.

IRC software is available at these sites:

Ftp to: cs-ftp.bu.edu

Look in the *irc/clients* area for subdirectories for DOS, Windows, and Mac versions

Ftp to: ftp.classroom.net

Look in the *wentworth/Internet-Software* subdirectories

You can access IRC in one of two ways. If you have a SLIP or PPP account, you'll be able to use IRC software such as Homer or WINIRC on your computer. To do so, you will need the Internet address of an Internet IRC server computer to connect with using your IRC software. Consult the following list for one near you.

Internet IRC sites

Alaska: **merlin.acf-lab.alaska.edu**
California: **nova.unix.portal.com**
Colorado: **irc.colorado.edu**
Florida: **irc.math.ufl.edu**
Illinois: **irc.uiuc.edu**
Louisiana: **sluaxa.slu.edu**
Massachusetts: **irc-2.mit.edu, cs-pub.bu.edu**
New York: **organ.ctr.columbia.edu**
North Carolina: **hobbes.catt.ncsu.edu**
Oregon: **irc.csos.orst.edu**
Pennsylvania: **irc.duq.edu**
Texas: **irc.bga.com**
Utah: **irc.math.byu.edu**
Virginia: **poe.acc.virginia.edu**

If you don't have a direct account and IRC software, start your IRC program by typing **IRC** at the prompt if you have a Unix shell account. If you have graphical access, you click on the appropriate icon.

More IRC servers

irc.gate.net

irc.uiuc.edu

irc.mit.edu

cs-pub.bu.edu

irc.indiana.edu

irc.uiuc.edu

ug.cs.dal.ca

irc.colorado.edu

(In Australia) **jello.qabc.uq.oz.au**

(In England) **stork.doc.ic.ac.uk**

(In Germany) **sokrates.informatik.uni-kl.de**

Once you're into IRC, you'll want a list of channels. A channel is like a room people drop into to talk about a certain subject, say England. Channels organize the thousands of people online at once—almost 15,000 people can simultaneously use Internet Relay Chat. Type **/LIST** to get a list of open channels. When you find the channel you want, type **/JOIN <channel name>** to join the conversation. You'll probably receive a message welcoming you to the group. From this point on, anything preceded with a forward slash is a command. Anything typed *without* a slash becomes a public message. All you need to do now is learn some simple commands.

Basic IRC commands

/help	Lists all commands
/list -min10	Lists active channels with at least 10 (or another number) users
/list -max10	Lists active channels with no more than 10 users
/join #Sports	Join the Sports channel
/who #Sports	Lists current Sports channel users
/whois JDoe	Gives more details about a user
/msg JDoe	Send a private message only to JDoe
/nick JDoe	Changes your online nickname to JDoe
/ignore ObNox1	Ignores all messages from ObNox1
/query JDoe	Opens a private channel with JDoe, no matter what channel he or she is on at the time
/quit, /bye, or /exit	End the IRC session

Educators need to know how to start or open a new channel. That way, they can create a channel just for their class or project. (Simply allowing students to dive into IRC without structure can be risky.) You can create your own channel by typing **/JOIN** followed by a channel name that doesn't already exist. Whoever opens a new channel becomes the *channel operator* (op, for short) by default. Ops have complete control over the channel they open: they can make it private, remove users, give other members ops rights, or entirely shut down the channel.

Basic operator commands

/kick JDoe	Kicks JDoe off the channel
/+i	Channel becomes invitation only
/+m	Channel is moderated—only op can talk
/l20	The maximum number of users is 20.
/o JDoe	Op gives JDoe operator privileges

Note: If you need to permanently remove someone from a channel, use the /whois feature to find the user's Internet address, then enter the following command: /mode +b JDoe <JDoe's Internet address>

IRC presents interesting possibilities for education, but some educators have expressed concern about easy access to some inappropriate chat areas. Certain IRC channels are home to the same kinds of inappropriate material found in unmoderated newsgroup postings. Since IRC activity takes place in real time, explicit language or other offensive behavior is difficult to control.

Students must be made aware that using IRC requires them to take personal responsibility, much as they're expected to show maturity and constraint when using the telephone. But there are ways to exercise control. Find a partner class for your project ahead of time (email and newsgroups are great ways to find them), agree on an IRC server and channel to "meet" in, and then set a time to chat (remember time zone differences). You can even start your own by-invitation-only channel, so that others surfing through IRC channels won't know of yours unless you give them the specific name. If you create a channel and get ops rights you can remove or permanently ban offending participants.

IRC safety tips

- Remind students not to reveal personal information they wouldn't give to strangers on the street, including home phone numbers and addresses, computer or security alarm passwords, or other sensitive information.
- Supervise "free time" on IRC, and immediately leave channels where abuses occur. Many programs let you log session activities, so save and print transcripts to monitor online behavior. You could also ask students to write brief reports about their online adventures.
- Forbid students to "cruise" IRC chat channels.
- Monitor how much time students spend using IRC—it can become somewhat addicting.

Internet searching tools

More than four million computers are connected to the Internet, and the number is growing rapidly. Each one is an independent library, putting more up-to-the-minute information at the fingertips of educators and students than ever before. These libraries, however, each have their own organizational system. Finding information on a given topic is a lot like trying to finding a needle in an earth-sized haystack.

While you could take a year's sabbatical to methodically search every Internet site for the educational information you need, there is an easier way—simply take advantage of the Internet's powerful searching tools. The whimsically named Veronica, Jughead, and Archie search tools, along with the full-text search features of WAIS, help you quickly find the information you need.

Veronica

Veronica is the premier search tool for the Internet's 5,000-plus gopher databases. Veronica searches for items by keyword from gopher menus around the world.

Let's say you were interested in finding information about biology. First, log on to the Internet. Start your gopher software or type **gopher** at the prompt. Then enter **veronica.scs.unr.edu** as your destination. This is the Veronica search program's home site.

First, a main menu appears. Select *Search ALL of Gopherspace using Veronica* from the list. A menu of eight main searching servers around the world will appear. It doesn't matter which site you use. All will return the same information.

To start your search, select one of the sites. Enter **biology** as the keyword, and hit enter. If one site is busy and denies you access, go back and select another. When Veronica finishes searching, it presents you with a single gopher menu of items containing that word. You can select any entry and be instantly transported to the computer containing that information.

You can give Veronica several keywords at once to narrow the search. Using biology as the keyword returned more than 2,000 individual items. Searching for molecular biology turned up half as many.

Jughead

While Veronica searches the entire planet for gopher resources, Jughead looks through a small segment of, or a single site in, gopherspace. Jughead is Veronica software scaled down to search one or a few specific gopher sites.

When you log on to most gopher sites, *Search this site using Jughead* is usually one of the items on the main menu. When you select Jughead and type in your keyword, it searches only that gopher server.

To get a feel for how Jughead works, gopher to **gopher.cc.utah.edu** and search the University of Utah's site.

Archie

In a way, the Net ranks as the largest disk drive in the world. Thousands of Internet sites offer free access to portions of their disk drive space, which hold millions of programs and computer files. Internauts can retrieve these files using ftp, or File Transfer Protocol.

Finding a specific file on one of thousands of ftp sites would be impossible. That's where Archie comes in. Archie is a gigantic database listing all files publicly available on the Internet and points you to where they're stored. As long as you know (or can guess at) part of the filename of the file you're looking for, Archie can help you locate it.

Let's say you wanted to find out where the latest version of the popular Web browser Mosaic was stored. Your first step is to find an archie server nearest to you. Consult the following list.

ARCHIE Sites

archie.internic.net	New York
archie.rutgers.edu	New Jersey
archie.sura.net	Maryland
archie.au	Australia
archie.uqam.ca	Canada
archie.ac.il	Israel
archie.wide.ad.jp	Japan
archie.luth.se	Sweden
archie.doc.ic.ac.uk	United Kingdom

Next, pick one of three ways to access the Archie database:

1. Telnet to the nearest Archie server. Use **archie** as your login.

2. Or, if you're logging on to a text-based Internet account, type **archie <archie server name>** at the first prompt and hit return.

3. Or, if you have a SLIP or PPP account, load your favorite Archie software and access the nearest server. (See the following box for software sources.)

(Note: Typing **help** after logging in to an Archie server will give you a list of commands and instructions.)

No matter which site you use or how you access it, the search results will be the same. In this example, we telnetted to **archie.sura.net** to do our search.

At the login prompt, type **archie**. You can type **help** to view a list of available commands and how to use them. Since you're searching for a specific program named Mosaic, type **prog Mosaic** to look for it. A few seconds later, a list of all the anonymous ftp sites with the file "Mosaic" scrolls onto the screen. Pick a site from the list, ftp to it, and grab the file.

You can also use email to search with Archie. To find out how, send email.

Email to: archie@archie.sura.net

Type **help** in the body of the message

Where to find Archie, WAIS, and WWW software online

AnArchie for Macintosh
Ftp to: ftp.classroom.net
Go to the *wentworth/Internet-Software/Mac* subdirectory

Archie for Windows
Ftp to: bcm.tmc.edu
Go to the *nfs* subdirectory

WAIS Station for Macintosh
Ftp to: ftp.oit.unc.edu
Go to the *pub/wais/clients/macintosh* subdirectory

OacWAIS for Windows
Ftp to: wais.com
Go to the *pub/freeware/windows* subdirectory

Netscape and Mac Web WWW browser software
Ftp to: ftp.classroom.net
Go to the *wentworth/Internet-Software* subdirectory

WAIS

While Archie can pinpoint the *location* of a file, it can't search the information *inside* it. That's a job for a Wide Area Information Server, or WAIS.

WAIS allows you to search for specific information in many databases on the Internet. You formulate a statement or question, such as "Recent developments in personal computers and education," tell WAIS where to search for relevant documents, and hit return. A list of files matching your search criteria is returned for you to read or print.

Each time you send a new question you can change the parameters of the search to narrow the focus of your request. In this way, WAIS is the most precise and efficient searching tool for hunting down online information.

WAIS is best used via a WAIS software program or client on your own computer. (See the above box for software sources.) You can also telnet to **sunsite.unc.edu** and login as **swais** to try out a simple WAIS interface. A new, powerful World Wide Web (WWW) interface to WAIS is now available as well.

URL: http://wais.com

World Wide Web searches

Several World Wide Web sites have become central indexes to Internet information. These "meta" sites are huge indexes of pointers to information on thousands of topics which can be searched by keyword.

URL: http://www.classroom.net/classroom/search.htm

URL: http://galaxy.einet.net/galaxy.html

URL: http://www.ncsa.uiuc.edu/SDG/Software/Mosaic/MetaIndex.html

URL: http://www.w3.org/hypertext

URL: http://www.lib.umich.edu/chhome.html

Save time when searching online

    Here are some tips that can help you use your time effectively when searching the Internet for information.

- Consider launching any search for information on the Internet by first reading an FAQ (Frequently Asked Questions) file on the topic. Thousands of FAQs are freely available online and cover just about any topic.

  Ftp to: rtfm.mit.edu

  Go to the *pub/usenet* subdirectory

- Try to narrow your search for gopher information when using Veronica. Use *and, not,* and *or* when composing your keyword queries (i.e., education *and* Internet). You can tack asterisks (*) onto the end of words or parts of words to act as wildcard characters. For example, the keyword **ship*** will search all gopher titles for words beginning with ship, such as ships, shipping, shipwreck, ship-to-shore, etc.

- Narrow your search when using Archie to search for ftp files. Several commands can help.

  set search maxhits 20: limits the number of responses to 20.

  set search sub: makes your search case insensitive.

  Asterisks (*): act as wildcards.

    Here's an example of a typical Archie search done via telnet. We're looking for Mosaic software. Each item would be typed on a separate line just after logging in as Archie, followed by a return.

  set search sub

  set maxhits 20

  prog mosaic*

    After entering these lines, Archie searches the world's ftp sites for the first 20 locations of a file named *Mosaic* or *mosaic*. It also looks for any filename containing the word Mosaic, such as *Mosaic.txt* or *mosaic-browser.exe*. Archie's **whatis <filename>** command will return a description of any program or file. When you're in an Archie site you can type **help** to get a list of commands and how to use them.

A C C E P T A B L E
U S E   P O L I C I E S

How to write a policy regulating Internet use in schools

E ducators worldwide know that bringing the Internet into the classroom promotes educational excellence and breathes new life and excitement into the educational experience.

But educators and parents are justifiably concerned about the appropriateness of some material online. They're becoming aware that regulating how Internet connections are used in schools is almost as important as getting connected. Such concerns are understandable, but don't let them keep the Internet out of your school or stall your district's move to full Net connectivity. The Internet's just too valuable.

Concern about content

Most schools and districts that are already online have taken measures to keep inappropriate material out of the classroom. Hardware and software controls are often used to limit student and faculty access to certain Internet resources, such as specific Usenet newsgroups. Sometimes computers are available to students only by appointment and under strict supervision. Whatever the control strategy, there's no guarantee that a knowledgeable, determined user won't find a way to access inappropriate material or misuse his or her time on the Net.

To protect the school and reassure parents, administrators and technology coordinators must create and implement an Acceptable Use Policy, or AUP. An AUP is a written agreement signed by students, their parents, and teachers that outlines the terms and conditions of Internet use. It specifically outlines acceptable uses of the Internet, rules of online behavior, and access privileges. It also defines the penalties for violations of the policy, including security violations and vandalism of the system. Anyone using a school's Internet connection should be required to sign an AUP and know that it will be kept on file as a legal, binding document.

What should be included in an AUP?

AUPs are still a relatively new concept, so your administrators and school solicitor may only now be learning of their existence. They can save time and gain the benefit of other schools' experience by reviewing AUPs already in use. (See resource list later in story.) To give you an idea of what should be included in your school's AUP, here's a detailed rundown of an AUP's contents along with sample wording.

1. Begin with basics

Explain what the Internet is, how students and teachers will access it, and how they'll use it in classrooms. Don't assume that parents know what the Internet is. Bring them up to speed with as little techno-jargon as possible, and be sure to cover all of the basics.

Sample wording: "Internet access is now available to students and teachers in our school district. The access is offered as a collaborative project involving your student's school and a local Internet Service Provider. Our goal in providing this service is to promote educational excellence in the district by facilitating resource sharing, innovation, and communication.

Our connection provides direct access to the Internet, an "electronic highway" connecting millions of computers and individuals all over the world. Your student will use it to communicate with fellow students all over the planet."

2. Emphasize student responsibility

Stress that students will be held responsible for their behavior while online. Explain that students will be taught about behavior that is impermissible on the network. Emphasize the importance of having the Internet in the classroom, but also make parents aware of the potential risks of students obtaining "objectionable" material. Be sure to mention the name and capabilities of special protection software, such as SurfWatch or CyberSitter, that your school may use.

Sample wording: "The smooth operation of the network relies upon the proper conduct of its users, who must adhere to strict guidelines. These guidelines are provided here so that you are aware of the responsibilities you are about to acquire. These responsibilities include not violating the privacy of other users, the right of all users to free expression, and not plagiarizing other users' works. With access to computers and people all over the world comes the availability of material that may not be considered of educational value in a school setting. We have taken precautions to restrict access to controversial materials by teaching students about responsible use and by using SurfWatch software to block student access to inappropriate materials."

3. List the penalties

Emphasize that use of the Net is a privilege, not a right. Consider including a short paragraph about Internet etiquette, called netiquette, which users adhere to while online. Outline the penalties and repercussions of violating the AUP. Some schools issue a warning letter to students and parents after the first violation. Subsequent violations may result in students having their access restricted or being suspended from the system.

Sample wording: "The use of our school district's Internet connection is a privilege, not a right. Inappropriate use will result in a cancellation of those privileges. Before receiving an Internet account and password, each student will meet with a faculty member to learn about proper use of the network, become familiar with netiquette, and review the AUP. The system administrators will deem what is inappropriate use and their decision is final. The administration, faculty, and staff may request the system administrator to deny, revoke, or suspend specific user accounts."

4. Sign on the dotted line

Provide space for everyone to sign. Students should sign to show that they have read the document and understand its contents. Parents sign to verify that they're aware that there's a remote chance their student could access potentially inappropriate material, and that they accept responsibility if their child accesses your school's Internet connection from home. Teachers should sign on behalf of the school. Many schools host a "technology night" to introduce families to the Internet. Teachers meet with students and their parents to talk about how the Net will be used, to explain the AUP and its ramifications, and have all parties sign.

Do your AUP homework

Before creating your own AUP, take the time to see what other schools have done. Many schools across the country make copies of their AUPs available online. Use these as a template for creating your own, modifying it as necessary to fit your particular needs.

• Boulder Valley School District's AUP is a great example of a successful AUP used at one of the United State's pioneering schools. For a copy, send an email message per the following directions.

Email to: info@classroom.net

Type **send aup-faq** in the body of your message

• ERIC (Educational Resource and Information Center)

Gopher to: ericir.syr.edu

Look in *Internet Guides & Directories, Acceptable Use Policies, Agreements for K–12*

• Rice University

Gopher to: riceinfo.rice.edu

Look in *Information by Subject Area, Education, Acceptable & Unacceptable Uses of Net Resources (K12)*

When doing your AUP homework, take full advantage of Internet mailing lists and Usenet newsgroups to discuss your needs, ask questions, and talk with other educators who have successfully implemented AUPs at their schools.

• Consortium for School Networking mailing list

Email to: listserv@listserv.net

Type **subscribe cosndisc <Your Full Name>** in the body of the message and leave the subject line blank

• Kidsphere mailing list

Email to: kidsphere-request@vms.cis.pitt.edu

Type **subscribe kidsphere <Your Name>** in the body of the message

• EDnet mailing list

Email to: listproc@lists.umass.edu

Type **subscribe ednet <Your Name>** in the body of the message

• Usenet newsgroups

alt.education.research

misc.education

k12.chat.teacher

Three books are now available on the subject of AUPs. They're filled with real-world examples of AUPs and tips for creating them.

Anthology of Internet Acceptable Use Policies
National Association of Regional Media Centers
$20 (Includes shipping and handling.)
(712) 722-4378

Plans & Policies for Technology in Education
National School Boards Association
$35
(800) 706-6722

Telecommunications and Education:
Surfing and the Art of Change
National School Boards Association
$28.95
(800) 706-6722

COMMERCIAL ONLINE SERVICES

Using their educational resources at school or at home

Before the Internet became easily available to computer users at large, people who wanted to join the online world used the commercial online services. More expensive, less global, and not as powerful as the Internet, they still give users the thrill of being in an online community full of people and information. And it's all at their fingertips.

Internet access is becoming easier and less expensive all the time. But these commercial services are often still a new user's first step into the online world. As these services continue to add Internet navigation tools to their menus, they will become many users' primary access method to the Internet.

America Online

America Online, or AOL, is one of the fastest growing commercial online services. Besides a sensible, easy-to-use graphical interface, AOL offers a massive conglomeration of content providers, from *The New York Times* to Disney.

In terms of K–12 educational content, AOL includes resources valuable to teachers, students, parents, and administrators. The Education section offers The NEA Public Forum, The Learning Channel, The Discovery

Channel, Library of Congress, National Council of Teachers of English, *Scientific American*, Smithsonian Online, and CNN Newsroom Online, to name just a few. Everything in AskERIC or Scholastic.com—both rich Internet sites for educators—is available through AOL.

A "Kids Only" section contains *TIME* for Kids, *Compton's Encyclopedia*, and Kids World, a "place to talk about issues that are important to you...and meet up with people your own age from all over the United States and beyond." The Reference Center includes a long list of resources, including the Career Center, College Handbook, Scholarships, Grants & Loans, and White House Information. Users can search all of America Online's contents by keyword.

One of the service's most popular features is its many public forums or "chat rooms" (similar to Internet Relay Chat channels). It also offers live classes, online homework help, and real-time conferences for teachers and parents.

Parents will appreciate AOL's control features. Master account holders control all screen names and can set parental filters for each. All account information is available online, including the current month's billing summary and remaining free time.

AOL recently added many Internet components and now offers Internet-compatible email, newsgroups, ftp, gopher, and World Wide Web access. Users can connect to AOL via Internet service providers for faster speeds without incurring long distance telephone charges. Most users should be able to find a local dial-in number, ranging from 9,600 baud to 28,800K baud.

America Online costs $9.95 a month and includes 5 free hours; additional online time costs $2.95 an hour. To join, install the free AOL software and fill out the online registration and credit card information. Call (800) 827-6364.

Prodigy

Prodigy offer an extensive selection of educational information for teachers and students of all grade levels. To keep up with a growing, highly competitive market, Prodigy cut its hourly rates, improved its graphical interface, and added new Internet components.

Most important, in early 1995 Prodigy became the first commercial online service to offer *complete* World Wide Web access. The Web browser is comparable to Internet Web tools such as Netscape and Mosaic. Users can interact with pages while they're downloading and can even launch gopher or ftp sessions via the browser.

Unlike the other services, Prodigy includes advertisements that appear on screen with other content. Most users shouldn't find them too distracting or cumbersome. Users must click on unobtrusive icons to get to full advertisement screens.

The main Prodigy screen isn't quite as well organized as that of America Online, but it does link users fairly easily to a number of departments, including news, business, sports, entertainment, and an extensive array of interactive bulletin boards.

Educators and students will find many helpful resources in Prodigy. The Education button under Home/Family/Kids includes sections such as Education Bulletin Board, *National Geographic*, NOVA, Sesame Street, and Space Challenge. Homework Helper, a new, commercial-free service created by Prodigy just for education, offers real-time, teacher-controlled "chat" areas, numerous electronic field trips such as MayaQuest, and online cooperative learning projects with accompanying lesson plans. Users can select "Jump" words to quickly navigate to their favorite locations.

Prodigy costs $9.95 per month for five free hours; online time after that costs $2.95 per hour. Call (800) 776-0845. Homework Helper is an additional $9.95 per month. Call (800) 776-3449, extension 176.

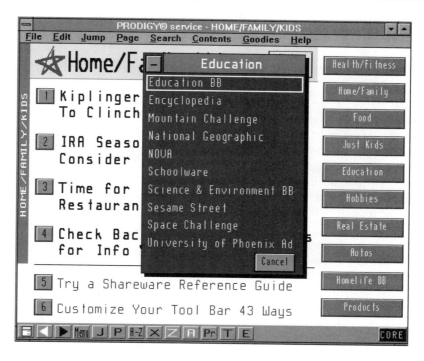

CompuServe

Although it's the most expensive online service, CompuServe continues to lead the pack in terms of specialized forums and databases. It provides something for everyone, from Fortune 500 CEOs to K–12 teachers. Among its offerings are the latest issues of more than 300 national magazines; access to the Knowledge Index and IQuest, a vast array of searchable information databases; the latest stock quotes and investment information; news wires from around the world; and a large Reference department.

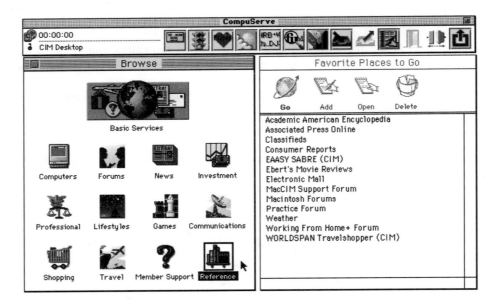

The Reference department is the area of most interest to educators. Here is the complete *Peterson's College Database*, the *Academic American Encyclopedia*, *American Heritage Dictionary*, and links to an Education InfoCenter with thousands of documents related to languages, science, math, English, even dinosaurs. Users can select Go words to quickly navigate to their favorite areas.

CompuServe costs $9.95 per month for 5 hours, and cost $2.95 per hour. CompuServe allows users to send and receive Internet email but charges ten cents per message for all incoming mail if you send or receive more than 90 messages per month. Call (800) 848-8199.

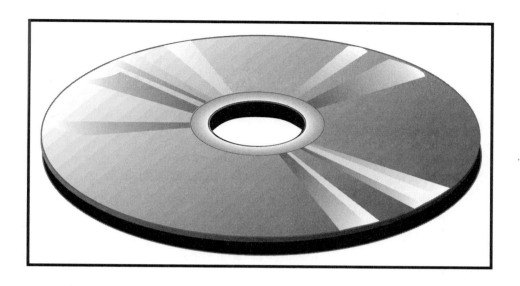

Educator's Internet Companion CD ROM

Free software to get you up and running on the Internet right away

In the back of this book you'll find a CD ROM jam-packed with free software to get you onto the Internet and using its resources in your classroom on minutes! There are five main items on the disc:

1. **Internet Access Software,** *including the incredible Netscape 2.0 Internet browser with built-in email,* from Concentric Network, a national (U.S.) Internet access provider. This software entitles you to 30 days FREE local dial-in access for only $1.00. For details on how to qualify for this special offer, see below.
2. **Educator's Internet Companion HotPage**, which contains "live" Internet links to nearly all of the online sites listed in Chapter 3 & 4 of the book.
3. **HyperStudio Multimedia software demo,** which will enable you to use the multimedia files you find on the Internet to create colorful, interactive slide shows. This demo also includes close to 200 mb of clip art, video clips, sounds and other multimedia files.
4. **Monstrous Media Kit for Macintosh**, multimedia authoring software that's perfect for students who are new to computers and want to create fun, informative interactive presentations with sounds and video.
5. **CyberPatrol Internet access filter software**, a highly flexible and effective means for blocking access to inappropriate online sites. The version on the CD enabled for a full 30 day free trial. (see details below)
6. **NASA K–12 Internet web site.**

How to I run the CD ROM, and what kind of computer do I need?

The CD-ROM is a hybrid CD, which means it will work with either an IBM-compatible PC running Windows 3.1/Windows 95, or a Macintosh computer running System 7.5. We recommend that you have at least 8 megabytes of RAM to navigate the Internet and use the included software.

Installing the CD-ROM

To install the CD, simply load the CD-ROM into your CD drive. Then, using any word-processing program, look for a file called READ ME (on the Mac), or README.TXT (on a PC). That file contains complete instruction s on how to load, and make the most of, all the programs on the CD.

Internet Access Software

Getting on the Internet has never been easier! Just install the Concentric Network Internet Access Software, and you're ready to go. The incredible Netscape Navigator 2.0 Internet browser is included! When you use Netscape Navigator through the Concentric Network, you can experience all the exciting opportunities available online, including the World Wide Web, electronic mail, online chat, and interactive games.

When you install the enclosed software and register for your Concentric Network account, you'll get your first month of Internet access for only $1. During the registration process, you'll have a chance to select from several convenient connection plans, with subscription rates as low as $7.95 per month!

Please note: The Internet access software on the CD is Windows version only. To get a free Mac version, please call Concentric at (800) 939-4CNC(4262) and mention the Classroom Connect Special.

Educator's Internet Companion HotPage

On the CD you'll find a file called **HOTPAGE.HTM**. This is a World Wide Web document which you can view in your Netscape or any Internet browser software. Just use the **Open File** command under the **File** menu of your browser, locate the HOTPAGE.HTM file on your CD, and double click to open it up and read it.

This HotPage contains "live" Internet links to almost all of the online sites listed in Chapter 3 & 4 of the book. Rather than typing in these address to get where you want to go, simply click on the places you want to go with your mouse! You may want to copy this file to your hard disk drive for faster, more convenient access.

HyperStudio

In this age of CD ROM and the Internet, the way we read and gather information has changed. If your students' references are in a multimedia format, isn't it time they delivered their research in that same style? Paper and pencil reports, even word processing, no longer prepare students for their future! Over a million students use HyperStudio as their multimedia writing tool — more than all the other multimedia authoring systems combined.

The HyperStudio demo on this CD contains a full working demo of HyperStudio 3.0 (Mac and Windows versions are on the CD), plus almost 200 megabytes of multimedia clip art (images, video clips, etc.) This version of the software doesn't expire, which means you can create an unlimited number of presentations. However, it does limit you to creating presentations that are only four "cards" in length. HyperStudio retails for $199, but under a special offer from Classroom Connect, you can call (800) HYPERSTUDIO and pay about $119 to upgrade to the full version. That's a savings of almost $80! Here are some other important facts about HyperStudio:

• Hyperstudio allows you to create your own CD ROM-style projects, Mac or Windows
• Free home use for students and teaching staff with the purchase of a 10-pack at your school
• Move projects between Windows and Mac effortlessly - no tricky conversions necessary

- Capture elements from the Internet, other CD ROMs, PhotoCDs, laser discs, and more!
- Includes tons of clip art, sounds, and read-made card templates
- Applicable across the curriculum and at all grade levels
- Compatible with virtually every graphic and sound file types
- Built-in capture of images with AV Macs, the Apple QuickTake Camera, or the Kodak DC-40 camera

Monstrous Media Kit

If you're an educator who works with students and Macintosh computers, then be sure to check out the Monstrous Media Kit right away! It's a fun, easy-to-use multimedia creation tool which is sure to energize your students to use the computer in exciting new ways.

The CD includes the full working version of the software for Mac computers — it's not limited in any way! Your students can easily create a multi-card presentation, and incorporate pictures, sounds and movie clips to create their own multimedia shows. The Monstrous Media Kit can even use the 150 megabytes of free clip art, sounds, and video clips included with HyperStudio!

Monstrous Media Kit is available in a commercial and educational version, on a hybrid CD-ROM for both Mac and Windows.

Special pricing for the CD-ROM version is: Home or School Edition—for one user $22; Lab Pack with 5 CDs—for up to five users $65; Classroom Pack with 5 CDs—for up to 30 users $185; Network Pack with 5 CDs—for up to 50 users $325; Site License with 5 CDs—unlimited use in one school building $400.

For more information, contact: CyberPuppy Software, 2248 Park Boulevard, Palo ALto, CA 94306. Telephone: (415) 326-2449. Fax (415) 326-6301. URL: http://www.cyberpuppy.com

CyberPatrol

CyberPatrol provides teachers, parents, and anyone who is responsible for children's access to the Internet with the tools they need to get block access to inappropriate materials online. Best of all, CyberPatrol's CyberNOT list is more comprehensive than competitive lists (such as SurfWatch), and includes comprehensive time and budget management functions to help you manage your online budget. And, it works great with both Macintosh and Windows computers.

Included on the CD is the CyberPatrol Enhanced Home Edition. Designed especially for readers of Classroom Connect books, this version of the software functions exactly like the full retail version for a full 30 days, and then drops back to the reduced feature Home Version. It is for home use only, and not for use in businesses or schools without payment of the registration fee.

The list price of CyberPatrol is $49.95 but through Classroom Connect, you only pay $29.95 to register and upgrade the software to the full-featured retail version. This price even includes a one-year subscription (retail value $17) to the CyberNOT access blocking list of inappropriate sites, so that the CyberPatrol software keeps up to date automatically.

Complete instructions for using this software are included with the program itself. For more details, see the full page CyberPatrol fact sheet below.

NASA K–12 Internet Web Site

We've also included a great Web site, of special interest to teachers—and students too.find the Web file on the CD-ROM called nasa.htm and view it using your web browser. This is a World Wide Web document which you can view with your Netscape or any Internet browser software. Just use the **Open File** command under the **File** menu of your browser, locate the nasa.htm file on your CD, and double click to open it up and read it. You'll enjoy dozens of megabytes of documents and images from NASA.

G L O S S A R Y

Definitions of terms in this book and on the Internet

Acceptable Use Policy (AUP) A binding document signed by all users that explains the rules of Internet use at an institution.

Anonymous ftp A publicly available Internet file site. Users must sign on as "anonymous" and enter their email addresses to connect to an anonymous ftp site.

Archie A program that locates files that are freely available on anonymous ftp sites across the Internet. To use Archie, telnet to one of these sites and logon as **archie**.

archie.internic.net
archie.ans.net
archie.rutgers.edu
archie.sura.net
archie.unl.edu
archie.au
archie.doc.ic.ac.uk
Type **help** to obtain full instructions.

Bitnet An autonomous network of academic and research sites.

Browser Software that allows users to access and navigate the World Wide Web. Some Web browsers, such as Mosaic and NetScape, are graphical. Lynx is a text-based browser used on Unix computers.

Bulletin Board Service (BBS) A forum for users to browse and exchange information. Computer BBSs are accessible by telephone via a personal computer and a modem. Many BBSs are small operations run by a single person that allow only several users to logon at the same time. Some are much larger and allow hundreds of users to logon simultaneously to use the system. Huge, commercial examples are America Online, CompuServe, and Prodigy.

Commercial online service A company that, for a fee, allows computer users to dial in via modem to access its information and services, which can include Internet access. Examples are America Online, CompuServe, and Prodigy.

Database A computer holding large amounts of information that can be searched by an Internet user. A storehouse of information on the Net.

Dialup Internet connection Lets a user dial into an Internet service provider using a modem and telephone line to access the Internet. The user is presented with a text-based set of menus which are used to navigate the Internet. (See **SLIP** or **PPP connections**)

Directory A list of files or other directories on a computer at an Internet site.

Download/upload To download is to transfer a file from another computer to the user's computer. To upload is to send a file to another computer.

Email Allows users to send and receive messages to each other over the Internet.

Emoticons Smileys and other character art used to express feelings in email communication.

File Transfer Protocol (FTP) Allows files to be transferred between Internet-connected computers.

Filter Hardware or software designed to restrict access to certain areas on the Internet.

Finger Software that allows the user to enter the address of an Internet site to find information about that system's users or a particular user. Some finger addresses return other topic-specific information.

Flame To send a harsh, critical email message to another user, usually someone who has violated the rules of netiquette.

Free-Net Any one of more than two dozen freely accessible Internet sites, primarily offering community and educational information.

Frequently Asked Questions (FAQ) FAQ files answer frequently asked questions on hundreds of Internet-related topics. They're freely available at many locations on the Net. This ftp site holds every FAQ on the Net.
> **Ftp to: rtfm.mit.edu**
> Go to the *pub/usenet/news.answers* subdirectory

Gopher A menu-based system for browsing Internet information.

Graphical interface Software designed to allow the user to execute commands by pointing and clicking on icons or text.

Hacker A computer user who illegally visits networked computers to look around or cause harm.

Home page The first page a user sees when visiting a World Wide Web site.

HTML (Hypertext Markup Language) Programming "language" of the World Wide Web, HTML software turns a document into a hyperlinked World Wide Web page.

Hypertext/hyperlink A highlighted word or graphic in a document that, when clicked upon, takes the user to a related piece of information on the Internet.

Infobot (or **mailbot**) An email address that automatically returns information requested by the user.

Internaut Anyone who uses the Internet.

Internet The global "network of networks" that connects more than four million computers, called hosts. The Internet is the virtual "space" in which users send and receive email, logon to remote computers (telnet), browse databases of information (gopher, World Wide Web, WAIS), and send and receive programs (ftp) contained on these computers.

Internet account Purchased through an Internet service provider, the account assigns a password and email address to an individual or group.

Internet Relay Chat (IRC) Interactive, real-time discussions between Internauts using text messages. Users logon to designated Net computers and join discussions already in progress. More information about IRC can be obtained via ftp.
> **Ftp to: cs.bu.edu**
> Go to the *irc/support* subdirectory

Internet server A computer that stores data that can be accessed via the Internet.

Internet Service Provider (ISP) Any organization that provides access to the Internet. Many ISPs also offer technical assistance to schools looking to become Internet information providers by placing their school's information online. They also help schools get connected to the Net. A list of ISPs can be retrieved via ftp.

Ftp to: **ftp.classroom.net**

Look in the *wentworth* subdirectory

Internet site A computer connected to the Internet containing information that can be accessed using an Internet navigation tool such as ftp, telnet, gopher, or a Web browser.

IP address Every computer on the Internet has a unique numerical address assigned to it, such as 123.456.78.9.

Jughead An Internet search tool that will scan one or a few gopher sites for material related to a keyword.

Keyword A word or words which can be searched for in documents or menus.

Knowbot Software that searches Internet "white pages," lists of users at large institutions, to find a person's name and address.

Logon To sign on to a computer system.

Mailing lists (or **Listserv**) There are more than 4,000 topic-oriented, email-based message bases that can be read and posted to. Users subscribe to the lists they want to read and receive messages via email. Mailing lists are operated using listserv software. Thus, many Internauts call mailing lists "listservers." There are two types of lists: moderated and unmoderated. Moderated lists are screened by a human before being posted to subscribers. Messages to unmoderated lists are automatically forwarded to subscribers.

Menu A list of information that leads to documents or other menus.

Modem An electronic device that attaches to a computer and links that computer to the online world via a phone line. Modems are available for any computer, can be internal or external, and come in several speeds, known as the baud rate. The higher the baud rate, the faster the modem. The most popular modem was 14,400 baud but 28,800 baud modems are now the standard. Most Internet service providers allow you to dial into their systems at 14,400, or even 28,800 baud.

Mosaic Internet navigation software that allows Internauts to access information through a graphical, point-and-click interface rather than text-only screens or menus. Mosaic is known as a Web browser because it accesses World Wide Web information formatted into special home pages using hypertext. Other graphical Web browsers include NetScape, WinWeb, InternetWorks, and Cello.

National Information Infrastructure (NII) The official U.S. government name for the Internet and other computer networks. Commonly known as the Information Superhighway.

Netiquette The rules of conduct for Internet users. Violating netiquette could result in flaming or removal from a mailing list. Some service providers will even cancel a user's Internet account, denying him or her access to the Net, if the violation is severe enough.

Net surfer Someone who browses the Internet.

Network A group of computers that are connected in some fashion. Most school networks are known as LANs, or Local Area Networks, because they are networks linking computers in one small area. The Internet could be referred to as a WAN, or a Wide Area Network, because it connects computers in more than one local area.

Online/Offline When you are logged onto a computer through your modem, you are said to be online. When you're using your computer but are not connected to a computer through your modem, you're said to be working offline.

Posts Email messages sent to a mailing list or Usenet newsgroup to be read by subscribers or others on the Internet.

Request for Comments (RFC) Online documents that have to do with technical standards for the Internet.

Serial Line Internet Protocol (SLIP) or Point to Point Protocol (PPP, a Dial-up IP) Internet connections Both allow a computer to connect to the Internet using a modem and telephone line. Users then navigate the Internet using software on their own computer. This is in contrast to using a Dialup Internet Connection, where users are forced to navigate the Net using text-based sets of menus.

Signature file Return address information such as name, phone number, and email address that users put at the bottom of email messages.

Telnet Allows users to access computers and their data at thousands of places around the world, most often at libraries, universities, and government agencies.

Text-based Internet account The user must use Unix commands to navigate the Internet.

Unix A computer operating system commonly used on the Internet.

URL (Universal Resource Locator) The address and method used to locate a specific resource on the Internet. A URL beginning with **http://** indicates that the site is a WWW resource and that a Web browser will access it.

Usenet newsgroups More than 13,000 topic-oriented message bases that can be read and posted to. Also called newsgroups.

Veronica Veronica is a computer program that helps Internauts find what they're looking for on gopher servers around the world. Instead of looking through menus, Veronica allows users to enter keywords to locate the gopher site that holds the information they want.
  Gopher to: veronica.scs.unr.edu

Virtual A computer-generated environment.

WAIS (Wide Area Information Servers) These servers allow users to conduct full-text keyword searches in documents, databases, and libraries connected to the Internet.

World Wide Web (WWW or **Web)** A revolutionary Internet browsing system that allows for point-and-click navigation of the Internet. The WWW is a spiderweb-like interconnection of millions of pieces of information located on computers around the world. Web documents use hypertext, which incorporates text and graphical "links" to other documents and files on Internet-connected computers.

INDEX

- C -

- H -

- I -

- M -

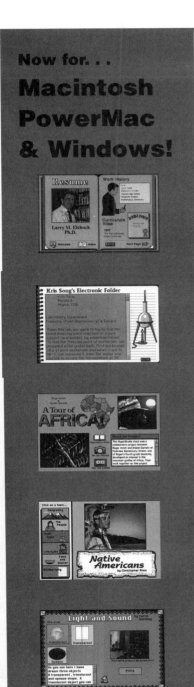

"TO SURF AND PROTECT"

Internet Access Management Utility

CyberPatrol lets parents and teachers control children's access to the Internet, providing:
- Automatic blocking of access to specified Internet sites
- CyberNOT block list—researched Internet sites that parents may find questionable
- First and only Internet filter that works with all browsers, including 32-bit browsers
- Built-in support for the SafeSurf system
- Restriction access to certain times of day
- Limit total time spent on-line
- Control local applications use

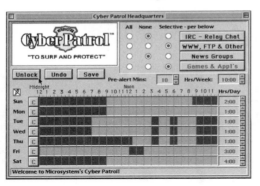

CyberPatrol's main administration screen lets parents, teachers, and others control children's use of a computer by hours of the day and by specific Internet locations.

CyberPatrol is an Internet access management utility which parents and teachers use to control children's access to the Internet.

It allows those responsible for children to restrict access to certain times of day, limit the total time spent online in a day and block access to Internet sites deemed inappropriate. CyberPatrol also can be used to control access to the major online services and to local applications such as games and personal financial managers.

CyberPatrol comes loaded with Microsystems Software's "CyberNOT Block List," a listing of researched Internet sites containing material which parents may find questionable. The list is divided into categories and access can be managed down to the file directory or page level. This means that appropriate material at an Internet address need not be blocked simply because there is some restricted material elsewhere at the address. Parents and teachers may select all or any of the categories to be blocked by content, time of day, or specific Internet site.

Parental Control

CyberPatrol allows parents to manage computer use in their own household(s). Cumulative duration of the use of the Internet and other applications is captured, allowing reporting. In addition to providing a useful overview of computer usage, these reports can also be used to verify online provider and telephone bills.

CyberPatrol is available for Windows and Macintosh systems. CyberPatrol 2.0 for

Windows provides control of children's access through Internet Applications and web browsers, including America Online, America Online's MegaWeb Internet access service, CompuServe/Spry Mosaic, Netcruiser, Netscape and Mosaic 2.0. CyberPatrol 2.0 also blocks sites accessed via a proxy server.

CyberPatrol 1.0 for Macintosh is capable of blocking direct Internet access. This core functionality is required by the education market. Currently, the Macintosh product will intercept calls to the Macintosh TCP driver, and will block access from the popular Mac browsers and Internet applications such as Netscape, Mosaic and NewsWatcher.

CyberPatrol loads during start-up and runs in the background, controlling access to all associated applications. CyberPatrol is accessed via password, and offers two levels of parental password control. Several safeguards include controls which prevent children from disabling CyberPatrol or simply renaming blocked applications.

CyberNOT Block List

The sites on the CyberNOT Block List are reviewed by a team of professionals at Microsystems software, including parents and teachers. They use a set of criteria that categorizes Internet sites and resources according to the level of possibly objectionable content. The categories include: Partial Nudity, Nudity; Sexual Acts/ Text: Gross Depictions; Racist/ Ethnic; Gambling; Satanic/ Cult; Militant/Extremist; Drugs and Drug

Culture; Alcohol, Beer, and Wine; Violence/ Profanity; and Questionable/Illegal.

Parents can select the categories of content they wish to block and allow access to any site on the CyberNOT List that they deem appropriate. Parents also can deny access to additional sites not included on the CyberNOT List and control or block access to major online services as well as applications (games, for example0.

The CyberNOT List is updated weekly and can be downloaded using CyberPatrol.

How to Purchase

The $49 list price for CyberPatrol includes a six-month subscription to the CyberNOT Block List. **But through special arrangement with Classroom Connect you can purchase CyberPatrol for only $29.95,** which includes a 12-month subscription to the CyberNOT Block List. You can download a free 14-day working demo from **www.classroom.net/cyberpatrol.** Call Classroom Connect at (800) 638-1639. Quantity discounts available

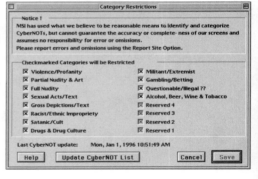

$1 Internet Access

Classroom Connect Offer Includes:
Netscape Navigator 2.0
Plus 30 Days FREE Internet Access

A limited time offer, courtesy of Classroom Connect

That's right! The latest version of Netscape Navigator 2.0, the world's most popular Internet browser (with built-in email), plus one month of unlimited local access from Concentric Network—all for A BUCK.

Too good to be true? After your 30-day period, take advantage of monthly plans that start at only $7.95 per month for 5 hours of access or $19.95 for unlimited access. Your account includes email and 5 MB of space for your own World Wide Web page.

Concentric's Internet service features customer support 24 hours a day, 7 days a week, and local dial access speeds of 28.8 kbps from more than 3,000 U.S. and Canadian cities.

Concentric Network Customer Support: (800) 745-2747
Available 24 hours a day, 7 days a week.

Internet made easy in the classroom™

For more information, call Concentric at (800) 939-4262

TM

◆ A complete online research library.

◆ Deep and broad consumer reference product.

◆ The best way for students and families to do research.

◆ Content is as safe as local public library.

◆ Accessible via the Internet.

◆ Updated daily via satellite.

The way you do research.™
http://www.k12.elibrary.com/classroom

Using The Electric Library, a student can pose a question in plain English and launch a comprehensive and simultaneous search through more than 150 full-text newspapers, over 900 full-text magazines, two international newswires, two thousand classic books, hundreds of maps, thousands of photographs as well as major works of literature and art.

In a matter of seconds, query results are returned to a user ranked in relevancy order, displaying reference data, file size, and grade reading level. With this easy-to-use product a researcher need only click on the document or image of interest and it is automatically downloaded. The materials can also be copied and saved into a word processing document with bibliographic information automatically transferred.

Included in The Electric Library database are materials from world renowned publishers such as Reuters, Simon and Schuster, Gannett, World Almanac, Times Mirror, and Compton's New Media. The Electric Library also incorporates a host of local, ethnic, and special interest publications.

All retrieved information can be downloaded and saved or transferred to a word processor in real time, and used for educational purposes. This includes both the text and images from The Electric Library's databases.

PARTIAL LIST OF ELECTRIC LIBRARY CONTENT

Magazines/Journals
Art Journal
The Economist
Editor & Publisher
Inc.
Lancet
Maclean's
Mother Jones
National review
New Republic
World Press Review

Books/Reference Works
3,000 Great Works of Literature
Monarch Notes
The Complete Works of Shakespeare
The World's Best Poetry
Compton's Encyclopedia
King James Bible
Thematic Dictionary
Webster's Dictionary
World Fact Book

Newspapers/Newswires
Baseball Weekly
Jerusalem Post
La Prensa
Los Angeles Times
Magill's Survey of Cinema
Newsbytes News Service
News India
New York Newsday
Reuters
USA Today

FREE 60-DAY TRIAL!
Offer made in special arrangement with Classroom Connect

PRICING
Individual User: 9^{95} per month
School Site License: $2,000 per year

1-800-638-1639

Infonautics Corporation
900 W. Valley Rd., Suite 1000
Wayne, PA 19087-1830
Voice: 800-304-3542
Fax: 610-971-8859
Email: k12@infonautics.com

Monstrous Media Kit

(formerly Kid's Studio)
The award-winning multimedia creativity tool for kids ages seven to twelve.

Produce, direct and star in your own multimedia productions. CyberPuppy's Monstrous Media Kit is an all-in-one multimedia application that offers children sophisticated tools for creating their own presentations. Kids can compose brilliant pages combining photo-realistic images with paint, text, and sound, and show off their work as full-screen slide shows, movies or printed stories. Features a "Treasure Chest" of images, Cookie-Cutter Technology, QuickTime or Video for Windows, and Kodak Photo CDs.

Minimum Requirements:

Macintosh: Mac LC or higher, CD-ROM Drive, System 7
5 mb RAM, 5mb free hard disk space
12-inch monitor with 256 colors/grays.

Windows: 486SX, CD-ROM Drive, Windows 3.1
8mb RAM, 5 mb free hard disk space
VGA+ (640 X 480 at 256 colors)

Price: $22 plus $3 shipping and handling
(California residents add sales tax.)

Classroom Connect Newsletter

Send for your <u>FREE</u> <u>trial</u> <u>issue</u> today!

Walk through the crater of a live volcano, visit the White House, watch astronauts explore the universe—that's the kind of student-involving activities the Internet brings to your classroom.

Each issue of the *Classroom Connect* newsletter is packed with articles you can read in minutes and immediately put to use. You'll find directions for finding free lesson plans, educational games, Internet trips, international classroom-to-classroom projects—and a host of other educational resources—all just a few keystrokes away. Whether you're an Internet veteran or a first-time user, you'll appreciate *Classroom Connect's* clear, easy-to-understand, jargon-free language.

Educator's special: $39 per year (regular $47)
Published 9 times yearly. Newsletter format. 20 pages per issue. Illustrated.

1866 Colonial Village Lane, Lancaster, PA 17601
Phone: **(800) 638-1639** Fax: **(717) 393-5752**
Email: **connect@classroom.net**

CLASSROOM CONNECT
FREE Trial Issue Offer

❑ Send my FREE trial issue of *Classroom Connect*. If I choose to subscribe, I'll honor your invoice for $39 for 9 monthly issues and you'll rush my FREE Bonus Gift: *The Educator's Internet Resource Handbook* If I choose not to subscribe, I'll return the invoice marked "cancel" and keep the trial issue free of charge.

Name: _____ Title: _____

School/Organization: _____

Address: _____

City: _____

State/Province: _____

Zip/Postal Code: _____

Address is: ❑ School ❑ Home

Phone: (_____)_____

Fax: (_____)_____

Email: _____

Classroom Connect
1866 Colonial Village Lane, Lancaster, PA 17605-0488
Phone: **(800) 638-1639** Fax: **(717) 393-5752**
Email: **connect@classroom.net**
URL: **http://www.classroom.net**

EIC0595

How to use the Internet in the K-12 classroom

The Internet Revealed video series

This landmark videotape production quickly delivers an A to Z understanding of what the Internet is and how to tap its limitless educational resources. It's the one place students and teachers can turn for a thorough orientation and how-to-do-it instructions that get the beginner online. Tim McLain, nationally known writer/surfer for *Classroom Connect,* is your host for this easy-to-understand series of four top-of-the-line, movie-quality video productions. Tapes can be viewed as a set or individually in any order.

Tape #1: The Amazing Internet gives teachers and students a taste of the tremendous global teaching and learning power. It introduces all of the communication, research and navigation tools and the phenomenal World Wide Web. Captures and holds student interest from start to finish! *Running time 17 minutes.*

Tape #2: Internet Email is the most versatile and commonly used communications tool. Here are clear step-by-step directions for using the power of electronic mail to join over 4,000 global discussion lists, collaborate on international projects, and communicate with teachers and students worldwide. *Running time 27 minutes.*

Tape #3: Searching the Internet teaches hands-on navigation skills and valuable searching techniques. Quickly and easily, learn to unlock the treasure trove of educational resources on the Internet. Includes gopher, Archie, Veronica, Jughead, principles of Boolean searching, and much more. Bonus section on WebWanderer, WebCrawler, Lycos, Yahoo, and other World Wide Web search engines. *Running time 24 minutes.*

Tape #4: Discovering the World Wide Web opens the door to an inexhaustible wealth of educational information. It's an up-to-the-minute teaching and learning tool of unparalleled scope. Easy to understand, it turns viewers into World Wide Web power users. *Running time 38 minutes.*

4 VHS videotapes, ~~complete set price $150~~
EDUCATOR'S SPECIAL ! $125
Individual tapes: $40 each.

To order, detach or photocopy coupon and send to address shown. For faster service:
Phone: **(800) 638-1639**
Fax: **(717) 393-5752**
Email: **connect@classroom.net**

❑ **YES!** Send me **The Internet Revealed** complete 4 videotape set at **$125.**

❑ Send only the individual tapes indicated at **$40 each**:
   ❑ Tape 1   ❑ Tape 2   ❑ Tape 3   ❑ Tape 4

I may review the tapes for 10 days. If satisfied, I will pay the invoice amount. If not, I will return the tapes in good condition with the invoice marked "cancel." If prepaid, I'll receive a full refund immediately.

Name:_____

School:_____

Title:_____

Address:_____

City:_____State:____Zip:_____

Phone: (_____)_____Fax: (_____)_____

Email:_____

EIC595

❑ Payment enclosed
   (Free shipping & handling)

❑ Bill my credit card
   (Free shipping & handling)
   ❑ Visa   ❑ M.C.   ❑ AmEx
   Card #:_____
   Exp.:_____
   Signature_____

❑ Bill me (Shipping & handling will be added: $6 U.S., $10 elsewhere)

CLASSROOM CONNECT

Classroom Connect
1866 Colonial Village Lane
Lancaster, PA 17601

A visual tour of over 150 exciting educational Web sites!

Educator's World Wide Web TourGuide™

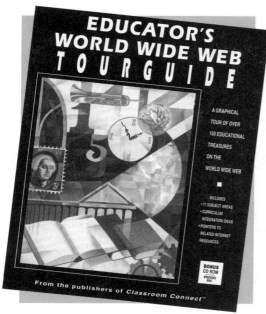

Find educational treasures instantly with this easy-to-use book/CD ROM package!

Over 150 of the most valuable and fascinating educational sites have been packaged into one convenient sourcebook covering eleven subject areas. Each Web site profile includes a large reproduction of the computer screen, address information, description of the contents, ideas on how to integrate the Web site information into your curriculum, PLUS pointers to related gopher, Web, and ftp sites—giving you literally thousands of resources.

Added bonus—FREE CD ROM with purchase of the book!

We've captured hundreds of sites on the CD ROM disk—it's like having the Internet at your fingertips without even going online! Multiple active hyperlinks allow you to sample each site's contents. As an added benefit, a World Wide Web browser is included on the CD.

$39.95
Completely revised for 1996, Softcover, Over 200 pages, Illustrated
Included FREE with purchase of the book, *CD ROM disk* and *Web browser*.
ISBN 0-932577-16-4
1866 Colonial Village Lane, Lancaster, PA 17605-0488
Phone: **(800) 638-1639** Fax: **(717) 393-5752**
Email: **connect@classroom.net**

The Educators' Essential Internet Training System

The easiest way to teach the Internet

Everything you need to conduct a complete Internet workshop for your staff — in one easy-to-use trainer's kit.

This complete kit includes:

- step-by-step trainer's manual
- over 150 color slides on diskette
- trainer slide follow-along
- two instructional videotapes
- FREE Internet service for 30 days

- 20 easy-to-follow participants' workbooks
- blackline masters of presentation
- Internet access and navigation software
- and more!

Topics include:

- Seven best uses of the Internet in education
- Overview of the most popular ways to get on the Internet
- How to effectively use email, gopher, telnet, ftp, mailing lists, Usenet newsgroups, World Wide Web, Internet Relay Chat, and more!
- Critical things to remember when creating an Acceptable Use Policy — *full text of sample AUP included*
- Shortcuts and tips busy teachers use to find lesson plans, create projects for the classroom
- Where to go and what to do to find the best educational resources on the Internet
- How to integrate the Internet into the curriculum — just the way you want it
- 50 classroom integration ideas
- Internet project list with complete contact information.

Also includes Internet lesson plans, training tips, and curriculum integration ideas!

Additional participant workbooks available.

Bonus: Complete sections of this system designed for use with hands-on Internet training workshops.

☐ **YES!** Please rush the *Educators' Essential Internet Training System* to me. My special limited-time price for the complete kit is **only $199** (Reg. $249) — **a $50 savings!** I understand that if I'm not completely satisfied with the *Educators' Essential Internet Training System,* I may return the kit within 10 days for a full refund.

Name: _____ Title: _____

School/Org: _____ Street: _____

City: _____ State/Province: _____ Zip/Postal Code: _____

Address is: ☐ Home ☐ School Phone: (___) _____

CLASSROOM CONNECT

1866 Colonial Village Lane,
P.O. Box 10488
Lancaster, PA 17605-0488
FOR FASTER SERVICE —
Phone: (800) 638-1639
Fax: (717) 393-5752
Email: connect@classroom.net
URL: http://www.classroom.net

Order	
Training Systems . (reg. $249) each $199	$ _____
Additional Seminar Participant Paks shipped in sets of 20 . . . . $50/set	$ _____
Subtotal	$ _____
PA residents add 6% sales tax	$ _____
Please add shipping and handling	$ _____
TOTAL	$ _____

Shipping & Handling

U.S.–$12

Canada–$22

Foreign–$37
Foreign orders allow 6-8 weeks for regular delivery. Additional charge for shipping by air.

❸ **Payment Options (Payable in US funds only, drawn on US bank)**

☐ My check is enclosed (Made payable to *Classroom Connect*)

☐ Charge to my credit card: ☐ VISA ☐ MasterCard ☐ AmEx

Card # : _____ Exp. Date: _____

Signature: _____

☐ P.O. # (if not attached): _____

☐ Bill me

8555 Printed in the U.S.A. ©1996 Wentworth Worldwide Media, Inc. **1234**

The Educator's Internet CD Club

Instantly enter the exciting educational world of the Internet on CD-ROM — no online access required!.

Discover how to:

- Integrate audio and video into classroom activities
- Gain immediate access to A+Web sites
- Increase student excitement using Internet technology
- Decrease lengthy planning time

• Your students can experience the feel and fun of cruising the Internet without needing actual on–line access which means you don't worry about expensive phone lines, modems, and monthly access fees.

• Design your lesson plans using the Internet CD Club and you can feel confident that your students will always have access to the sites you've designated. You'll not only save processing time but you won't have to worry about your students accessing any "inappropriate material".

• Every iCD issue you receive includes a "Curriculum Integration" section where you can access lesson plans designed to help you integrate the CD Web sites into your classroom. In addition, there are dozens of lesson plan extensions, project ideas, and teacher resources.

✂ **Cut Here**

CHARTER MEMBERSHIP APPLICATION

iCD
CD Club

☐ **Yes**, *I'd like to become a Charter Member of the Educator's Internet CD Club.*
Please enroll me in the iCD Club at the special Charter Member rate of ONLY $79 ($50 savings off the regular $129 price). I'll receive four CD-ROMs during the school year, loaded with Web sites and lesson plans. Also, as a member, I'll have the opportunity to purchase additional CD-ROMs at the special member price of ONLY $19.95 each - a 50% savings off the regular price of $39.95. **And, as a special BONUS, upon receipt of my iCD membership payment, you'll send me absolutely FREE, the Teachers Resource PowerPak CD** chock full of Internet lesson plans, teaching tips, Internet sites designed for use by teachers only, and a working demo of Hyperstudio for multimedia presentations, complete with 150 mb of multimedia clip art.

PAYMENT METHOD

☐ My check is enclosed. (Payable to iCD Club, in US funds, drawn on US bank)
☐ Charge my credit card: ☐ VISA   ☐ MasterCard   ☐ AMERICAN EXPRESS

Card Number: _____

Expiration date: _____

Signature: _____
☐ Bill me. Purchase Order Number: _____ (if not enclosed)
(Bonus Teacher's Resource PowerPak CD will be shipped upon payment)

iCD Charter Membership $ 79.⁰⁰

Sales Tax $_____
PA residents add 6% sales tax ($4.80)

Shipping and Handling $_____
US - No Charge
Canada - $6
Foreign - $12

Total $_____

SATISFACTION GUARANTEED!
If, at any time, I'm not completely satisfied with the Educator's Internet CD Club, I may cancel my membership and receive a full refund for the CD-ROMs that have not been shipped.

Detach and mail this order card to:
iCD Club
P.O. Box 10488, Lancaster, PA 17605-0488

For Faster Service C
(800) 638-163
Fax: (717) 393
Email
connect@cla
http://www.cla

Special Pri
Site Licenses
Call for more in

SHIP TO ADDRESS

Address is: ☐ Home ☐ School
Name _____   Title _____
School _____
Address _____
City _____
State/Province _____   Zip/Postal Code _____
Phone _____   Fax _____
Email Address
_____